CHEIRO'S *BOOK OF PALMISTRY, NUMEROLOGY AND ASTROLOGY*

ASTROLOGICAL SYMBOLS

Each of the ten planets and 12 signs of the zodiac has its own identifying symbol (sometimes called a glyph) used to show its position on a birth chart. Some specific angles between planets (called "aspects") are also identified by a symbol. These symbols are among the conventions of astrology with which you will need to become familiar.

Planets	Zodiac signs	Aspects
☉	♈	☌
Sun	Aries	Conjunction

Aries हेमेष
March 22 – April 20

Taurus वृष
April 21 – May 21

Gemini मिथुन
May 22 – June 22

Cancer कर्क
June 23 – July 23

Leo सिंह
July 24 – August 23

Virgo कन्या
August 24 – September 23

Libra तुला
September 24 – October 23

Scorpio वृश्चिक
October 24 – November 22

Sagittarius धनु
November 23 – December 22

Capricorn मकर
December 23 – January 19

Aquarius कुम्भ
January 20 – February 19

Pisces मीन
February 20 – March 21

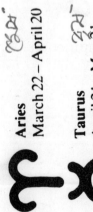

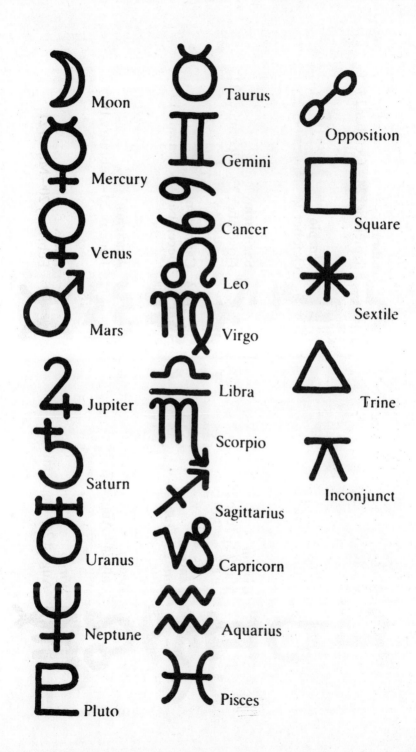

Moon

Mercury

Venus

Mars

Jupiter

Saturn

Uranus

Neptune

Pluto

Taurus

Gemini

Cancer

Leo

Virgo

Libra

Scorpio

Sagittarius

Capricorn

Aquarius

Pisces

Opposition

Square

Sextile

Trine

Inconjunct

CONTENTS

Introduction

PART ONE : PALMISTRY

PART TWO: NUMEROLOGY

PART THREE: NUMEROLOGY

PART ONE

PALMISTRY

16

A DEFENCE OF PALMISTRY

IN this introduction, which constitutes a defence of Cheiromancy I have endeavoured to collect the many facts, both medical and scientific, which can be brought forward to demonstrate that, as the hands are the servants of the system, so all that affects the system affects them. In following out the ideas of many famous men on the subject of the nerve-connection between the brain and the hand, I have in every case given my authority for whatever statement I have adopted. I trust that in this way even the greatest sceptic in such matters will be led to see that the study of the hand has not been confined alone to the attention of those he has so often been pleased to call 'weak-minded,' but on the contrary, that men of learning, both among the philosophers of Greece and the scientists of the present, have considered the subject worthy of their time and attention.

In presenting with this work the hands of famous people, I have done so with the object of enabling the student to study the hands of those with whose lives and characteristics he is probably acquainted, and also to show the reader at a glance the difference that exists between the hands of different temperaments. It would not be in keeping with the purpose of this book if I were to give a delineation of such hands. In the first place, their owners were too well known to make the readings of value as a test; and in the second, the student will derive greater benefit by tracing out for himself the lines and formations that exhibit each well-known characteristic.

I have endeavoured to place clearly and candidly before the intelligence of the reader the rules and theories that I have proved to be true, and those from whose foundations I have built up whatever success I may have achieved. I have done so for two reasons: the first—and most important—being, that I *believe in* cheiromancy and wish to see it acknowledged as it deserves to be; the second is, that the time is not far distant when, from considerations of health and demands from other fields of labour, I must perforce retire from the scene and leave others—I trust more competent— to take my place.

To endeavour to show the solid and sufficient foundation that this study rests upon, I will merely ask my readers to follow the pages of this defence, with curiosity if they wish, but, I hope, with curiosity tempered by common sense and patience.

To consider the origin of this science, we must take our thoughts back to the earliest days of the world's history. and furthermore to the consideration of a people the oldest of all, yet one that has survived the fall of empires, nations, and dynasties, and who are today as characteristic and as full of individuality as they were when thousands of years ago the first records of history were written, I allude to those children of the East, the Hindus, a people whose philosophy and wisdom are every day being more and more revived.

In endeavouring to trace the origin of palmistry, we are carried back to the confines of a prehistoric age. History tells us that in the remotest period of the Aryan civilisation it had even a literature of its own. Beyond this we cannot go; but as fragments of this literature are even now extant, we must therefore conclude that it had a still more remote infancy; but into that night antiquity we dare not venture.

As regards the people who first understood and practised this study of the hand, we find undisputed proofs of their learning and knowledge. Long before Rome or Greece or Israel was even heard of, the monuments of India point back to an age of learning beyond, and still beyond. From the astronomical calculations that the figures in their temples represent, it has been estimated that the Hindus understood the precession of the equinoxes centuries before the Christian era. In some of the ancient cave temples, the mystic figures of the Sphinx silently tell that such knowledge had been possessed and used in advance of all those nations afterward so celebrated for their learning. It has been demonstrated that to make a change from one sign to another in the zodiacal course of the sun must have occupied at the least 2,140 years, and how many centuries elapsed before such changes came to be observed and noticed it is impossible even to estimate.

The intellectual power which was necessary to make such observations speaks for itself; and yet it is to such a people that we trace the origin of the study under consideration. With the spread of the Hindu teachings into other lands do we trace the spread of the knowledge of palmistry. The Hindu Vedas are the oldest scriptures that have been found, and according to some authorities they have been the foundation of even the Greek schools of learning.

When we consider that palmistry is the offspring of such a race, we should for such a reason alone at least treat it with respect, and be more inclined to examine its claims for justice than we are at present. In the examination of these points we therefore find that this study of the hand is one of the most ancient in the world. History again comes to our assistance, and tells that in the north-west province of India, palmistry was practised and followed by the Joshi caste from time immemorial to the present day.

It may be interesting to describe here, in as few words as possible, an extremely ancient and curious book on the markings of hands, which I was allowed to use and examine during my sojourn in India. This book was one of the greatest treasures of the few Brahmans who possessed and understood it, and was jealously guarded in one of those old cave temples that belong to the ruins of ancient Hindustan.

This strange book was made of human skin, pieced and put together in the most ingenious manner. It was of enormous size, and contained hundreds of well-drawn illustrations, with records of how, when, and where this or that mark was proved correct.

One of the strangest features in connection with it was that it was written in some red liquid which age had failed to spoil or fade. The effect of those vivid red letters on the pages of dull yellow skin was most remarkable. By some compound, probably made of herbs, each page was glazed, as it were, by varnish; but whatever this compound may have been, it seemed to defy time, as the outer covers alone showed the signs of wear and decay. As regards the antiquity of this book there could be no question. It was apparently written in three sections or divisions: the first part belonged to the earliest language of the country, and dated so far back that very few of the Brahmans even could read or decipher it. There are many such treasures in Hindustan; but all are so jealously guarded by the Brahmans that neither money, art, nor power will ever release such pledges of the past.

As the wisdom of this strange race spread far and wide across the earth, so the doctrines and ideas of palmistry spread and were practised in other countries. Just as religion suits itself to the conditions of the race in which it is propagated, so has palmistry been divided into systems. The most ancient records, however, are those found among the Hindus. It is difficult to trace its path from country to country. In far-distant ages it had been practised in China, Tibet, Persia, and Egypt; but it is to the days of the Grecian civilisation that we owe the present clear and lucid form of the study. The Greek civilisation has in many ways been considered the highest and most intellectual in the world, and here it was that palmistry, or cheiromancy—from the Greek *cheir*, the hand - grew, flourished, and found favour in the sight of those whose names are as stars of honour in the firmament of knowledge. We find that Anaxagoras taught and practised it in 423 B.C. We find that Hispanus discovered, on an altar dedicated to Hermes, a book on cheiromancy written in gold letters, which he sent as a present to Alexander the Great, as 'a study worthy the attention of an elevated and inquiring mind.' We find it also sanctioned by such men of learning as Aristotle, Pliny, Paracelsus, Cardamis, Albertus Magnus, the Emperor Augustus, and many others of note.

Now, as in the study of mankind there came to be recognised a natural position on the face for the nose, eyes, ears, etc., so also on the hand there came to be recognised a natural position for the line of head, the line of life, and so on. The time and study devoted to the subject enabled these students to give names to these marks; as the line of head, meaning mentality; the line of heart, affection; the line of life, longevity; and so on, with every mark or mount that the hand possesses. This brings us down to the period when the power of the Church was beginning to be felt outside the domain and jurisdiction of religion. It is said that the early Fathers were jealous of the power of this old-world science. Such may or may not have, been the case; but even in the present day we find that the Church constitutes itself in all matters, both spiritual and temporal, the chosen oracle of God. Without wishing to seem intolerant, one connot help but remark that the history of any dominant religion is the history of the opposition to knowledge, unless that knowledge proceed from its teachings. Palmisty, therefore, the child of pagans and heathens, was not even given a trial. It was denounced as rank sorcery and witchcraft. The devil was conjured up as the father of all palmists, and the result was that men and women, terrified to acknowledge such a parentage, allowed palmistry to become outlawed and fall into the hands of vagrants, tramps, and gipsies.

During the Middle Ages several attempts were made to revive this ancient study; as, for instance, *Die Kunst Ciromanta*, published in 1475, and *The Cyromantia Aristotelis* cum *Figuris*, published in 1490, which is at present in the British Museum. These attempts were useful in keeping the ashes of the study from dying out; but it is in the nineteenth century that once more it rises, a Phoenix from the fire of persecution which has tried in vain to destroy it. The science of the present has come to the rescue of the so-called superstition of the past.

We will now see what science has done for palmistry, and whether or not it has any foundation beyond that of mere speculation and hypothesis.

I publish the following letter which appeared in the *Student*, a paper belonging to the University of Edinburgh, Scotland.

CHEIROMANCY

SIR: Some years ago I was walking through one of the wards in the Royal Infirmary when suddenly the idea occurred to me that I would examine the lines on a patient's hands.

I went to the nearest bed, and without pausing to look at the patient, I examined his hand. I knew little of palmistry, and believed still less; in fact, I hardly knew more than the names of the five principal lines, and that breaks in those lines meant misfortune. I examined the hands, and saw the life-line broken in both hands, and the fate-line, before it had reached a quarter of its natural length, stopped and replaced by a large cross. I questioned the patient, and found that he was twenty-three years old, and far gone in phthisis. He died in a few days. I could multiply instances, but space forbids. Would you then allow me to offer a few suggestions as to the possible relations of these lines to processes carried on in the cells of the grey matter? I am well aware that palmistry is considered quackery and humbug; but, after all, facts are stubborn things, even if they do not rest on any *known* scientific basis.

[A few suggestions on the possible relation of linear markings on the palm of the hand to certain physiological and psychical processes in the brain.]

1. The hand is a high stage of development peculiar to man as a reasonable being.

2. Tendencies, such as eloquence, anger, and affection, are shown by movements.

3. These movements are coarse and fine, and so produce large and small creases or lines.

4. Creases and lines, therefore, bear a definite relation to movements, and so to tendencies.

5. There are four well-marked creases or lines on every hand, found by experience to bear a definite relation to the tendencies of affection, mental capacity, longevity, and mental bent, or what cheiromants call 'fate'.

6. A line crossing the longevity line, a branch or break in it, interferes with its uniformity, and therefore interferes with the uniformity of the tendency to live.

7. Nerves regulating coarser and finer motions, and so creases or lines, contain chiefly motor fibres; but probably also other filaments transmitting in vibrations the resultant or combined effect of acquired and constitutional tendencies, and determining it to that part of the longevity line that will be affected, and there causing a crease resembling a cross by its junction with the main line or a branch, as the case may be.

25

8. The same train of reasoning obviously applies to *avoidable accidents*—that is, accidents caused by carelessness.

9. *Unavoidable accidents*. Certain tracts of cells in the conical grey matter are, incredible as it may seem, probably affected by coming events, and made to vibrate; hence, vague fears, intuitive perception, but no actual train of reasoning. The vibrations excited in these cells cannot awaken the activity of the cells engaged in reasoning processes that adjoins them, but merely cause protoplasmic vibrations in them, these vibrations being transmitted and marked on the hand by creases of different shapes. According to cheiromants, the left hand is what you are constitutionally; the right hand, what you make yourself or acquire. We may, therefore, reasonably expect to see in the right hand the resultant of acquired and constitutional tendencies.

As regards futurity, I think it not impossible that Professor Charcot's researches on the higher functions of the nervous system will demonstrate that tracts of cells, or a pathological condition of these cells, enables a perception of futurity, but no memory of it.　　　　(Signed) SPERANUS.

In will thus be seen that it requires but a little study of the subject to convince even the most sceptical that there is something in the lines'; and if a little, why not a great deal, if a sufficient amount of study be devoted to it?

Almost all medical men admit now that the different formations of nails indicate different diseases, and that it is possible from the nails alone to predict that the subject will suffer from paralysis, consumption, heart disease, and so on. Many a well-known doctor has told me that he has read more from the hand than he dared acknowledge, and that it was but the old-time prejudices which kept many a man from admitting the same thing.

At this point let me also draw a comparison between the way a doctor treats his patient and the way a palmist treats his client. I draw this comparison on account of the unfair manner in which medical men as a rule treat the palmist.

In the first place, the doctor has a recognised science to go by; he has scientific instruments with the most modern improvements to assist his researches; but how many can tell the patient what he is suffering from, unless the patient first tells the doctor all about himself and his symptoms; and even then, how often can the doctor arrive at a correct diagnosis?

Now, in the case of palmist, the client, without giving his or her name, without telling his occupation, or whether married or single, simply holds out his hands, and the palmist has to tell him past events in his life, present surroundings, health past and present; and having, by accuracy only, gained his confidence, he proceeds to read the future from the same materials that he has told the past. Now, if the palmist, without one particle of the help that the doctor gets, should make one mistake, the client immediately considers that he is a charlatan, and palmistry a delusion and a snare. If, however, the doctor makes a blunder, it is never known, but the result is that the patient has been 'called away by Providence' to another sphere.

I leave my readers to draw their own conclusions.

Among the testimony and ideas given by scientific men we find the greatest possible arguments in favour of the cheiromantic use of the lines, formations, mounts, and so forth, In the first place, the markings, of no two hands have ever been found alike. This is particularly noticeable in the case of twins; the lines will be widely different if the natures are different in their individuality, but at least some important difference will be shown, in accordance, with the different temperaments. It has also been noted that even with the lines of the hand a certain peculiarity will run in families for generations, and that each succeeding race will also show in temperament whatever that peculiar characteristic is. But again, it will be found that in the markings of the hand some children bear very little resemblance, in the position of the lines, to those of the parents, and that, if one watches their lives, they will, in accordance with this theory, be found very different from those who gave them birth. Again, one child may resemble the father, another the mother, and the markings of the hand will also be found to correspond with the markings on the hand of the particular parent the child resembles.

It is a very popular fallacy that the lines are made by work. The direct opposite, however, is the case. At the birth of the infant the lines are deeply marked (Plate VIII). Work, on the contrary, covers the hand with a coarse layer of skin and so hides instead of exposes them; but if the hand is softened, by poulticing or other means, the entire multitude of marks will be shown at any time from the cradle to the grave.

The superiority of the hand is well worth our attention. Scientists and men of learning in all ages have agreed that it plays one of the most important parts of all the members of the body. Anaxagoras has said: 'The superiority of man is owing to his hands'. In Aristotle's writings we find: 'The hand is the organ of organs, the active agent of the passive powers of the entire system'. More recently, such men as Sir Richard Owen, Humphrey, and Sir Charles Bell all call attention to the importance of the hand. Sir Charles Bell wrote: 'We ought to define the hand as belonging exclusively to man. *corresponding in its sensibility and motion, to the endowment of his mind'*.

Sir Richard Owe, in his work on *The Nature of Limbs*, said: 'In the hand every single bone is distinguishable from one another; each digit has its own peculiar character.'

29

It has long been known and recognised that the hand can express almost as much by its gestures and positions as the lips can by speech. Quintilian, speaking of the language of hands, says; 'For the other parts of the body assist the speaker, but these, I may say, speak for themselves; they ask, they promise, they invoke, they dismiss, they threaten, they entreat, they deprecate, they express fear, joy, grief, our doubts, our assents, our penitence, they show moderation, profusion, they mark number and time.

We will now give our attention to the skin, the nerves, and the sense of touch. Speaking of the skin, Sir Charles Bell once said: 'The cuticle is so far a part of the organ of touch that it is the medium through which the external impression is conveyed to the nerve. The extremities of the fingers best exhibit the provisions for the exercise of this sense. The nails give support to the tips of the fingers,' and in order to sustain the elastic cushion that forms their extremities they are made broad and shield-like. This cushion is an important part of the exterior apparatus. Its fullness and elasticity adapt it admirably for touch. It is a remarkable fact that we cannot feel the pulse with the tongue, *but that we can with the fingers*. On a nearer inspection we discover in the points of the fingers a more particular provision for adapting them to touch. Wherever the sense of feeling is most exquisite, there we see minute spiral ridges of the cuticle. These ridges have corresponding depressions on the inner surface, and they again give lodgement to soft, pulpy processes of the skin called papillae, in which lie the extremities of the sentient nerves. Thus the nerves are adequately protected, while they are at, the same time sufficiently exposed to have impressions communicated to them through the elastic cuticle and thus give rise to the sense of touch'.

As regards the nerves, medical science has demonstrated that the hand contains more nerves then any other portion of the system, and the palm contains more than any other portion of the hand. It has also been shown that the nerves from the brain to the hand are so highly developed by generations of use, that the hand, whether passive or active, is in every sense the immediate servant of the brain. A very interesting medical work states 'that every apparent single nerve is in reality two nerve cords in one sheath; the one conveys the action of the brain to the part, and the other conveys the action of the part to the brain'.

That the lines are not produced by work we have noted earlier. If, therefore, as has been demonstrated, they are not produced by work, they likewise are not produced by constant folding. It is true that the hands fold on the lines, but it is also true that lines and marks are found where no folding can possibly take place, and if so in one case, why not in all? Again, there are many diseases (as, for example, paralysis) in which the lines completely disappear, although the hands continue to fold as before. The folding argument, it will therefore be observed does not hold ground.

31

As regards the question: Is the study of phrenology and physiognomy to be considered as an aid in a cheiromantic examination?—a little thought will convince the inquirer that such is not by any means necessary. A thorough study of the hand will combine both. The hand, by its direct communication with every portion of the brain, tells not only the qualities active, but those dormant, and those which will be developed. As regards physiognomy, the face allows itself to be too easily controlled to be accurate in its findings, but the lines cannot be altered to suit the purposes of the moment.

It is Balzac who has said, in his *Comèdie Humaine:* 'We acquire the faculty of imposing silence upon our lips. upon our eyes, upon our eyebrows, and upon our foreheads; the hand alone does not dissemble—no feature is more expressive than the hand'.

We will now turn to the question of the future as revealed by this study, and carefully examine the reasons advanced for such a belief.

In the first place, we must bear in mind that the meaning of the different lines in conjunction with the different types of hands dates back to that period already referred to when this study lay in the hands of men who devoted their lives to its cultivation. Now, as there came to be recognised a natural position for the nose or the lips on the face, so in the study of the hand there came to be recognised a natural position for the line of head or the line of life, as the case might be. How such a thing was originally discovered is not our province to determine, but that the truth of such designations has been proved, and can be proved, will be admitted by any person who will even casually examine hands for himself. Therefore, if proved in one point that certain marks on the line of head mean this or that mental peculiarity, or that certain marks on the line of life have relation to length of life or the reverse, the same course of observation, if is not illogical to assume, can predict illness, health, madness, and death. If persisted in, it may be also accurate in its observation that marriage will occur at this or that point, with this or that result, and also in regard to prosperity or the reverse. It is beyond my power to answer why such a thing should be, but it is surely not beyond my jurisdiction to advance the following theory: That as the hidden laws of nature become more revealed by each century of time, so does man become more cognisant of the fact that things before called mysteries are but produced by the action of certain laws that beforetime he was ignorant of.

Is it hard to believe in some unseen law, some mysterious cause or power that thus shapes and controls our lives? If at first sight it seems so, we must consider the hundred and one things we have believed in with less foundation. To be consistent, we must remember the multitudious variety of religions, creeds, and theories that have not only been accepted by the masses, but have been the solid beliefs of intellectual minds. If, therefore, people can so easily believe in that which is beyond this state of life, of which no actual facts exist, is there anything so very absurd in supporting a doctrine of fate, which it is logical to suppose exists, if we only take it from the standpoint of the repetition of events from natural causes? On this question I would draw attention to the words of Dugald Stewart in his *Outlines of Moral Philosophy,* in which he says: 'All philosophical inquiry, and all that practical knowledge which guides our conduct in life presupposes such an established order in the succession of events as enables us to form conjectures *concerning the future from the observation of the past.*'

Man therefore becomes both the maker and the servant of destiny, bringing into force, by his existence alone, certain laws that react upon himself, and, through him, upon others. The present is therefore the effect of a heretofore cause; and again, *the present is the cause of a hereafter effect.* The deeds of the past are the karma of the present, as in 'the sins of the fathers,' and in the effect of hereditary laws. As we, therefore, work out our own fate, so do we make fate for those to follow, and so on in every degree from stage to stage in the world's progress.

The true fatalist will not close his hands and wait, he will open them and work, earnestly and patiently and well, remembering that the burden he bears has been made for him to teach him to make lighter the burdens of others. He will feel that he is a link in life's chain, which is eternal; that no matter how small that link may be, it still has its purpose—to be borne with patience, to be served with honour. Tis naught to him the clash of creeds, 'tis naught the success of the moment, or the failure of the year, he will do wrong in his life, as well as right—we all do evil is as necessary as good—but he will do his best, that is all. And at the end—well, there is no end, for even if there be no life beyond, he lives again in the particles of clay from whence he came; but if there be a spirit, then is his spirit part of the eternal spirit of all things, and so in the success of all is he successful. This is, to my mind, the doctrine of fate as preached by this study of the hand.

2

OF THE SHAPES OF HANDS AND FINGERS

PALMISTRY should really mean the study of the hand in its entirety. It is, however, divided into two sections: the twin sciences of cheirognomy and cheiromancy. The first deals with the shape of the hand and fingers, and relates to the hereditary influence of character and disposition; and the second to the lines and markings of the palm, to the events of past, present, and future.

It will therefore be readily understood that the second portion of this study cannot be complete without the first; and as in the study, so in the reading of the hand—the student should first observe the shape and formation, skin, nails, etc., before proceeding to judge the lines and markings of the palm. Some people consider this portion of the subject too uninteresting to merit much attention, and books on palmistry frequently ignore its importance, and commence too quickly with the more interesting details of cheiromancy.

A little thought will, however, convince the student that such a plan is a mistake, and can only result is error; that if the subject is worth any study at all, it is certainly worth going into thoroughly; besides, the shape of the hand can be more readily observed than the lines of the palm, and it is therefore all the more interesting, as by this means one can read the character of strangers while sitting in the railway train, the church, the concert, or the salon.

The characteristics of various nations as shown by the shape of the hand is also a fascinating branch of the study, and one very much neglected. Later, I will endeavour to point out the leading characteristics that I myself have observed in relation to this portion of the subject. The varying shape of hands and their suitability to various kinds of occupation is also worthy of note, and although by the exercise of will we can alter and make up, in a certain degree, for almost any constitutional defect, yet it is undoubtedly the case that certain types are more suited for one work than another, which it is the more immediate province of cheirognomy to determine. We will therefore at once proceed to consider the different types of hands with their various modifications, in their relation to temperament and character.

There are seven types of hands, each of which may again be subdivided into seven varieties.

The seven types are:

I   The elementary, or the lowest type.

II   The square, or the useful hand.

III   The spatulate, or the nervous active type.

IV   The philosophic, or the knotty hand.

V	The conic, or the artistic type.
VI	The psychic, or the idealistic hand.
VII	The mixed hand.

The seven varieties are formed by the blending of the seven types. Among civilised nations the elementary being rarely found in its purity, we therefore commence with the square, divided into seven heads, as, for example: the square with square fingers, short; the square with square fingers, long; the square with knotty fingers; the square with spatulate fingers; the square with conic fingers; the square with psychic fingers; and the square with mixed fingers.

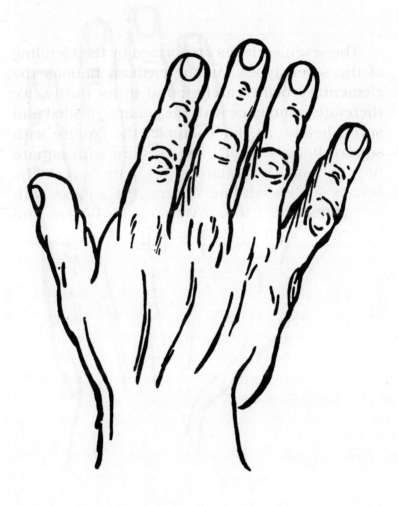

FIG. 1

THE ELEMENTARY HAND

39

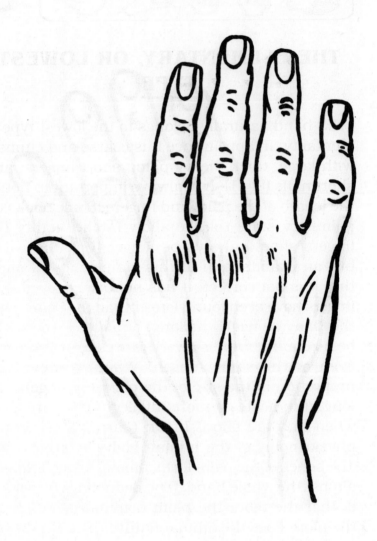

FIG. 2

THE SQUARE, OR USEFUL HAND

3

THE ELEMENTARY, OR LOWEST <u>TYPE</u>

THIS hand naturally belongs to the lowest type of mentality. In appearance it is coarse and clumsy, with large, thick, heavy palm, short fingers, and short nails (Fig. 1). It is always important to notice the length of the palm and fingers. Some books on palmistry state that to show intellectuality the fingers should always be longer than the palm; but an examination of this statement will show that it is not correct. It has not been proved that fingers have been found longer than the palm. That they may be nearly as long, or as long, there can be no doubt; but it is a very rare case to find them even of the same length. When, however, in proportion to the size of the palm the fingers are long, it indicates a more intellectual nature than when they are short. In Dr. Cairn's work on the physiognomy of the human body, he states that 'the bones of the palm form, among brute animals, almost the whole hand.' The deduction, therefore, is that the more the palm dominates the hand, the more does the animal nature rule. This is the important point in the elementary hand; the palm is always thick and coarse, and the fingers short and clumsy. There are also very few lines to be seen on the palm. The people possessing such a type have very little mental capacity, and what they do possess leans more to the order of the brute. They have little or no control over their passions; love of form, colour, and beauty does not appeal to them. The thumb of such hands is short and thick, with the upper part or nail phalange heavy, full, and generally square, Such people are violent in temper, passionate but not courageous. If they commit murder, it is in the fury and in the spirit of destruction. They possess a certain low cunning, but the cunning of instinct, not reason. These are people without aspirations; they but eat, drink, sleep, and die. (see also *The Hands of Nations*, Chapter 17)

4

THE SQUARE HAND AND ITS <u>SUBDIVISIONS</u>

THE square hand means the palm square at the wrist, square at the base of the fingers, and the fingers themselves square (Fig.2). Such a type is also called the useful, because it is found in so many walks of life. With this type the nails as well are generally short and square.

People with such a hand are orderly, punctual, and precise in manner, not, however, from any innate grace of nature, but more from conformity with custom and habit. They respect authority, they love discipline, they have a place for everything and everything is kept in its place, not only in their household, but in their brains, They respect law and order, and are slaves to custom; they are not quarrelsome, but are determined in opposition; they prefer reason to instinct, peace to war, and are methodical in work and in habit. They are endowed with great perseverance, but are tenacious, not resigned; they are not enthusiastic over poetry or art; they ask for the material, they win success in practical things. In religion they will not go to extremes; they prefer substance to show, and dogma to ideas. They are not adaptable to people, or versatile; they have little originality or imagination, but in work they have great application, force of character, strength of will, and often outdistance their more brilliant and talented rivals. They naturally love the exact sciences, and all practical study. They encourage agriculture and commerce; they love home and the duties of home, but are not demonstrative in affection. They are sincere and true in promises, staunch in friendship, strong in principle, and honest in business. Their greatest fault is that they are inclined to reason by a twelve-inch rule, and disbelieve all they cannot understand.

THE SQUARE HAND WITH SHORT SQUARE FINGERS

This peculiarity is often found, and very easily recognised. The subject with such a type is materialistic in every sense of the term. He would be the kind of man who would say; 'Except I hear with my ears and see with my eyes, I cannot believe,' And even then I very much doubt if such a man would be convinced. It also denotes an obstinate kind of nature, as a rule, narrow-minded. These people make money, but by plodding; they may not be miserly, but they are business-like and practical; they like to accumulate wealth; it is the material they seek.

THE SQUARE HAND WITH LONG SQUARE FINGERS

The next modification is the square hand with very long fingers. This denotes a greater development of mentality than the square hand with short fingers. It denotes logic and method, but in a greater degree then possessed by the purely square type, which, tied down by rule and custom, must follow the beaten track. This hand, on the contrary, though submitting everything to scientific examination, will not be so influenced by prejudice, but will proceed cautiously and thoroughly to logical conclusions, and will find its vocation in a scientific career, or in one involving logic and reason.

THE SQUARE HAND WITH KNOTTY FINGERS

This type is generally found with long fingers, and gives in the first place, extreme love of detail. It is also fond of construction; it builds plans from any *given* point to any *known* possibility; it may not produce great inventors, but it will produce good architects, mathematicians, and calculators, and if it applies itself to medical work, or to science of any kind, it will choose some speciality and use its love of detail in the perfection of its own particular study.

THE SQUARE HAND WITH SPATULATE FINGERS

This is the hand of invention, but always on practical lines. Men with this formation run the gamut in invention, but on a practical plane. They make useful things, instruments, and household articles, and are, as well, good engineers. They love mechanical work of almost every kind, and the finest useful mechanism has been turned out by men with square hand and the spatulate fingers.

Now, though at first sight it may appear strange to say that musical composition comes under this head, yet a little consideration will show that such not only is the case, but that there is a logical reason that it should be so. In the first place, the square hand is more the hand of the student. It gives more the power of application and continuity of effort, while the conic fingers give the intuitive and inspirational faculties. The musical composer, no matter how imaginative, no matter how inspired in ideas, is certainly not without the student's side to his character. If we consider, for a moment, the quality of brain and the disposition which is absolutely necessary, we will understand more clearly why the hand must be thus wonderfully balanced—why the inspirational, imaginative nature must be linked to that of the thoughtful, the solid, the methodical, and that which also proceeds from the foundation of the known—as, for instance, harmony and counterpoint—to reach the world of the unknown, through the gates of imagination and idealism. I have given great study to the hands of musical people, and I find this rule invariable. I find that the same also applies to literary people, those who from the foundation of study build up the ivy-clad towers of romance. It is here that the student of palmistry is often discouraged. He imagines that because a man or woman leads an artistic life, be it musical or literary, that the shape of the hand must be what is commonly called the conic or artistic; but the smallest observation of life will show that though the people with the purely conic or artistic hands have the artistic nature and the appreciation of what is artistic, yet they may not have —and I have more often observed that have not —the power or the ability to bring their ideas before the world in the same masterful way in which the mixed square and conic do. A man of a very artistic spirit, with the conic hand, once said to me: 'It is sufficient for the artist to be the artist to his own inner nature; the approbation of the world is, after all, only the vulgar hall-mark on what he knows is gold.' 'Yes.' I reply, 'sufficient for you own nature, perhaps, but not sufficient for the world that expects the diamond to shine and the gold to glitter. If the flower made itself, then might it refuse to allow its perfume to scent the earth.' On the contrary, the square type will exert its powers to the great advantage of all mankind.

THE SQUARE HAND WITH PSYCHIC FINGERS

The square hand with purely psychic fingers is rarely found, but an approach to it is often seen in the form of the square palm combined with long, pointed fingers and long nails. Such a formation causes people to start well, and mean well, but makes them subservient to every mood and caprice. An artist with such a type will have studio of unfinished pictures, and the business man will have his office filled with unfinished plans. Such a blending of types the extreme opposite of each other makes a nature too contradictory ever to succeed.

THE SQUARE HAND WITH MIXED FINGERS

This is a type that is very often seen, and more so among men than among women. It consists of every finger being different in shape, sometimes two or three, sometimes all. It is often found that the thumb of such a hand is supple, or bends back very much in the middle joint; the first finger is generally pointed, the second square, the third spatulate, and the fourth pointed. Such a hand indicates great versatility of ideas; at times such a man will be full of inspiration, again he will be scientific and extremely logical; he will descend from the most imaginative idea to the most practical; he will discuss any subject with the greatest ease; but from want of continuity of purpose, he will rarely, if ever, rise to any great height of power or success.

I have not space at my disposal to give the subdivisions of every type, but this is an example for the student of how the seven types may be divided.

THE SPATULATE HAND

THE spatulate hand is so called not only because the tip of each finger resembles the spatula which chemists use in mortars, but also because the palm instead of having the squareness of the preceding type, is either unusually broad at the wrist or at the base of the fingers (Fig. 3).

When the greater breadth of formation is at the wrist, the palm of the hand becomes pointed toward the fingers; when, on the contrary, the greatest breadth is found at the base of the fingers, the shape of the hand slopes back toward the wrist. We will discuss these two points a little later, but we must first consider the significance of the spatulate hand itself.

In the first place, the spatulate hand, when hard and firm, indicates a nature restless and excitable, but full of energy of purpose and enthusiasm. When soft and flabby, which is often the case, it denotes the restless but irritable spirit. Such a person works in fits and starts, but cannot stick to anything long. Now, in the first place, the peculiar attribute that the spatulate hand has is its intense love of action, energy, and independence. It belongs to the great navigators, explorers, discoverers, and also the great engineers

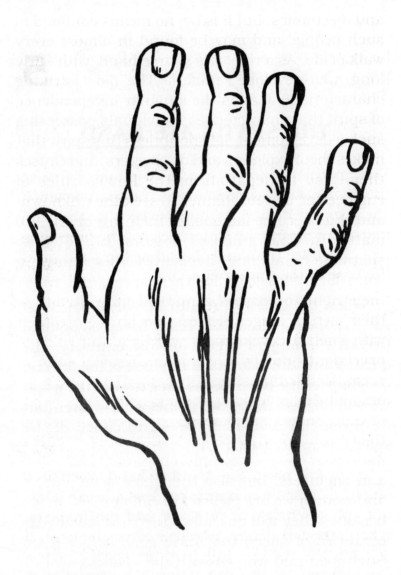

FIG. 3

THE SPATULATE OR ACTIVE HAND

and mechanics, but it is by no means confined to such people, and may be found in almost every walk of life. As a rule, it is a large hand, with fairly long, well-developed fingers. The most striking characteristic of all is the singular independence of spirit that characterises individuals possessing such a development. It is doubtless this spirit that makes them explorers and discoverers, and causes them also to depart from the known rules of engineering and mechanics to seek the unknown, and thus become famous for their inventions. No matter in what grade or position in life these spatulate hands find themselves, they always in some form strike out for themselves, and assert their right to possess a marked individuality of their own. A singer, actress, doctor, or preacher with such a development will break all rules of precedent—not by any means for the sake of eccentricity, but simply because they have an original way of looking at things, and their sense of independence inclines them to resent suiting their brain to other people's idea. It is from this hand that we get not only our great discoverers and engineers, but also the whole army of men and women we are pleased to call cranks, simply because they will not follow the rut made by the centuries of sheep that have gone before them. Such men and women with the spatulate hands are the advance agents of thought. They are, it is true, very often before their time; they are often wrong in the way they set about their work; but they are, as a rule, the heralds of some new thought or life that will, years later, give life to their fellow men.

This brings us down to the two divisions I have just mentioned. We will now consider their meaning.

The spatulate hand with the broad development at the base of the fingers is the more practical of the two. If he be an inventor, he will use his talents for making locomotives, ships, railways, and all the more useful things of life, for the simple reason that he comes nearer the formation of the square type. But if he has the greater angular development at the wrist, his bent will be for action in the domain of ideas. He will invent if he has the inventive talent, hunt for new flowers if he be a botanist, be the demigod of some new gospel if he be a priest. These people wonder that God took six days to make the earth—with the little power that they possess they would revolutionise the world in a day. But they all have their purpose in the evolution of life; they are necessary, therefore they are created.

THE PHILOSOPHIC HAND

THE name of this type explains itself, the word philosophic' being derived from the Greek *philos*, live, and *sophia*, wisdom. This shape of hand is easily recognised: it is generally long and angular, with bony fingers, developed joints, and long nails (Fig. 4). As far as success in the form of wealth is concerned, it is not a favourable type to have; it gleans wisdom, rarely, if ever, gold. People with such a type are, as a rule, students, but of peculiar subjects. They study mankid; they know every chord and tone in the harp of life; they play upon it, and are gratified with its responsive melody more then with the clink of coin. In this way they have as much ambition as other types of humanity, only theirs is of a different kind, that is all. They like to be distinct from other people, and they will go through all kinds of privations to attain this end; but as knowledge gives power, so does the knowledge of mankind give power over man. Such people love mystery in all things. If they preach, they preach over the heads of the people; if they paint, they are mystic; if they are poets, they discard the dramatic clash and colour of life for the visionary similes and vapourish drapings of the spirit. Theirs is the peace of the aesthetic; theirs

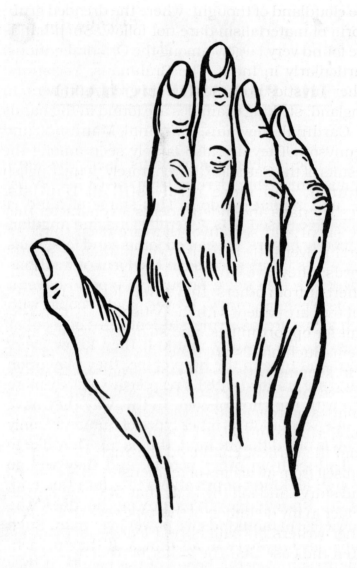

FIG.4

THE KNOTTY, OR PHILOSOPHIC HAND

the domain beyond the border land of matter; theirs the cloudland of thought, where the dreaded grub-worm of materialism dare not follow. Such hands are found very largely among the Oriental nations, particularly in India. The Brahmans, Yogis, and other mystics possess them in great numbers. In England, striking examples are found in the hands of Cardinal Newman, Cardinal Manning, and Tennyson, They are also largely seen among the Jesuits of the Catholic Church, rarely in the English Church, and more rarely still in Baptists, Presbyterians and Independents. In character they are silent and secretive; they are deep thinkers, careful over little matters, even in the use of little words; they are proud with the pride of being different from others; they rarely forget an injury, but they are patient with the patience of power. They wait for opportunities, and so opportunities serve them. Such hands are generally egotistical, which is in keeping with the life they lead. When in any excess of development they are more or less fanatical in religion or mysticism. Of this the most wonderful examples are found in the East, where from the earliest childhood the Yogi will separate himself from all claims of relationship and kindred, and starve and kill the body that the soul may live

I differ in my definition of this type very largely from other writers on palmistry. I fear if has been too often the case that the writer on this subject has followed too closely what other authorities have said, without taking the trouble to follow out his own observations. When I have come in contact with an opinion in opposition to my own, I have carefully considered all points for and against, and before deciding in any direction I have taken time to examine often hundreds of hands before coming to a conclusion on even the smallest point. When one considers the opportunities placed at my disposal, not only in one country, but in almost every country in the world, he will more readily understand that there is some likelihood of my being, not infallible, but fairly accurate.

With these hands, therefore, it must be borne in mind that the developed joints are the peculiar characteristic of thoughtful people, while the smooth, pointed fingers are the reverse. Again, such a development gives the love of analysing, but it is the shape or type of hand which determines whether that power of analysis be for chemicals or for mankind. The end of the finger being square and conic combined gives the solemn tone to their inspiration and fits them specially for the religious thought or the mysticism with which, as a rule, they become associated. Again, these hands in the pursuit of what they consider truth, will have the patience of the square type, with that love of self-martyrdom which is the characteristic of the conic. It is the blending of these almost opposite characteristics which brings about the peculiar ideas that makes man and women with the philosophic type of hands so different from the practical drones in the vast hive of humanity.

7

THE CONIC HAND

THE conic hand, properly speaking, is medium-sized, the palm slightly tapering, and the fingers full at the base, and conic, or slightly pointed, at the tip or nail phalange (Fig.5) It is often confounded with the next type, the psychic, which is the long, narrow hand, with extremely long, tapering fingers.

The main characteristics of the conic hand are impulse and instinct. People with the conic hand are often, in fact, designated 'the children of impulse.' There is a great variety in connection with this type, but it is more usually found as a full, soft hand, with pointed fingers, and rather long nails. Such a formation denotes an artistic, impulsive nature, but one in which love of luxury and indolence predominate. The great fault with people possessing this type is, that though they may be clever and quick in thought and ideas, yet they are so utterly devoid of patience and tire so easily, that they rarely, if ever, carry out their intentions, Such people appear to their greatest advantage in company, or before strangers. They are good conversationalists, they grasp the drift of a subject quickly, but they are more or less

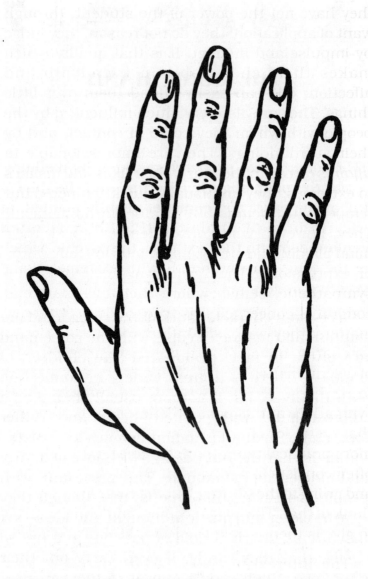

FIG. 5

THE CONIC, OR ARTISTIC HAND

58

superficial in knowledge, as also in other things; they have not the power of the student, through want of application; they do not reason, they judge by impulse and instinct. It is that quality which makes them changeable in friendship and affection; one can easily offend them over little things. They are also very much influenced by the people with whom they come in contact, and by their surroundings. They are impressionable in *affaires de coeur*, they carry their likes and dislikes to extremes; they are usually quick-tempered but temper with them is but a thing of the moment. They, however, when out of temper, speak their mind plainly, and are too impetuous to study words or expressions. They are always generous and sympathetic, selfish where their own personal comfort is concerned it is true, but not in money matters; they are easily influenced to give money for charity, but alas! here they have not the power of discrimination, consequently the money is given to anybody or anything which may rouse their sympathies at the moment. These hands never get that credit for charity which falls to the lot of the more practical types. To get credit for charity very often consists in saving what we give to the beggar and giving to the Church, but the conic fingers never think of that. The beggar comes, and if the impulse to give is there—well, they give, and that is all.

The interesting type has been called, and deservedly so, the artistic, but such relates more to temperament than to the carrying out of the artistic ideas. It would really be more correct to say that the owners of such hands are influenced by the artistic, than that they are artistic. They are more easily influenced by colour, music, eloquence, tears, joy, or sorrow, than any other type. Men and women possessing this class of hand respond quickly to sympathetic influences; they are emotional, and rise to the greatest heights of rapture, or descend to lowest depths of despair, over any trifle.

When the conic hand is hard and elastic, it denotes all the good qualities of the first-mentioned, but accentuated by greater energy and firmness of will. The hard conic hand is artistic in nature, and if encouraged for an artistic life the energy and determination will go far toward making success. It will have all the quickness of the first, with all the brilliancy and sparkle in company and before strangers, and it is for that reason that the conic hand has been chosen to represent those who lead a public life, such as actors, actresses, singers, orators, and all those who follow a purely emotional career. But it must not be forgotten that such people depend more upon the inspirational feeling of the moment than thought, reason, or study. They will do things well, but will not know why or how they do them. The singer will carry away her audience by her own individuality more than by study of the song; the actress, from her own emotional nature, will stir the emotions of others; and the orator will move multitudes by the eloquence of his tongue—not by the logic of his words. It must, therefore, be remembered that the type of hand but relates to the natural temperament and disposition of the individual; it is the foundation upon which the talent rises or falls. For instance, a woman with square fingers can be as great a singer, and may often be capable of rising to greater things than the woman with the pointed formation; but she will reach that point by different means—by her application, by her study, by her conscientious work, and by the greater power of endurance and patience that she possesses. Study and development are one half the ladder of fame. Genius sits on the rungs to dream, Study works and rises rung by rung; it is the earthworms alone who, dazzled by the heights above them, confound the two, and oft crown Study and call it Genius. The artistic type as a type but relates to temperament; the variety of fingers indicates only where that temperament is strongest: as, for instance, the artistic hand with square fingers indicates more the student, and, consequently, more exactness in foundation, method, and correctness; such persons will try and try again until they are successful.

The spatulate fingers on the artistic hand will give, say, to a painter the greater breadth of design and colour, the more daring ideas that will make the man famous for his originality. They philosoplic will give the mystical treatment of the idea—the tones, and semitones that subdue the already subdued colours. The lights and shades that creep across the canvas, the poem in the petals of the asphodel, the *Benedictus* in the hands that soothe the dying—all will be detail, but detail leading to the regions of the spirit, all will be calm, but with that calmness that awes one with the sense of the mysterious.

8

THE PSYCHIC HAND

THE most beautiful but the most unfortunate of the seven is what is known as the psychic (Fig.6). This in its purity of type is a very rare hand to find. But although the exact type may be hard to find, yet there are hundreds of men and women who so approach the psychic that they must be considered part of it, particularly when the customs that control our present-day life are taken into consideration. The psychic is the most beautiful hand of all. If is in formation, long, narrow, and fragile-looking, with slender, tapering fingers and long, almond-shaped nails. Its very fineness and beauty, however, indicate its want of energy and strength, and one instinctively pities such hands if they have to try to hold their own in the battle of life.

Individuals with the psychic hand have the purely visionary, idealistic nature. They appreciate the beautiful in every shape and form; they are gentle in manner, quiet in temper; they are confiding, and they instinctively trust every one who is kind to them. They have no idea of how to be practical, business-like, or logical; they have no conception of order, punctuality, or discipline;

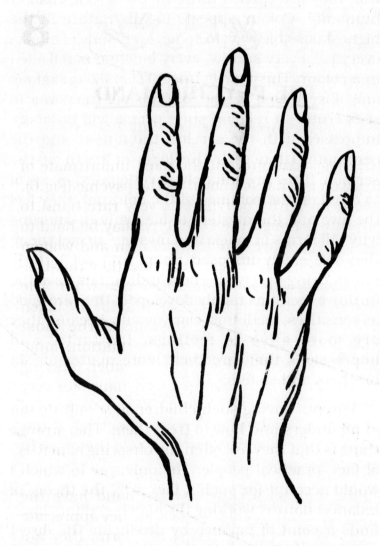

FIG.6

THE PSYCHIC. OR IDEALISTIC HAND

they are easily influenced by others; against their will, they are carried away by the strong rush of humanity. Colour appeals to this nature in the highest possible way; to some, every tone of music, every joy, every sorrow, every emotion is reflected in a colour. This type is unconsciously a religious one; if feels what is true, but has not the power to seek truth. In religion such people will be more impressed with the service, the music, and the ceremony than with the logic or truth of the sermon. They are innately devotional, they seem to dwell on the confines of the spiritual, they feel the awe and the mystery of life, without knowing why. All forms of magic and mystery attract them; they are easily imposed upon, and yet bitterly resent being deceived. These individuals have the intuitive faculties highly developed; they are good as sensitives, mediums, clarivoyants, because they are more alive to feelings, instincts, and impressions than are their more matter-of-fact brothers and sisters.

Parents having such children generally do not at all understand how to treat them. The strange thing is that they are often the offspring of matter-of-fact, practical people. The only way in which I would account for such a fact is by the theory of balance; nature, working through hereditary laws, finds a point of balance by producing the direct opposite of the parent; thus the law of reaction produces the type under examination. Alas! too often a temperament of this kind, by the ignorance and stupidity of the parents, is forced into some business life, simply because the father is in business.

Possessors of these beautiful, delicate hands, the indicators of the purely sensitive nature, usually feel their position in life so keenly that they too often consider themselves useless, and become morbid and melancholy in consequence. Such, however, is not the case; there is nothing useless that nature calls into creation; the beauty and sweetness of such temperaments are often of more use and do more good than those who, by the accumulation of this worlds goods, build a convent or endow a church. They may be placed here to establish a balance in the laws of humanity; they may be here to increase our love and appreciation of the beautiful; but they are not useless—of that we may be assured; therefore let us encourage and help them, instead of crushing and destroying them as we too often do. Alas! in the worldly sense they are generally left far behind in the race for fame and fortune.

9

THE MIXED HAND

THE mixed hand is the most difficult of all to describe. In the chapter on the square hand I gave an illustration of that type with mixed fingers. In that case, however, the mixed fingers have the foundation of the square hand, whereas with the true mixed type no such foundation can be cited for the student's guidance.

The mixed type is so called because the hand cannot possibly be classed as square, spatulate, conic, philosophic, or psychic; the fingers also belong to different types—often one pointed, one square, one spatulate, one philosophic, etc.

The mixed hand is the hand of ideas, of versatility, and generally of changeability of purpose. A man with such a hand is adaptable to both people and circumstances, clever, but erratic in the application of his talents. He will be brilliant in conversation, be the subject science, art, or gossip. He may play some instrument fairly well, may paint a little, and so on; but rarely will he be great. When, however, a strong line of head rules the hand, he will, of all his talents, choose the

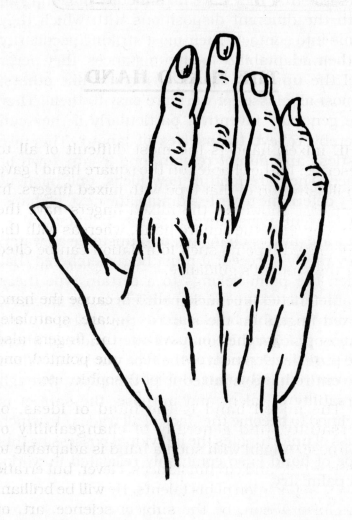

FIG. 7
THE MIXED HAND

best, and add to it the brilliancy and versatility of the others. Such hands find their greatest scope in work requiring diplomacy and tact. They are so versatile that they have no difficulty in getting on with the different dispositions with which they come into contact. Their most striking peculiarity is their adaptability to circumstances: they never feel the ups and downs of fortune like others; almost all classes of work are easy to them. They are generally inventive, particularly if they can thereby relieve themselves of labour. They are restless and do not remain long in any town or place. They are fond of new ideas: one moment they determine to write a drama, the next, perhaps, they invent a gas-stove or go into politics; but as they are always changing, and unstable as water, they rarely succeed. It must be remembered that when the palm belongs to a certain type these characteristics are much modified; as, for instance, mixed fingers on the square, the spatulate, the philosophic, or the conic will often succeed where the pure development of the type would fail. When the entire hand is mixed it is then that, through versatility of talent and purpose, the subject is inclined to become the 'Jack of all trades,' to which class of unfortunates the individual possessing this type of hand is so commonly relegated in works on palmistry.

 **10**

THE THUMB

THE thumb is in every sense so important that it calls for special attention, not only in the domain of cheirognomy, but also in its relation to cheiromancy. The truth of palmistry could rest upon the solid foundation given by the study of the thumb alone, in its relation to the most important characteristics of the subject.

In every age the thumb has played a conspicuous part, not only in the hand, but also in the world itself, It is a well-known fact that among many of the tribes of Oriental nations, if the prisoner, when brought before his captors, cover his thumb by his fingers, he is in this dumb but eloquent fashion giving up his will and independence, and begging for mercy. We find in the war annals of the children of Israel instances of their cutting off the thumbs of their enemies. Gipsies, in their judgment of character, make the thumb the great foundation for all their remarks. Being interested with gipsies in my early life, I know this for a fact, for I have seen and watched them from the position, angle, and general appearance of the thumb make their calculations accordingly.

In India they have a variety of systems by which they read the hand, but here, again, they make the thumb the centre and foundation, no matter what system they work out. The Chinese also believe in palmistry, and they, too, base their remarks on the position of the thumb itself. Again, it is an interesting fact to notice that even in Christianity the thumb has played an important role, the thumb representing God; the first finger Christ, the indicator of the will of God, and the only finger on the hand that has by virtue of its position, the power to point, or to stand upright independent of the rest; the second representing the Holy Ghost, as the attendant to the first. In the Greek Church the bishop alone gives the blessing by the thumb and first and second fingers, representing the Trinity; the ordinary priest has to use the whole hand. And, again, in the old ritual of the English Church, we find that in baptism the cross must be made by the thumb. Another very interesting point is the old idea of the midwives—an idea, by the way, that can easily be seen to contain a good deal of truth. They believed that if the child, some days after birth, was inclined to keep the thumb inside the fingers, if foreshadowed great physical delicacy, but if, seven days after birth, the thumb was still covered, then there was good reason to suspect that the child would be delicate mentally, If one will visit the asylums of the country, he cannot fail to notice that all congenital idiots have very weak, poor thumbs; in fact, some are so weak as not to be properly developed, even in shape. All weak-minded individuals have weak thumbs, and the man or woman who will stand talking with the fingers covering and concealing the thumb has little self-confidence or self-reliance. It is D'Arpentigny who has said, 'The thumb individualises the man.' This is remarkably true, particularly when one follows out Sir Charles Bell's discovery that in the hand of the chimpanzee, which is the nearest approach to the human, though well formed in every way, yet the thumb, if measured, does not reach the base of the first finger. The deduction to be made is, therefore, that the higher and better-proportioned the thumb, the more the intellectual faculties rule, and vice versa. This point the student will prove by the most casual observation. The man with the short, clumsy, thick-set thumb is coarse and brutish in the ideas and animal in his instincts, while the man or woman with the long, well-shaped thumb is intellectual and refined, and in the attainment of a desire, or the carrying out of an object, such a person will use the strength of intellectual will, as opposed to that of brute force, which will be applied by the man with the thick, short formation. The thumb, therefore, should be long and firm upon the hand. It should not stand at right angles to the palm, nor yet should it lie too close to the side. It should have a slope toward the fingers, and yet not lie down on them. When it stands off the hand, at right angles to it, the nature will fly to extremes, from sheer independence of spirit. It will be impossible to manage or control such natures; they will brook no opposition, and they will be inclined to the aggressive in their manner and bearing. When the thumb is well formed, but lying down, cramped toward the fingers, it indicates the utter want of independence of spirit. It denotes a nervous, timorous, but cautious nature; it will be impossible to find out what such a person is thinking about or what he intends to do, he cannot be outspoken, because his nature is the reverse. If the thumb, however, is a long one, he will use his intellectual faculties to outwit his opponent, but if it be short and thick he will cautiously await his opportunity for any deed of violence that he may meditate. When a well-formed thumb, therefore, strikes the happy medium of these two extremes, the subject will have sufficient independence of spirit to give him dignity and force of character; he will also be properly cautious over his own affairs, and have strength of will and decision. It therefore stands: the long, well-formed thumb denotes strength of intellectual will; the short, thick thumb, brute force and obstinacy; the small, weak thumb, weakness of will and want of energy.

From time immemorial the thumb has been divided into three parts, which are significant of the three great powers that rule the world—love, logic and will.

The first or nail phalange denotes will.

The second phalange, logic.

The third, which is the boundary of the Mount of Venus, love.

When the thumb is unequally developed, as for instance, the first phalange extremely long, we find that the subject depends upon neither logic nor reason, but simply upon will.

When the second phalange is much longer than the first, the subject, though having all the calmness and exactitude of reason, yet has not sufficient will and determination to carry out his ideas.

When the third phalange is iong and the thumb small, the man or woman is a prey to the more passionate or sensual side of the nature.

One of the most interesting things in the study of the thumb is to notice whether the first joint is supple or stiff. When supple, the first phalange is allowed to bend back, and forms the thumb into an arch; when, on the contrary, the thumb is stiff, the first phalange cannot be bent back, even by pressure; and these two opposite peculiarities bear the greatest possible relation to character.

The supple thumb (Fig. 8). is the distinctive peculiarity of the Latin races; the stiff joint is more the property of the Northern. The supple joint, for instance, is very rare among the Danes, Norwegians, Germans, English, and Scotch, whereas it is found in large numbers among the Irish, French, Spanish, Italians, and wherever these races have congregated. I hardly think that the theory of climatic influence bears out this point. I am more inclined to consider that the unconscious influence of the surroundings, prenatal or otherwise, has more to do with this peculiarity, for the characteristics that it shows in the individual are also the characteristics of the nation to which that individual belongs.

THE SUPPLE-JOINTED THUMB

For example, the supple-jointed thumb, bending from the hand, is the indication of the extravagant person, not only in matters of money, but in thought; these are life's natural spend-thrifts—improvident of time, improvident of wealth. They have adaptability of temperament for both people and circumstances; they are quickly at home in whatever society they are thrown; they have the sentimental love of kindred and country, as opposed to the practical; they settle down easily to new work and new surroundings, and consequently they quickly make a home in whatever country they are placed.

THE FIRM-JOINTED THUMB

Again, in a general way, the exact opposite of all this is found among the people with the stiff, firm joint (Fig. 8). In the first place, they are more practical; they have a strong will and a kind of stubborn determination which makes them rather stronger in character, and which is a large element in their success. They are more cautious and secretive; they advance by slow steps where the other nature will act by leaps and bounds. Again, they are not erratic like the first-mentioned; they stick to one thing; they carry out their purpose with a kind of resistless stubbornness; they have the practical idea of making the most out of their own home and their own country; they rule with strength; they have a keen sense of justice; they control self as they would control machinery; in war they are solid, strong, and resistless; in love they are undemonstrative, but firm and staunch; in religion their churches are plain, but solid; in art they have the strength of their own individuality.

THE SECOND PHALANGE

The next important characteristic of the thumb is the shape and make of the second or middle phalange. It will be found that this varies greatly and is a decided indicator of temperament. It has two noticeable formations, namely, the narrow moulded centre or waist-like appearance (Fig. 8, *d*), and its opposite, which is full and more chumsy (Fig. 8, *f*).

In an earlier work I called attention to the great difference, as far as character is concerned, shown by these two formations. My statement that the waist-like appearance indicated tact aroused a good deal of interest, and as it was taken exception to by some of my critics, I will here endeavour to show in a logical way why such should be the case. In the first place, the student has by this time seen the truth of my remarks about the finer formation of the thumb being the indication of the greater development of the intellectual will, and the coarse formation that of the nature that will use more brute force in the accomplishment of an object. It therefore follows that the waist-like appearance, which is a portion of the finer development, indicates the tact born of mental power, whereas the fuller, coarser development indicates force in the carrying out of a purpose, in keeping with the characteristics of each nature.

When the first or nail phalange is thick and heavy, with a short, flat nail, it is a sure indication of the ungovernable passion of the subject. All brutal animal natures have such clubbed formations, the force of blind passion completely dominating whatever reason they possess. Such people, as a rule, also have the first joint stiff, and the two points together give that terrible obstinacy of purpose that drives the subject, once out of temper, into deeds of violence and crime. The flat first phalange, consequently, whether short or long, is more calm in matters of temper and more controlled by reason.

When the hand is hard the natural tendency toward energy and firmness indicated by the thumb is increased; consequently the subject with the hard, firm hand and the first phalange of the thumb well developed will be more resolute of purpose and more determined in the execution of his ideas than is the subject with the soft hand.

When the hand is soft the subject will be more inclined to use his will by fits and starts, but cannot

(A)   THE CLUBBED THUMB

(B) SUPPLE-JOINTED THUMB   (C) FIRM-JOINTED THUMB

(D)   (E)   (F)

FIG. 8

THE THUMB

be so much depended upon in the execution of his plans.

One very striking peculiarity to be found in this study of human nature through the medium of the hand is shown in the case of people with the supple or bending-back thumb. They rarely have the same keenness of moral consciousness that is found with those of the straight, firm development. They are generally more those impulsive children of nature in whom conscience in morals does not play so important a part.

11

THE JOINTS OF THE FINGERS

THE development or non-development of the joints of the fingers is a very important consideration in the reading of the hand. The joints are, figuratively speaking, walls between the phalanges, and are important indications of the peculiarities as well as of the temperament of the subject.

When the subject has what are known as smooth joints he is more inclined to be impulsive in thought and to arrive at conclusions without using the reasoning faculties. With square hands this is very much modified, but not by any means eradicated. Consequently a scientific man with square fingers, but with smooth joints (Fig.9, *a*), will jump at conclusions without being always able to account for them. Such a doctor will diagnose a patient in the same way; if the man be really talented he may be very accurate in his conclusions, but such a man is more apt to make mistakes than the man with the square type with developed joints. With the pointed hands the smooth joints are purely intuitive (Fig.9, *b*); they cannot be troubled with details of any kind; they are also careless in dress, appearance, and in little matters. Such a person in business affairs could not keep papers and little things in their places, although he would be very particular in insisting upon order in other people.

The opposite is found in the case of people with the developed joints (Fig.9, c), work has nothing to do with the increase or diminution of such formations; the smooth joints are as often found among men who do the hardest kind of manual labour as the knotty or developed joints among men who do nothing but mental work. They are sometimes found running in families for generations, or appearing in one child and but slightly found in all the others. In the breeding of animals it may be observed, *en passant*, how often little peculiarities of this kind occur, and also how significant they are. Thus, when one considers how wonderful are the laws of heredity, he will study these 'little things' with greater interest. For instance, there is that well-known fact that if a woman gives birth to a child by her first husband, children who follow by the second, third, or even fourth husband, as the case may be, all in some slight way exhibit the peculiarities of the first husband.

The developed joints being the opposite of the smooth, it follows that they show more exactness in method and work. In this case, a man with the square hand and developed joints, engaged in some scientific pursuit, does not care how much time he spends in working out details in connection with any science in which he is engaged. It is the same reason that makes the philosophic hands

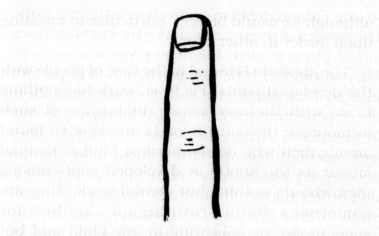

(A) SQUARE WITH
SMOOTH JOINTS

(B) POINTED WITH
SMOOTH JOINTS

(C) DEVELOPED JOINTS

FIG. 9

THE JOINTS OF THE FINGERS

so exact about detail in connection with their work. The owners of these joints notice the slightest thing out of place in even the arrangement of a room. They worry over little things, though in important matters they will be cool and calm. Men with these developed joints have an almost feminine instinct in matters of dress—they class and blend colour well, and nothing will irritate them more than to accompany a woman the colours of whose esteem do not harmonise. In dramatic work, people with such joints are careful and accurate in the delineation of character, but lack dramatic breadth and force. Outside of science, they perhaps make their best mark in literature, because of their extraordinary power of analysing human nature, and because of the true instinct and knowledge of humanity which seems to come to them without effort. We must therefore draw the deduction that these developed walls or joints between the phalanges, figuratively speaking, stop the tide of impulse, and make the nature more observant, thoughtful, and analysing.

12

THE FINGERS

FINGERS are either long or short, irrespective of the length of the palm to which they belong.

Long fingers give love of detail in everything— in the decoration of a room, in the treatment of servants, in the management of nations, or in the painting of a picture. Long-fingered people are exact in matters of dress, quick to notice small attentions; they worry themselves over little things, and have occasionally a leaning toward affectation.

Short fingers are quick and impulsive. They cannot be troubled about little things; they take everything *en masse;* they generally jump to conclusions too hastily. They do not care so much about appearances, or for the conventionalities of society; they are quick in thought, and hasty and outspoken in speech.

Fingers thick and clumsy, as well as short, are more or less cruel and selfish.

When the fingers are stiff and curved inward, or naturally contracted, they denote an excess of caution and reserve, and very often indicate a cowardly spirit.

When they are very supple and bend back like an arch, they tell of a nature charming in company, affable and clever, but curious and inquisitive.

Naturally crooked, distorted, twisted fingers on a bad hand indicate a crooked, distorted evil nature; on a good hand they are rarely found, but if found they denote a quizzical, irritating person.

When a small fleshy ball or pad is found on the inside of the nail phalange, it denotes extreme sensitiveness and tact through the dread of causing pain to others.

When the fingers are thick and puffy at the base, the subject considers his own comfort before that of others; he will desire luxury in eating, drinking, and living. When, on the contrary, the fingers at the base are shaped like a waist, it shows an unselfish disposition in every way, and fastidiousness in matters of food.

When, with the fingers open, a wide space is seen between the first and second, it indicates great independence of thought. When the space is wide between the third and fourth, it indicates independence of action.

THE LENGTH OF THE FINGERS IN RELATION TO ONE ANOTHER

The first finger on some hands is very short; again, on others, it is as long as the second, and so on.

When the first, or index finger, is excessively long,

84

it denotes great pride, and a tendency to rule and domineer. It is to be found in the hands of priests as well as politicians. Such a man, literally speaking, will 'lay down the law'.

When this finger is abnormal, namely, as long as the second, it indicates great pride of disposition, a desire for power, the 'one man, one world' creed. Napoleon was a striking example of this rule; on his hand the first finger was abnormal, it being fully equal to the second.

When the second finger (the finger of Saturn) is square and heavy, it shows a deeply thoughtful, almost morbid nature.

When pointed, the reverse—callousness and frivolity.

When the third finger (the finger of the Sun) is nearly of the same length as the first, it denotes ambition for wealth and honour through its artistic leanings, and a great desire for glory. If excessively long, almost equal to the second, it denotes the nature that looks at life in the light of a lottery, one that gambles with all things—money, life, and danger—but one endowed withal with strong artistic instincts and talents.

The spatulate termination for this third finger is an excellent sign for the actor, orator, or preacher. It indicates that his artistic gifts are strengthened by the dramatic or sensational power, the breadth, the coslour necessary to appeal to audiences.

When the fourth, or little finger, is well shaped and long, it acts as a kind of balance in the hand to the thumb, and indicates the power of the subject to influence others. When very long— almost reaching to the nail of the third—it shows great power of expression in both writing and speaking, and the owner is more or less the savant and philosopher; one who can converse with ease on any subject; one who interests and commands people by the manner in which he will apply facts and knowledge to the treatment of anything brought under his notice.

13

THE PALM, AND LARGE AND SMALL HANDS

A THIN, hard, dry palm indicates timidity, and a nervous, worrying, troubled nature.

A very thick palm, full and soft, shows sensuality of disposition.

When the palm is firm and elastic, and in proportion to the fingers, it indicates evenness of mind, energy, and quickness of intellect.

When not very thick, but soft and flabby, it denotes indolence, love of luxury, and a tendency toward sensuality.

A hollow palm has been proved to be an unfortunate sign; such people usually have even more disappointments than fall, as a rule, to the lot of mortals. I have also noticed a peculiarity which has not been mentioned in other works on the subject, namely, that the hollow inclines more to one line or portion of the hand than to another.

If it inclines to the line of life, it promises disappointment and trouble in domestic affairs, and if the rest of the hand denotes ill-health, it is an added sign of delicacy and trouble.

When the hollow comes under the line of fate,

it indicates misfortune in business, money, and worldy affairs.

When under the line of heart it tells of disappointment in the closest affection.

I do not hold with other works on the subject, that the fingers must be longer than the palm to show the intellectual nature. The palm of the hand is never, properly speaking exceeded in length by the fingers. How can we expect this to be the case with the square, spatulate, and philosophic types? The statement that in every case the fingers must be longer than the palm is erroneous and misleading.

LARGE AND SMALL HANDS

It is a thing well worth remarking, that, generally speaking, people with large hands do very fine work and love great detail in work, while those with very small hands go in for large things, and cannot bear detail in employment. I once examined the hands of the diamond setters and engravers' engaged in some of the largest goldsmiths establishments in Bond Street, London, and out of nearly a hundred, I did not find a single exception to this rule. One man—and I have the cast before me now—had extraordinarily large hands, yet he was famed for the fineness and minutiae of the work which those great hands turned out.

Small hands, on the contrary, prefer to carry

out large ideas, and, as a rule, make plans for too large for their power of execution. They love to manage large concerns and govern communities, and, speaking generally, even the writing of small hands is large and bold.

 **14**

THE NAILS

PARTICULARLY as regards health, and the diseases likely to affect the subject, the nails will be found to be remarkably sure guides. Medical men in both London and Paris have taken up this study of the nails with great interest. Often a patient does not know, or for the moment forgets, what his parents have suffered or died from; but an examination of the nails will in a few seconds disclose important hereditary traits. I will first treat of the health side of the question, then of the disposition, as shown by this study.

In the first place, the care of the nails does not alter or affect their type in the slightest degree; whether they are broken by work or polished by care, the type remains unchanged. For instance, a mechanic may have long nails, and the gentleman at ease may have very short, broad ones, though he manicure them every morning.

Nails are divided into four distinct classes; long, short, broad, and narrow.

LONG NAILS

Long nails never indicate such great physical strength as the short, broad type. Very long-nailed persons are more liable to suffer from chest and lung trouble, and this is more accentuated if the nails are much curved, both from the top back toward the finger and across the finger (Fig. 10, *g*). This tendency is even more aggravated if the nail is fluted or ribbed. This type of nail when shorter, indicates throat trouble, such as laryngitis and bronchial affections (Fig. *10*).

Long nails, very wide at the top and bluish in appearance, denote dead circulation proceeding from ill-health, or nervous prostration. This is very often the case with the hands of women between the ages of fourteen and twenty-one and forty-two and forty-seven.

SHORT NAILS

Short, small nails run in whole families in which there is a tendency toward heart trouble

Short nails, thin and flat at the base, with little or no moons, are signs of weak action of the heart.

Large moons Indicate good circulation.

Short nails, very flat and sunken, as it were, into the flesh at the base, show nerve disorders (Fig. *11*).

Short nails, very flat and inclined to curve out or lift up at the edges, may be forerunners of paralysis.

Short-nailed people have a greater tendency to suffer from heart trouble and from complaints affecting the trunk and lower limbs than those with long nails.

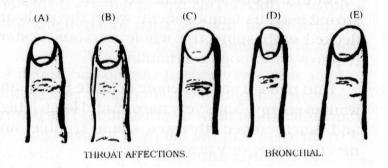

THROAT AFFECTIONS.　　　　BRONCHIAL.

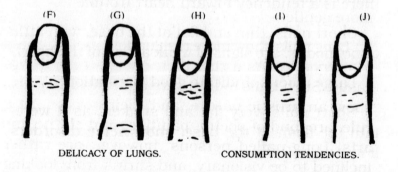

DELICACY OF LUNGS.　　　CONSUMPTION TENDENCIES.

FIG. 10

NAILS

Long-nailed persons are more liable to trouble in the upper half of the system—in the lungs, chest, and head.

Natural spots on the nails are signs of a highly-strung nervous temperament; when the nails are flecked with spots the whole nervous system requires a thorough overhauling.

Thin nails, if small, denote delicate health and want of energy. Nails very narrow and long, if high and much curved, threaten spinal trouble, and never promise very great strength.

DISPOSITION AS SHOWN BY THE NAILS

In disposition, long-nailed individuals are less critical and more impressionable than those with short nails. They are also calmer in temper and more gentle.

Long nails show more resignation and calmness in every way. As a rule their owners take things easily. Such nails indicate great ideality; they also show an artistic nature, and their owners, as a rule, are fond of poetry, painting, and all the fine arts. Long-nailed persons, however, are rather inclined to be visionary, and shrink from looking facts in the face, particularly if those facts are distasteful.

Short-nailed individuals, on the contrary, are extremely critical, even of things relating to self; they analyse everything with which they come into

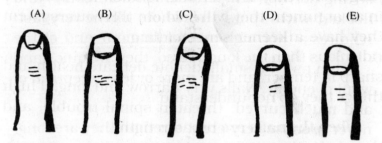

(A) (B) (C) (D) (E)

SHOWING BAD CIRCULATION AND TENDENCY TOWARDS HEART TROUBLE

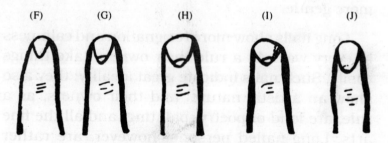

(F) (G) (H) (I) (J)

SHOWING TENDENCY TOWARDS NERVE WEAKNESS NAILS

FIG. 11

NAILS

contact; they incline to logic, reason, and facts, in opposition to the visionary qualities of the long nailed. Short-nailed individuals make the best critics; they are quicker, sharper, and keener in their judgement; they are, as well, fond of debate, and in an argument they will hold out till the very last; they have a keener sense of humour and of the ridiculous than the long-nailed; they are quick and sharp in temper, and are more or less sceptical of things they do not understand.

When the nails are broader than they are long, they indicate a pugnacious disposition, also a tendency to worry and meddle and to interfere with other people's business.

Nails short by the habit of biting indicate the nervous, worrying temperament.

15

THE HAIR ON THE HANDS

A SUGGESTED THEORY

IF the exponent of palmistry has to read hands through a curtain, without seeing his subject, the hair growing on the hand, although seemingly unimportant, to a thorough student becomes a study of very great note and magnitude. A slight knowledge of the laws that govern the growth of hair will not, therefore, be out of place. The hair is used by nature to fulfil a great many useful purposes in connection with the body. I will give those only that are necessary to the student of this particular study, namely, the cause of the colour of the hair, of its coarseness and fineness, as illustrative of disposition.

In the first place, each hair is in itself a fine tube; these tubes are in connection with the skin and the skin nerves. These hairs or tubes are, literally speaking, escape-valves for the electricity of the body, and by the colour they take in the passage of that electricity, so should the student be able to determine certain qualities of temperament of which he would otherwise be ignorant. For example: If there is a large amount of iron or pigment in the system, the flow of this electricity through the hair forces it into these tubes and makes the hair black, brown, blond, grey, or white, as the case may be. Individuals with blond or fair hair, therefore, have less iron and dark pigment in the system. As a rule they are more languid, listless, gentle, and more influenced by people and surroundings than those of the darker type.

People with very dark hair, although often less energetic in work, will have more passion in temper, will be more irritable and more energetic in affection than those of the fairer type, and so in every degree of shade until we come to the extreme opposite of the dark type, namely, those with red hair. If we will examine hair, we will find that red hair is coarser in quality as a rule than either black, brown, or blond. Now, being coarser or larger, the tube itself is, consequently, wider, and therefore shows the greater quantity of electricity that escapes, and of which these natures have the greatest amount. It is not that they have as much pigment as the dark people, but having the greater supply and force of electricity, they are consequently the more excitable and quicker to rouse to action than either the black, brown, or blond.

When the system gets old, or becomes enfeebled by excess or dissipation, the electricity, not being generated in such large quantities, is nearly or entirely consumed by the system itself; the pigment is no longer forced into these hair tubes, and consequently they commence to grow white at the outer ends, and so on, till the entire hair or tube becomes white, It is the same in the case of a sudden shock or grief—the hair often stands on end from the force of the nervous electric fluid rushing through these tubes; reaction naturally sets in immediately, and the hair often becomes white in a few hours. Very rarely can the system recover from such a strain, and consequently very rarely will the hair resume its colour.

In America more people are to be found with white hair than, I think in any other country in the world. It has been suggested that this fact may be due to the high pressure at which many Americans live.

 **16**

THE MOUNTS, THEIR POSITION AND THEIR MEANINGS

THE Mounts of the Hand (Fig. 12) vary in the most remarkable manner in accordance with the character and dispositions of races and their different temperaments.

In almost all the Southern and more emotional races, these Mounts are more noticeable than those belonging to Northern countries. It has been observed that all people with the Mounts apparent or prominent are more swayed by their feelings and emotions than those people who have flat palms and undeveloped Mounts.

The names given to the Mounts of the Hand are those also given to the seven principal planets that sway the destiny of our earth, viz., the Sun, Moon, Venus, Mercury, Mars, Jupiter, and Saturn.

These names were given to the Mounts by the Greek students of this subject, and were associated by them with the qualities attributed to these seven planets, such as:

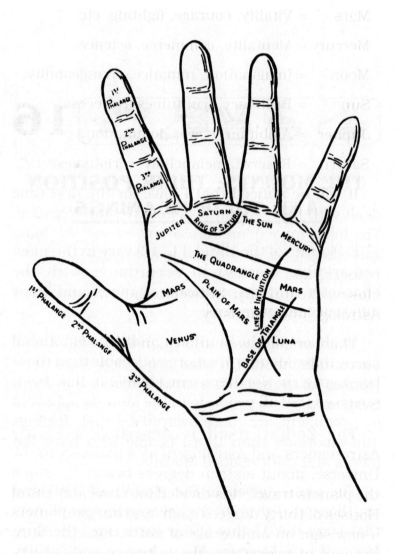

FIG. 12
THE MOUNTS OF THE HAND.

Venus   = Love, sensuality and passion.

Mars   = Vitality, courage, fighting, etc.

Mercury = Mentality, commerce, science.

Moon   = Imagination, romance, changeability.

Sun   = Brilliancy, fruitfulness, success.

Jupiter = Ambition, power domination.

Saturn   = Reserve, melancholy, seriousness.

It will be noticed that I have for the first time dealt with these Mounts as Positive and Negative. The following explanation of my reason for doing this should be of the greatest assistance of my readers, and will also be useful in showing the close relationship between the two sciences Astrology and Palmistry.

There are, it is well-known, in the Zodiac which surrounds our earth, what are called "the twelve Houses" of the seven principal planets of our Solar System.

The Zodiac itself is described both by Astronomers and Astrologers as a pathway in the Universe, about sixteen degrees broad, in which the planets travel. It is divided into twelve Signs of Houses of thirty degrees each, and our Sun enters a new sign on an average of every thirty days, At the end of twelve months it has completed the zodiacal circle of 360 degrees, or one Solar year.

The sun, the creator of life, and itself the greatest mystery of our Universe, is in bulk

330,000 times larger than our earth, It therefore follows that in entering a new sign of the Zodiac, it changes the magnetic vibrations of the effect of each sign towards our earth. Consequently it is reasonable to presume that a person born, say in April, and another in May, would have very different characteristics and naturally a distinct destiny, because character is Fate or Destiny.

THE MOUNT OF MARS

The Mount of Mars has two positions on the palm (Fig. 12); the first is to be found immediately under the upper part of the Line of Life, and the other opposite to it in the space lying between the Line of Heart and the Line of Head. The first relates to the physical characteristics and the second to the mental.

The first if large is Positive, and it has more importance when the person is born between the dates of March 21st and April 21st, and in a minor way until April 28th, which portion of the year in the Zodiac is called the House of Mars (Positive).

The second is considered Negative, and it has more importance when the person is born between October 21st and November 21st. and in a minor way until November 28th, because in the Zodiac this portion of the year is denoted as the House of Mars (Negative).

We will now consider the difference of these two positions, how distinctly they affect the mind and temperament, and also their relation as to health and tendency towards disease.

THE FIRST MOUNT OF MARS

In the first Mount of Mars, at the commencement of the Line of Life, and especially when the subject is born in the House of Mars (March 21st to April 21st, and in a minor way until the 28th), he possesses a strong martial nature.

They have great obstinacy of purpose and determination, they resent all criticism, they are decided and dogmatic in all their views, and seldom ask the advice of others, until it is too late to alter their pupose for good or evil.

They can only be handled or managed by kindness, patience, tact, or by their affections.

As a rule these people are good-natured and generous, but spasmodic and impulsive in all their actions. Their greatest fault lies in their impulsiveness and lack of self-control, and unless a good long Line of Head by shown on the hands, they rush madly into all kinds of difficulties and dangers.

Such people should be advised to cultivate repose, self-control, and above all to avoid wines, spirits, and stimulants of all kinds, to which as a rule these natures are very much inclined.

THE SECOND MOUNT OF MARS

The second Mount of Mars, lying between the Heart and Head Line (Fig.12). is more important when the subject is born between the dates of 21st October to the 21st November and until November 28th. In the Zodiac this period of the year is called the House of Mars Negative or Mental.

In character they are the complete opposite of the former types, all the Mars qualities being in the mind and in the mental attitude very courageous, and possess *moral courage* more than physical.

When not highly cultivated or developed, they employ cunning and craft of every description to carry out their plans. They will stop at nothing to carry out their purpose.

Mars Negative people are generally so versatile and many-sided that they are the most difficult of all to place in some special career. If a good Line of Head be found on the hand, then there is nothing in the world of mentla endeavour in which they will not make a success.

Their period in the Zodiac has from time immemorial been symbolised in their lower development as the figure of a scorpion wounding its own tail, and in their higher development that of an eagle with its head pointing upwards to the sky. Such symbols perfectly illustrate the dual nature of the type under consideration.

The Mount of Jupiter if found at the base of the first finger (Fig. 12). When large, it shows a desire to dominate, to rule others, to lead and organise, and to carry out some distinct object. But these good qualities will only be employed if the Line of Head is clear and long. When the line is poor and badly formed, then a large Mount of Jupiter gives pride, excess of vanity, a self-confident and self-opinionated person. But on what is known as a good well-marked hand, there is no Mount more excellent and no surer indication of success from sheer strength of character and purpose.

This Mount may be considered positive when a person is found born between November 21st to December 20th, and in a minor way until the 28th. These persons are naturally ambitious, fcarless and determined in all they undertake.

They concentrate all their attention on whatever they may be doing at the moment and see no way but their own, especially if they feel the least opposition to their plans. They are, however, honourable and high principled.

They have great enterprise in business and all matters requiring organisation.

The great fault of this class is that they are inclined to go to extremes in all things, and in doing so exhaust their efforts.

THE MOUNT OF JUPITER (NEGATIVE)

The Mount of Jupiter may be considered negative or mental when the subject is born between the dates of February 19th and March 20th, and in a slighter degree until the 28th.

In this case the ambition takes rather the mental form than what might be termed material.

They seem to possess a kind of natural understanding of things and easily acquire all sorts of knowledge about a large variety of things, especially the history of countries, races, peoples, geographical, botanical, and geological researches.

In spite of this mental ability, these people are very sensitive and lacking in self-confidence. It is again a strong clear Line of Head which, if found on the hand, will determine whether the mental will-power is sufficient to make this type overcome its natural sensitiveness and use the qualities they have carry out their aims and ambitions.

THE MOUNT OF SATURN AND ITS MEANING

The Mount of Saturn is found at the base of the second finger (see Fig. 12). Its chief characteristics are love of solitude, prudence, quiet determination, the study of serious sombre things, the belief in fatalism and in the ultimate destiny of all things.

A complete absence of this Mount indicates a more or less frivolous way of looking at life, while an exaggeration of it denotes an exaggeration of all the qualities it represents.

The Mount of Saturn may be considered Positive when the subject is found to be born between the follwing dates, December 21st to January 20th, and during the subsequent seven days while this period is fading out and being overlapped by the period following.

People born in these dates have strong will force and mentality, but they usuallly feel exceptionally lonely and isolated.

In character they are usually remarkable for their independence of thought and action, they also detest being under the restraint of others.

For kindness and sympathy they will do almost anything, but they have strange ideas of love and duty, and for this reason they are usually called somewhat peculiar by those few who attempt to penetrate their isolation.

They have a deeply devotional nature, even when appearing not to be religious, and they make every effort to do good.

Such people as a rule feel the responsibilites of life too heavily and in consequence often become despondent and gloomy.

THE MOUNT OF SATURN (NEGATIVE)

The Mount of Saturn may be considered negative or mental when the person is found born between the dates of January 21st to February 18th, and also for the seven days following.

These prople are like the preceding type in almost all things, except that the same things appear to affect them more mentally than physically.

These latter types are more sensitive and very easily wounded in their feelings.

They read character instinctively and seem to "see through" people too easily to be really happy.

They make loyal, true friends if their feelings are once aroused, and they will undergo any sacrifice for the sake of a friend.

They are very different from the previous type in that they usually take a keen interest in public meetings and large gatherings of people. They love theatres, concerts, and places of amusement.

THE MOUNT OF THE SUN AND ITS MEANING

The Mount of the Sun is found under the base of the third finger. To this Mount the Greeks also gave the name of Mount of Apollo (Fig. 12).

When large or well developed it indicates glory, publicity, a desire to shine before one's fellows. It is always considered a good Mount to have large.

It also indicates enthusiasm for the beautiful in all things, whether one follows an artistic calling or not. People with this Mount large also have an expansive temperament, are generous and luxurious in all their tastes. They are sunny by nature and have a forceful personality.

This Mount may be considered positive when the subject is found to be born between the dates of July 21st and August 20th, and generally until the 28th of this month, which portion of the Zodiac is called the "House of the Sun".

These people represent what may be called the heart force of the human race, and as a rule are generous and sympathetic even to an extreme.

They have great force of character and personality.

At heart they are really most sympathetic, though they often seem to hide this quality on account of their strong sense of trying to force people to do what is right towards others.

Many of these people who have cheered others, who have brough. Their grand sunshine of good into the hearts of others, connot cheer themselves when the twilight comes, and so they often fall victims to gloom and melancholy.

MOUNT OF THE SUN (NEGATIVE)

This Mount may be considered Negative when the subject is found born between January 21st and February 18th, and for the seven days following.

They seldom attract wealth as do those of the Positive type.

109

In strange apparent contradiction to this, these people are usually excellent in business and in their financial plans, but it is more for othere than for themselves.

As a rule, they find great pleasure in public ceremonies, and meetings of all kinds. They love theatres and all places where large numbers of people congregate, and when wound up to the occasion they can display great eloquence, power of argument and influence in debates.

Very dry climates and plenty of sunlight is their greatest safeguard against all their maladies.

THE MOUNT OF MERCURY AND ITS MEANING

The Mount of Mercury is found under the base of the fourth finger (Fig. 12). On a good hand it is a favourable Mount to have, but on a hand showing evil tendencies, especially mental, it increases the bad indications.

It seems to relate more to the mind than anything else. It gives quickness of brain, wit, thought, eloquence. It also relates to adaptability in science and commerce, but if evilly afflicted, it denotes mental excitability, nervousness, lack of concentration, trickiness in business.

This mount should always be considered with the kind of Line of Head found on the Hand.

With a Line of Head long and well marked, it increases all the promise of mental aptitude and success, but with a weak, badly marked, or irregular Head line, it augments all its weak or bad indications.

THE MOUNT OF MERCURY (POSITIVE)

This Mount can be considered positive when the subject is found to be born between the dates of May 21st June 20th, and until the 27th of that month, but during the last seven days its influence is considered dying out and not so strong.

People born in this period are represented in the Zodiac by the symbolism of the twins. It is a curious fact that all persons born in this part of the year are singularly dual in character and temperament. One side of their nature may, in fact, be described as perpetually pulling against the other, and although nearly always possessed with unusual intelligence, they often spoil their lives by lack of continuity in their plans and in their purpose.

They seldom seem to have a fixed idea of what they really want. They change their plans or their occupations at a moment's notice, and unless they chance to be very happily married, they are just as uncertain in marriage.

They are the most difficult of all classes to understand. In temperament they are hot and cold in the same moment, they may love passionately with one side of their nature and just as quickly dislike with the other.

In all business dealings or affairs where a subtle, keen mentality is useful, they can out-distance all rivals.

If taken as they are and with their moods, they are the most delightful people imaginable, but one must never expect them to be the same today that they were yesterday.

THE MOUNT OF MERCURY (NEGATIVE)

This Mount may be considered negative when the persons are born between August 21st to September 20th, and until the 27th but these last seven days of this period are not so marked, but take more from the characteristics of the incoming sign.

People belonging to this negative type of the Mount of Mercury have all the good points of the positive class, and even some added in their favour. For example, they stick longer and with more continuity to whatever study or career they adopt.

They are also more materialistic and practical in their views of life.

Women born in this period are especially curious puzzles. They are either extremely virtuous or the direct opposite, either extremely truthful and conventional or the reverse; but whether good or bad, they are all a law unto themselves, and in all things they usually think of themselves first.

Again, as in the positive type, it is the Line of

Head that must be carefully considered if one should endeavour to form an estimate of what they will eventually become.

If it be clear and straight, their best qualities will, as a rule, come to their rescue; but if weak or poorly marked, it is more than likely, especially with this class, that the evil side of the nature will in the end predominate.

THE MOUNT OF THE MOON AND ITS MEANING

The Mount of the Moon, or as it is also called the Mount of Luna, is found on the base of the hand under the end of the Line of Head (Fig. 12).

This Mount relates to everything that has to do with the imaginative faculties, the emotional artistic temperament, romance, ideality, poetry, change of scenery, travel, and such like.

This Mount may be considered positive when it looks high or well-developed, and also when the subject is found to be born between the dates of June 21st to July 20th, and until July 27th.

People who belong to this positive class are gifted with strong imagination which tinges everything they do or say. They are intensely romantic, but idealistic in their desires, and have not that passionate or sensual nature that is given by the Mount of Venus on the opposite side of the palm.

As a rule they have the inventive faculties well

developed, and succeed in inventions and in all new ideas in whatever careers they may have entered.

People born in this period are seldom hidebound by any rule of thumb or set convention. They love what is new in everything, and perhaps for this reason they love travel and change.

They should, if possible, avoid marrying early in life unless they are absolutely sure they have met their affinity.

THE MOUNT OF THE MOON (NEGATIVE)

This Mount is considerd negative when it appears very flat on the hand, and it may also be taken as negative when people are found to be born between the dates of January 21st and February 20th, and in a minor degree, until about February 27th.

People born between these dates have good mental powers, but their imaginative faculties are seldom as much in evidence as is so strongly the case with the positive period.

They are high-minded and have very decided views on love, duty and social life. They make great efforts to do good to others, but as a rule their best work is done towards helping the masses more than individuals.

They are strongly inclined to be religious and generally bring their religious views into all they do.

The portion of the palm under the base of the Thumb and Line of Life is called the Mount of Venus (Fig. 12).

When well-formed and not too large, it denotes a desire for love and companionship, the desire to please, worship of beauty in every form, the artistic and emotional temperament, and it is usually very prominent in the hands of all artists, singers and musicians.

This Mount is called Positive when high or large, and Negative when small or flat.

With the rest of the hand normal, this Mount well shaped is an excellent sign to have, as it denotes magnetism and attraction of one sex to the other, but if found together with vicious or abnormal signs in the hand, it increases those tendencies.

When considered with the birth date it helps to throw considerable light on characteristics that might otherwise be overlooked.

The student may consider it Positive when the subject is born between April 20th and May 20th, and in a minor way until May 27th, the chief characteristics of this period being as follows.

These persons have a curious dominating power over others, and are found rather inclined to be too dogmatic in their opinions, but the strange thing is that when they love they become the most abject slaves of all to the object of their devotion.

115

They are hospitable and generous, and especially love to entertain their friends.

They dress with great taste, are impulsive in their likes and dislikes, rather too frank and outspoken quick in temper.

Their passion or temper is, however, quickly over. They are so independent in character that, especially if they marry early and find their mistake, they lead unconventional lives and get severely criticised in consequence.

THE MOUNT OF VENUS (NEGATIVE)

This Mount may be considered Negative when the subject is born between the dates of September 21st to October 20th, and in a minor way until October 27th, and with people born in this period it is seldom found so prominent. The fact is, that the affections these subjects possess may be just as intense as those of the positive type, but their love is spiritual rather than sensual.

All mental characteristics rule, however, very strongly. Those born in this latter period have keen intuition and a mental balance of all things not given to the other class. They have presentiments and psychic experiences which they often spoil by their reasoning faculties.

In love they are nearly always unhappy. They cannot "let themselves go", like the Positive Venus type. They hesitate and miss their opportunities whilst they think or reason.

They make excellent doctors, judges, lawyers, but are more concerned with being master of some particular branch than with seeking worldly advantage.

17

THE HANDS OF NATIONS

THAT different types of faces and bodies are characteristic of different nations is a well-known fact. There is a familiar statement which I would quote here: 'The law which rounds a dewdrop shapes a world', Therefore, if certain laws produce different types in different races they also produce different shapes of hands and bodies as illustrative of the different characteristics. The intermingling and intermixing by marriage, etc., must naturally modify the pureness of the different types; but that it does not destroy the entire individuality cannot for a moment be doubted.

THE ELEMENTARY HAND

Starting with the elementary hand, it is rarely if ever found in its purity among civilised nations. We find this type among the primitive races in extremely cold latitudes, as, for instance, among the Esquimaux and the inhabitants of Iceland, Lapland, and the northern portion of Russia and Siberia.

Such people are phlegmatic and emotionless; even the nerve centres of the body are not in a high state of development, therefore they do not feel pain as keenly as the other types. They are more animal in their instincts and brutal in their desires; they are devoid of aspirations, and have only sufficient mentality to make them distinct from the brute creation. In a slightly more developed form the elementary hand is found in more southern and civilised nations.

THE SQUARE HAND AND THE NATIONS REPRESENTED BY IT

The square hand, generally speaking, is found among the Swedes, Danes, Germans, Dutch, English, and Scots. The chief characteristics which it denotes are love of method, logic, reason, respect for authority and law, and conformity to conventionality and custom. It shows an undemonstrative and more or less unemotional nature; it will follow life's beaten track with dogged stubbornness and tenacity of purpose, will build solid houses, railways, and Churches; will kneel at the shrine of the useful and will pay homage to the practical side of life.

THE PHILOSOPHIC

This is essentially the hand of the Oriental nations. In European countries, it is to this type or to the possessors of its modifications that we are indebted for the modernised principles of Buddhism, Theosophy, and all doctrines and ideas that tend in that direction. It is essentially the hand of the mystic or of the religious devotee. Individuals with these hands will endure any privation or self-denial in defence of the religion they follow. The world may call such people cranks; but the world crucified its Chirist, and mocked and persecuted its greatest teachers. Its opinion, therefore, should only affect the scales of dross, not the balance of thought.

THE CONIC

This type, properly speaking, is peculiar to the South of Europe, but by the intermingling of races it has been carried far and wide over the world. It is largely found among Greek, Italian, Spanish, French, and Irish races. The distinctive characteristics which it denotes are a purely emotional nature, impulse in thought and action, artistic feeling, impressionability and excitability. It has been designated 'The Hand of Impulse.' Such hands are not the hands of money-makers, like the square or the spatulate. They show a lack of practical business sense, but nature compensates their owners with the poetic, the visionary, and the romantic.

THE SPATULATE

With all the varieties of national types that have found their way at some time or another to America; with all the admixture of races found in that enormous continent, the spatulate hand is the type which has to a great extent swallowed up all the others. This hand, and . consequently, the characteristics that it represents, has to my mind played the important role in the history of that great country. As I may claim to be a cosmopolitan in every sense of the word, I can therefore take an unbiased stand-point in reading the character of nations as I would that of the individual. The spatulate hand, as I stated before, is the hand of energy, originality, and restlessness. It is the hand of the explorer and the discoverer, which terms can also be applied to discoveries in science, art, or mechanics. Spatulate hands are never conventional; they have little respect for law, less for authority. They are inventors, more from the quickness of their ideas than from the solidity of earnest work as exemplified by the square; they may utilise other men's ideas, but they will try to improve upon them; they love risk and speculation; they are versatile, and their chief fault is their changeability—they shift from one thing to another with the mood of the moment; they are fanatics in their fads, enigmas in their earnestness; but, even with such faults, it is to a people many-sided and many-talented like this that the world must look for her new ideas, for the inventions and discoveries in science, religion, or materialism which must in years to come work out the evolution of humanity.

THE PSYCHIC

This peculiar type is not confined to any particular country of kindred; it is evolved sometimes among the most practical, sometimes among the most enthusiastic. Yet is it neither practical nor enthusiastic in itself; it may be an evolution of all the types, reaching into that plane in which there may be seven senses instead of five. Certain it is that its owners are not of the earth, earthy, nor yet of heaven—for they are human; they make up no distinct community, but are found in all and of all. It may be that, as their beautiful hands are not formed for the rough usage of this world, so their thoughts are not suited to the material things of life. Their place may be in giving to mankind that which is but the reflection of mankind. Thus in the shadow may we find the substance and, in the speculation that this type gives rise to, may we find that wisdom which sees the fitness and the use of all things.

18

ON READING THE HAND

I HAVE gathered whatever information this book contains from, I may say, the four corners of the earth, and in presenting this information to those who desire to learn, I do so with the knowledge that I have proved whatever statements I make to be correct. The one point I would, however, earnestly desire to impress upon the student is the necessity for conscientious study and patience. As there are no two natures alike, so there are no two hands alike. To be able to read the hand is to be able to read the book of nature—there is no study more arduous, there is none more fascinating or that will repay the time and labour spent upon it with more interest.

To do this study justice, I cannot, and will not pretend, as do the generality of writers on this subject, that it is an easy matter, by following this, that, or the other map of the hand, or by taking some set rules as a guide, to be able to 'read the hand' without any exercise of the student's mentality. On the contrary, I shall show that every line, without exception, is modified by the particular type to which it belongs as, for instance, a sloping line of head on a square hand has a completely different meaning from the same sloping line on a conic, or philosophic type and so on. I have written this book with the object of making it not only interesting to the reader, but useful to the student. I have endeavoured to make every point as clear and concise as possible, but the student must bear in mind the enormous difficulties that lie in the way of making a clear explanation of every point in connection with such an intricate study.

The chief point of difference between my teachings and those of other writers lies in the fact that I class the various lines under different heads, treating of each particular point.

This will be found not only more easy and less puzzling for the student, but also more in accordance with reason. For instance, I hold that the line of life relates to all that affects life, to the influences which govern it, to its class as regards strength; to the natural length of life, and to the important changes of country and climate. I regard the line of head as related to all that affects mentality, and so on with every other line, as will be seen later. This plan I have found to be the most accurate, as well as the simplest, and more in accordance with those teachers whose ideas we have every reason to respect.

As regards dates, I depart from the usual formula, and instead advance a theory which has been considered 'at least interesting and reasonable,' in the dividing of the life into sevens, in accordance with the teachings of nature. I will illustrate this when I come to that portion of this work dealing with time and dates.

 **19**

THE LINES OF THE HEAD

THERE are seven important lines on the hand, and seven lesser lines (Fig. 13). The important lines are as follows:

The Line of Life, which embraces the Mount of Venus.

The Line of Head, which crosses the centre of the hand.

The Line of Heart, which runs parallel to that of the head, at the base of the fingers.

The Girdle of Venus, found above the line of heart and generally encircling the Mounts of Saturn and the Sun.

The Line of Health, which runs from the Mount of Mercury down the hand.

The Line of Sun, which rises generally on the Plain of Mars and ascends the hand to the Mount of the Sun.

The Line of Fate, which occupies the centre of the hand, from the wrist to the Mount of Saturn.

The seven lesser lines on the hand are as follows:

The Line of Mars, which rises on the Mount of

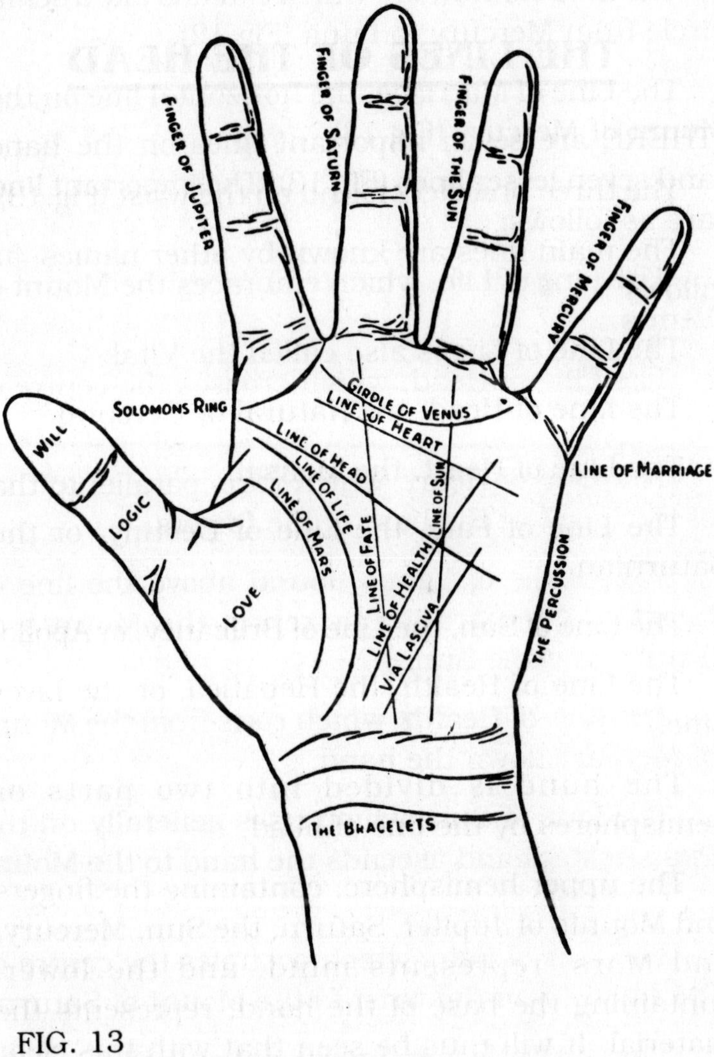
FINGER OF JUPITER
FINGER OF SATURN
FINGER OF THE SUN
FINGER OF MERCURY
SOLOMONS RING
GIRDLE OF VENUS
LINE OF HEART
LINE OF HEAD
LINE OF LIFE
LINE OF MARS
LINE OF MARRIAGE
WILL
LOGIC
LOVE
LINE OF FATE
LINE OF SUN
LINE OF HEALTH
VIA LASCIVA
THE PERCUSSION
THE BRACELETS

FIG. 13

THE MAP OF THE HAND

Mars and lies within the Line of Life (Fig. 13).

The *Via Lasciva*, which lies parallel to the line of health (Fig. 13).

The Line of Intuition, which extends like a semicircle from Mercury to Luna (Fig. 12).

The Line of Marriage, the horizontal line on the Mount of Mercury (Fig. 13),

The three bracelets found on the wrist (Fig. 13).

The main lines are known by other names, as follows:

The Line of Life is also called the Vital.

The Line of Head, the Natural or Cerebral.

The Line of Heart, the Mensal.

The Line of Fate, the Line of Destiny, or the Saturnian.

The Line of Sun, the Line of Brilliancy, or Apollo.

The Line of Health, the Hepatica, or the Liver Line.

The hand is divided into two parts or hemispheres by the line of head.

The upper hemisphere, containing the fingers and Mounts of Jupiter, Saturn, the Sun, Mercury, and Mars, represents mind, and the lower, containing the base of the hand, represents the material. It will thus be seen that with this clear point as a guide the student will gain an insight at once into the character of the subject under examination. This division has hitherto been ignored, but it is almost infallible in its accuracy; as, for example, when the predisposition is toward crime the line of head rises into the abnormal position shown by Plate XIII which, taken from life, is one instance in the thousands that can be had of the accuracy of this statement.

20

IN RELATION TO THE LINES

THE rules in relation to the lines are, in the first place, that they should be clear and well marked, neither broad nor pale in colour; that they should be free from all breaks, islands, or irregularities of any kind.

Lines very pale in colour indicate, in the first place, want of robust health, and, in the second, lack of energy and decision.

Lines red in colour indicate the sanguine, hopeful disposition; they show an active, robust temperament.

Yellow lines, as well as being indicative of biliousness and liver trouble, are indicators of a nature self-contained, reserved, and proud.

Lines very dark in colour, almost black, tell of a melancholy, grave temperament, and also indicate a haughty, distant nature, one usually very revengeful and unforgiving.

Lines may appear, diminish, or fade, which must always be borne in mind when reading the hand. *The province of the palmist, therefore is to warn the subject of approaching danger by pointing out the evil tendencies of his nature. It is purely a matter of the subject's will whether or not he will*

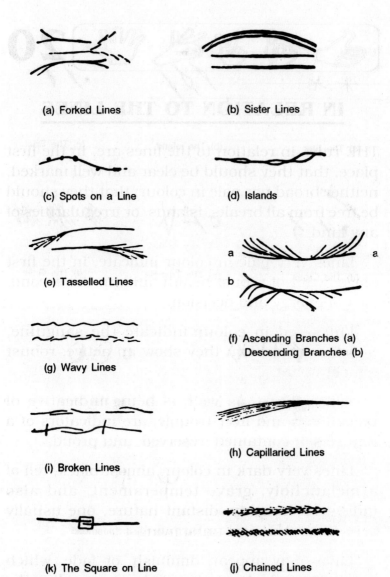

(a) Forked Lines

(b) Sister Lines

(c) Spots on a Line

(d) Islands

(e) Tasselled Lines

a   a

b

(f) Ascending Branches (a)
Descending Branches (b)

(g) Wavy Lines

(h) Capillaried Lines

(i) Broken Lines

(k) The Square on Line

(j) Chained Lines

FIG. 14
LINE FORMATIONS

129

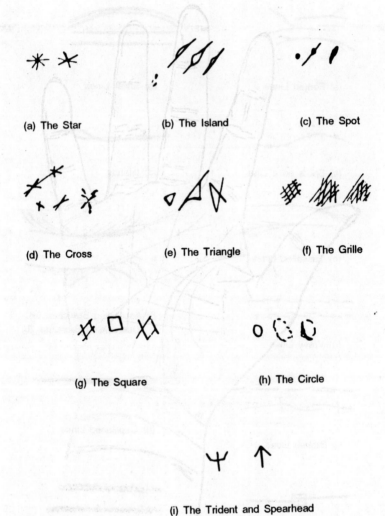

(a) The Star

(b) The Island

(c) The Spot

(d) The Cross

(e) The Triangle

(f) The Grille

(g) The Square

(h) The Circle

(i) The Trident and Spearhead

FIG. 15

SIGNS FOUND IN THE HAND

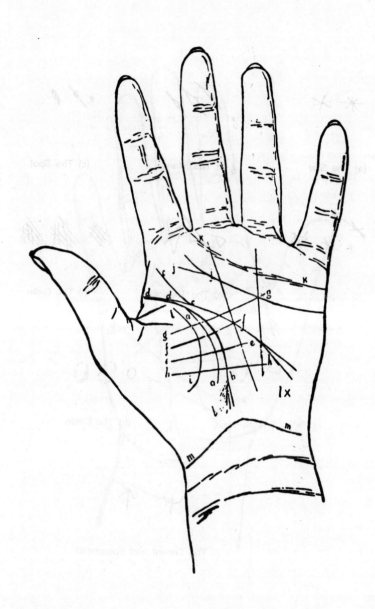

FIG. 16

MODIFICATIONS OF THE PRINCIPAL LINES

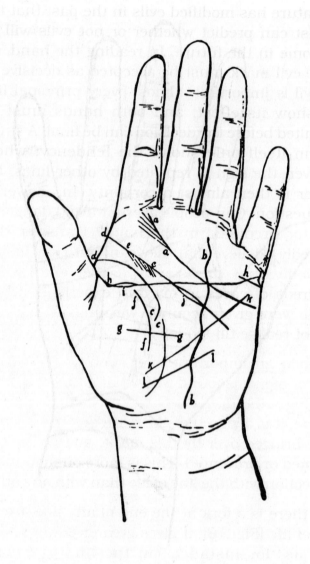

FIG. 17

MODIFICATIONS OF THE PRINCIPAL LINES

overcome these tendencies, and it is by seeing how the nature has modified evils in the past that the palmist can predict whether or not evils will be overcome in the future. In reading the hand, no *single* evil mark must be accepted as decisive. If the evil is important, almost every principal line will show its effect, and both hands must be consulted before the decision can be final. A single sign in itself only shows the tendency; when, however, the sign is repeated by other lines, the danger is then almost a certainty. In answer to the question, Can people avert or avoid danger or disaster predicted in the hand? I answer that decidedly I believe that they can; but I say just as decidedly that they rarely if ever do. I know hundreds of cases in my own experience where people were given accurate warnings which they did not realise till too late.

When an important line, such as the line of head or of life, is found with what is called a sister line (Fig. 16, *a-a*), namely, a fine line running by its side, it is a sign that the main line will be, as it were, bridged over by this mark, and the danger lessened or prevented. This is more often found in connection with the line of life than with any other.

If there is a fork at the end of any line, except that of life (Fig. 16), it gives greater power to that line; as, for instance, on the line of head it increases the mentality, but makes more or less of a double nature.

When however, the line ends in a tassel (Fig. 16,*b-b*), it is a sign of weakness and destruction to any line of which it forms part, particularly at the end of the line of life, where it denotes weakness and the dissipation of all the nerve qualities.

Branches rising from any line (Fig. 14, *a-a*) accentuate its power and strength, but all branches descending denote the reverse.

At the commencement of the line of heart, these lines are most important when considering the success of marriage for the subject; the ascending lines at this point indicate vigour and warmth of the affections (Fig. 17,*a-a*); the descending, the opposite.

On the line of head ascending branches denote cleverness and ambitious talent (Fig.16,*c-c*), and on the line of fate they show success in all undertakings made at that particular point.

A chained formation in any line is a weak sign (Fig.14): if on the line of heart it denotes weakness and changeability of affection; if on the line of head, want of fixity of ideas, and weakness of intellect.

Breaks in any line denote its failure (Fig. 17, *c-c*).

A wavy formation weakens the power of the line (Fig. 17, *b-b*).

Capillary lines are those little hair-lines running

by the side of the main line, sometimes joining it, sometimes falling from it; they denote weakness, like the chained formation (Fig. 14, *h*).

When the entire hand covered with a network or multitude of little lines running aimlessly in all directions, it betrays mental worry, a highly nervous temperament, and a troubled nature.

As the little grains make mountains, so do these little points make this study great. I therefore recommend their close consideration.

 **21**

THE RIGHT AND LEFT HANDS

The difference between the right and left hands is another important point to be considered. The most casual observer, looking at even a limited number of hands is generally struck by the marked difference which as a rule exists in the shape and position of the lines in the right and left hands of the same person.

This is an important point to be observed by the student. In practive, my rule is to examine both hands, but to depend more upon the information given by the right then that given by the left. There is a well-known old saying on this point. "The left is the hand we are born with; the right is the hand we make.' This is the correct principle to follow, the left hand indicating the natural character, and the right showing the training, experience, and the surroundings brought to bear on the life of the subject. The old idea of reading the left hand simply because it is nearest to the heart belongs to the many superstitions which degtraded the science in the Middle Ages. The heart at that time was regarded as the supreme organ-hence this medieval superstition. If, however, we examine this study from a logical and scientific standpoint, we find that the greater use of the right hand for long generations has placed it, as regards both nerves and muscles, in a more perfect state of development than the left. It is usually exercised in carrying out the thoughts of the brain, being, as it were, the more active servant of the mind. If, therefore, as has been demonstrated, the human body passes through a process of slow and steady development, and every change it undergoes affects and marks its effect upon the entire system, if follows that it is more logical and reasonable to examine the right hand for those changes which even at that moment are taking place, and upon which the development of the future depends.

My advice, therefore, is place both hands side by side, examine them, and see what the nature has been, see what it si find the reason by your examination for this or that change; and in forecasting what willb be, depend upon the development of the lines in the right hand.

It is very interesting to note that left-handed people have the lines more clearly marked on the left hand, and vice versa. Some people change so completely that hardly two lines are alike on both hands again, some change so slightly that the difference in the lines is barely perceptible. The general rule to follow is, that when a marked difference is shhown by bothe hands the subject has had a more interesting, eventful life than the person with both alike. The more interesting details as to a subject's past life, and even the very changes

in his method of work and ideas, can be brought
to light by a careful examination conducted in this
way.

 **22**

THE LINE OF LIFE

What we know as life is but existnce.

A waiting -place, a haven by the sea,

A little space amit immeasured distance,

A glimpse, a vista, of that life to be.

CHEIRO.

AS I remarked earlier, as there came to be recognised a natural position on the face fo9r the nose, eyes, etc., so also on the nand there came ot be recogniised a natural position for the line of life.

the line of head, and every other mark that the hand possesses.Thus, if the lines take abnormal courses it is only reasonable that abnormal characteristics are to be expected. and if so as regards temperament, why not in relation to health?

The line of life (Fig. 13). is theline which, rising under the Mount of Jupiter, goes down the hand and embraces the Mount of Venus, On it is marked time, also illness and death, and events foreshadowed by the other important lines are verified.

The line of life should be lon, narrow, and deep. without irregularities, breaks, or crosses of any kind. Such a formation promises long life, good health, and vitality.

When the line is linked (Fig.14,)or made up of little pieces like a chain, it is a sign of bad health, and particularly so on s soft hand, When the line recovers its evenness and continuity, health also is regained.

When broken in the left hand and joined in the right, it threatens some dangerous illness; bit if broken in both hands it could signify death. This is more decidedly confirmed when one branch turns back on the Mount of Venus (Fig. 17, *c-c*).

When the line starts from the base of the Mount of Jupiter, instead of the side of the hand, it denotes that from the earliest the life has been one of ambition.

When the line is chained at the commencement under Jupiter, bad health in early life is foreshadowed.

When the line is closely connected with that of the head, life is guided by reason and intelligence, but the subject is extremely sensitive about everything which affects self, and more or less cautious in enterprises for sell (Fig. 16,d-d).

When there is a medium space between the line of life and that of head, the subject is more free to carry out his plans and ideas; it also denotes energy

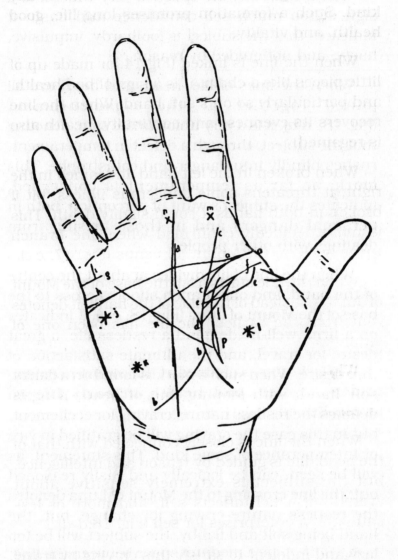

FIG. 18

MODIFICATIONS OF THE PRINCIPAL LINES

141

and a very go-ahead spirit (Fig. 17, *d-d*).

When, however, the space is very wide, it is a sign of too much self-confidence and dash; it indicates that the subjcet is foolhardy, impulsive, hasty, and not guided by reason.

When the lines of life, head, and heart are all joined together at the commencement (Fig. 18, *a-a*), it is a very unfortunate sign, denoting that the subject, through a defect in temperament, rushes blindly into danger and catastrophe. This mark, as far as temperament is concerned, indicates the subject's want of perception, both in personal dangers and in those arising from dealings with other people.

When the line of life divides at about the centre of the hand, and one branch shoots across to the base of the Mount of Luna (Fig. 18, *e-e*), it indicates on a firm, well-made hand a restless life, a great desire for travel, and the ultimate satisfaction of that desire, When such a mark is found on a flabby, soft hand, with sloping line of head, it again denotes the restless nature, craving for eccitement, but in this case the craving will be gratified in vice or intemperance of some kind. This statement, as will be seen, can be logically and easily reasoned out; the line crossing to the Mount of Luna denotes the restless nature craving for change, but, the hand being soft and flabby, the subject will be too lazy and indolent to satisfy this craving by travel, and the sloping line of head in this case showing a

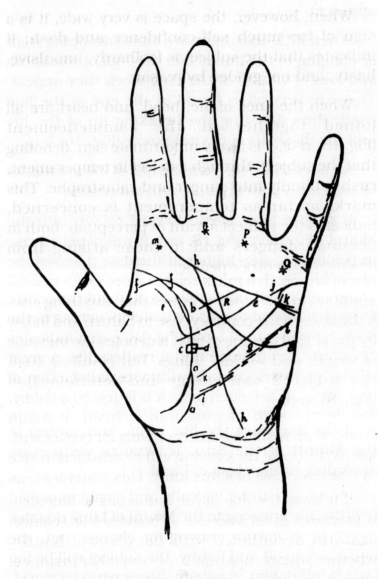

FIG. 19

MODIFICATION OF THE PRINCIPAL LINES

143

weak nature, the reason for this statement is apparent.

When little hair-lines are found dropping from or clinging to the line of life, they tell of weakness and loss of vitality at the date when they appear. They are very often found at the end of the line itself, thus denoting the breaking up of the life and the dissipation of vital power (Fig. 16, b-b).

All lines that rise from the line of life are marks of increased power, gains, and successes,

If such a line ascend toward or run into the Mount of Jupiter (Fig. 18, c-c), it will denote a rise in position or step higher at the date it leaves the line of life. Such a mark relates more to successful ambition in the sense of power than anything else. If the line, on the contrary, rise to Saturn and follow by the side of the line of fate, it denotes the increase of wealth and worldly things, but resulting from the subject's own energy and determination (Fig. 18, a-a).

If the line leave the line of life and ascend to the Mount of the Sun, if denotes distinction according to the class of hand.

If it leave the line of life and cross to Mercury, it promises great success in business or science, again in accordance with the class of hand— whether square, spatulate, or conic. For instance, such a line of the square would indicate success in business or science; on the spatulate, in invention or discovery; and on the conic it would foretell success in money matters, reached by the impulsive action of such a nature, as in sudden speculation or enterprise.

When the line of life divides toward the end and a wide space is shown between the lines, it is an indication that the subject will most probably end his life in a country different from that if his birth, or at least that there will be some great change from the place of birth to the place of death (Fg. 19, *a-a*).

An island on the line of life means an illness or loss of health while the island lasts (Fig.19, *b*), but a clearly formed island at the commencement of the line of life denotes some mystery connected with the subject's birth.

The line running through a square (Fig. 19, *c*), indicates preservation from death, from bad health when it surrounds an island, from sudden death when the life-line running through is broken, and from accident when a little line cutting the life-line rises from the Plain of Mars (Fig. 19, *d*).

A square, whenever found on the line of life, is a mark of preservation.

Of the great attendant line (Fig. 13) found parallel to and within the line of life, otherwise called the line of Mars, I shall speak later. This attendant line, the line of Mars, which rises on the mount of Mars, must not be confounded with those springing from the line of life itself, nor with

145

those that rise upon the Mount of Venus. The simplest rule to bear in mind is, that all even, well-formed lines following the line of life indicate favourable influences over the life (Fig. 17, *f-f*), but that all those rising in the opposite direction and cutting the life-line show worries and obstacles, caused by the opposition and interference of others (Fig. 17, *g-g*). Where these lines end and how they terminate is, therefore, an important point in this study.

When they cut the line of life only (Fig. 17, *g-g*), they denote the interference of relatives—generally in the home life.

When they cross the life-line and attack the line of fate (Fig. 16, *e-e*), they denote people who will oppose us in business or worldly interests, and where they cut the fate-line the point of junction gives the date.

When they reach and cut the line of heart (Fig. *16, g-g*), they denote interference in our closest affections, and here the date of such interference is given where the line cuts the life-line, and not where it touches the line of heart.

When they cut and break the line of sun (Fig. 16, *h-h*), they denote that others will interfere and spoil our position in life, and that the mischief will be causesd by scandal or disgrace at the point of junction.

When the line crosses the hand and touches

146

the line of marriage (Fig. 17, *h-h*), it signifies divorce, and will occur to the person on whose hand it appears.

When this crossing-line has in itself a mark like an island or any approach to it, it denotes that the person who will cause the trouble has had either scandal or some such trouble in connection with his or her own life, (Fig. 17, *f-f*).

I draw special attention to this system, as it prevails among the Hindus, and dating back to time immemorial. The following points have been obtained by close study of the precepts and their practical application by the Hindus themselves, and not a few of them have been translated almost verbatim from the quaint leaves of that ancient work before mentioned. When minuteness of detail is required, the remarkable accuracy of this system makes it especially valuable.

I will give the leading points only, as the subject is well-nigh inexhaustible.

In the first place, if the ray-line rise on the Mount of Mars (Fig. 18, *e-e*). and lower down touch or attack the life-line in any way, it denotes on a woman's hand some unfavourable attachment in her early life which will cause her much trouble and annoyance.

If the same line, however, send only offshoots or rays to the line of life (Fig. 18, *f-f*), it denotes a similar influence, but one that will continue to persecute her at different intervals. Again, such a line on a woman's hand is illustrative of the nature of the man who influences her, as denoting a fiery, passionate, animal temperament.

If, however, the ray-line should rise by the side of the line of life and travel by the side of it (Fig. 17, *f-f*), it shows, on the woman's hand, that the man who enters into her life has the gentler nature, and that she will strongly influence him.

If the ray-line, rising at any point, in travelling with the life-line, retreats farther in on the Mount of Venus, thus away from the life, it indicates that the person with whom the woman is connected will more and more lose sympathy with her, and will eventually drift out of her life altogether (Fig. 16, *i-i*).

When the ray-line, however, runs into an island or becomes one itself, it foretells that the influence over her life will run into disgrace, and that something scandalous will result.

When the attendant line fades out by the side of the life-line, but renews itself later, it tells that the person influencing the life will cease his influence at that particular point, but that it will be renewed again.

When the line of influence fades altogether, total separation—possibly death—will be the result of such companionship.

When one of these attendant lines joins a cross-line and runs over the hand with it, it foretells that through the instrumentality of another the affection of the person influencing the life will change to hate, and that this will cause injury at whatever point it touch the life, the fate, the head, or the line of heart (Fig. 19, *e-e*).

The farther the ray-lines lie from the line of life, the farther removed from our lives will those influences be. But, as before remarked, one could easily fill a volume on these lines and cross-lines, which with the Hindus are the foundation for all systems connected with palmistry.

By this system alone, then, it is reasonable to assume that the student can predict marriages by considering the relation which these lines bear to the life-line. We will again refer to this point when we consider the question of marriage.

Another interesting phase of this subject is the consideration of the number of these lines of influence (it being remembered that only those near the line of life are important). Numerous lines indicate a nature dependent upon affection. Such people are what is called passionate in their disposition; they may have many *liaisons*, but in their eyes love redeems all. On the other hand, the full, smooth Mount of Venus indicates that the individual is less affected by those with whom he is associated.

When the line of life sweeps far out into the hand, thus, allowing the Mount of Venus a greater scope, it is in itself a sign of good physical strength and long life.

When, on the contrary, it lies very close to the Mount of Venus, health is not so robust or the body physically so well built. The shorter the line the shorter the life.

That the line of life does not always show the exact age at which death takes place I am quite convinced. This line merely denotes the natural term of the subjcet's life apart from accidental influence. Catastrophes indicated by other lines of the hand may cut short a life that would otherwise be long. I may, however, here remark that, when it is of equal strength with that of life, where these lines meet willl be the point of death, even hand may cut short a life that would otherwise be long. Such may be caused by whatever disease is indicated by the health-line, and the province and one of the many uses of this study is to find out and warn the subject of that germ of disease which is even then the enemy of the system.

In addition to the information I have given here concerning islands, squares, etc., I refer the student back to Chapter 19, which treats of them more fully. As regards time and the calculation of events, a special chapter will be devoted to these subjects.

23

THE LINE OF MARS

THE line of Mars (Fig. 13) is otherwise known as the inner vital or inner life-line. It rises on the Mount of Mars, and sweeps down by the side of the line of life, but is distinct in every way from those faint lines known as the attendant lines, of which I spoke a little earlier.

The general characteristic of the line of Mars is that it denotes excess of health on all square or broad hands; to a man of this type it gives a martial nature, rather a fighting disposition, and robust strength. It also denotes that while it runs close to the life-life the individual will be engaged in many quarrels, and will be subject to a great deal of annoyance which will bring all his martial or fighting qualities into play. It is always an excellent sign on the hand of a soldier.

When a branch shoots from this line out to the Mount of Luna (Fig. 20, *b-b*), it tells that there is a terrible tendency toward intemperance of every kind, through the very robustness of the nature, and the craving for excitement that it gives.

The other type of the line of Mars is found on the long, narrow hand, and here it is generally by the side of a delicate, fragile line of life. Its characteristics in such a hand are that it supports the life-line, carrying it past any dengerous breaks, and giving vitality to the nature.

A broken line of life with such a line beside it will, at the point of the break, indicate closeness to death but helped by this mark the subject will recover, through the great vitality given by the line of Mars.

24

THE LINE OF HEAD

'To know is power'—let us then be wise,
*   And use our brains with every good intent*
That at the end we come with tired eyes
*   And give to Nature more than what she lent.*

CHEIRO.

THE line of head (Fig. 13) relates principally to the mentality of the subject—to the intellectual strength or weakness, to the temperament in its relation to talent, and to the direction and quality of the talent itself.

It if of extreme importance in connection with this line that the peculiarities of the various types be borne in mind; as, for instance, a sloping line of head on a psychic or conic hand is not of half the importance of a sloping line on a square hand. We will, however, take general characteristics first, and proceed to consider variations afterward.

The line of head can rise from three different points—from the centre of the Mount of Jupiter, from the commencement of the line of life, or from the Mount of Mars, within the life-line.

Rising from Jupiter (Fig. 20, *c-c*) and yet touching the line of life, it is, if a long line of head, the most powerful of all. Such a subject will have talent, energy, and daring determination of purpose, with boundless ambition combined with reason. Such a man will control others, yet not seem to control them; he will have caution even in most daring designs; he takes pride in his management of people or things, and is strong in rule, but just in the administration of power.

There is a variation of this which is almost equally strong. This again rises on Jupiter, but is slightly separated from the line of life. Such a type will have the characteristics of the first, but with less control and diplomacy. He will be hasty in decision, impetuous in action. As a leader in a crisis such a man would find his greatest opportunity. When, however, the space is very wide, the subject will be foolhardy, egotistical, and will rush blindly into danger.

The line of head from the commencement of the line of life, and connected with it (Fig. 16, *d-d*), indicates a sensitive and more nervous temperament; it denotes excess of caution; even clever people with this mark rein themselves down too tightly.

The line of head rising from the Mount of Mars, within the life-line (Fig. 19, *f-f*), is not such a favourable sign, it being the extreme on the inside of the life-line, as the wide-spaced head-line is the extreme on the outside. This indicates a fretful, worrying temperament, inconstant in thought, inconstant in action; the shifting sands of the sea are more steadfast than are the ideas of such an

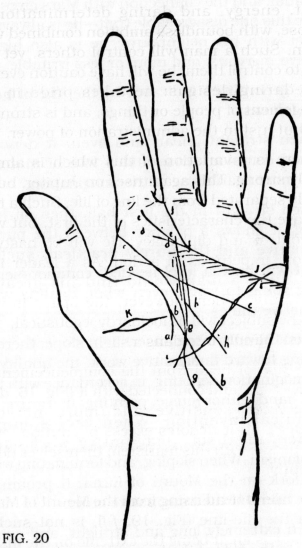

FIG. 20

MODIFICATIONS OF THE PRINCIPAL LINES

155

individual, and the connection with Mars gives his nature this one disagreeable trait—he is always in conflict with his neighbours; he is also highly sensitive, nervous, and more or less irritable.

The generalities indicated by the line of head are as follows:

When straight, clear, and even, it denotes practical common sense and a love of material things more than those of the imagination.

When straight in the first half, then slightly sloping, it shows a balance between the purely imaginative and the purely practical; such a subject will have a level-headed, common-sense way of going to work, even when dealing with imaginative things.

When the entire line has a slight slope, there is a leaning toward imaginative work, the quality of such imagination denoting, in accordance with the type of hand, either music, painting, literature, or mechanical invention. When very sloping, romance, idealism, imaginative work, and Bohemianism. When sloping, and terminating with a fine fork on the Mount of Luna, it promises literary talent of the imaginative order.

When extremely long and straight, and going directly to the side of the hand (the percussion), it usually denotes that the subject has more than ordinary intellectual power, but is inclined to be selfish in the use of that power.

When this line lies straight across the hand and slightly curves upward on Mars (Fig, 19, *g-g*), the subject will win unusual success in a business life; such a man will have a keen sense of the value of money—it will accumulate rapidly in his hands. Such a sign, however, denotes the taskmaster of life—the Pharaoh who expects his work-people to make bricks without straw.

When the line is short, barely reaching the middle of the hand, it tells of a nature that is thoroughly material. Such a man will utterly lack all the imaginative faculties, although in things practical he will be quite at home.

When linked, or made up of little pieces like a chain, it denotes want of fixity of ideas, and indecision.

When full of little islands and hair-lines, it tells of great pain to the head and danger of brain disease.

When the line of head is so high on the hand that the space is extremely narrow between it and the line of heart, the head will completely rule the heart, if that line be the strongest, and vice versa.

If the line should turn at the end, or if, in its course down the hand, it sends an offshoot or branch to any particular mount, by so doing it partakes of the qualities of the mount.

Toward the Mount of Luna, imagination, mysticism, and a leaning toward occult things.

157

Toward Mercury, commerce or science.

Toward the Sun, the desire for notoriety.

Toward Saturn, music, religion, and depth of thought.

With a branch to Jupiter, pride and ambition for power.

If a branch from the line of head rises up and joins the line of heart, it foreshadows some great fascination, or affection, at which moment the subject will be blind to reason and danger.

A double line of head is very rarely found, but when found it is a sure sign of brain power and mentality. Such people have a perfectly double nature—one side sensitive and gentle, the other confident, cold and cruel. They have enormous versatility, great command of language, a peculiar power for playing and toying with human nature, and generally great will and determination.

When the line of head is broken in two on both hands, it foretells some accident or violence to the head.

An island is a sign of weakness (Fig. 17, *j*). When clearly defined, if the line does not extend farther, the person may never recover.

If the line of head sends an offshoot to or runs into a star on the Mount of Jupiter, it is a sign of wonderful success in all things attempted.

When a number of little hair-lines branch

158

upward from the line of head to that of heart, the affections will be a matter of fascination, not of love.

When the line of head runs into or through a square, it indicates preservation from acccident or violence by the subject's own courage and presence of mind.

When there is a space found between the line of head and that of life, it is beneficial when not too wide; when medium, it denotes splendid energy and self-confidence, promptness of action and readiness of thought (Fig. 21, *f-f*). this is a useful sign for barristers actors, preachers, etc., but people with such a mark would do well to sleep on their decisions—they are inclined to be too hasty, self-confident, and impatient. When this space is extremely wide, it denotes foolhardiness, assurance, excessive effrontery, and self-confidence.

When the line of head, on the contrary, is very tightly connected with that of life, and low down in the hand, there is utter wnat of self-confidence. Such individuals suffer greatly from extreme sensitiveness, and the slightest thing will wound and grieve them.

25

THE LINE OF HEAD IN RELATION
TO THE SEVEN TYPES

THE general rules to be observed in connection with this most remarkable point are as follows:

The line of head is usually in accordance with the type of hand on which it is found—namely, practical on a practical type, imaginatives, on an artistic, and so on. It therefore follows that signs contrary to the nature are more important than characteristics indicated in accordance with it.

These peculiarities, it is therefore more reasonable to assume, relate to the development of the brain outside and beyond its natural characteristics. Such a divergence might be accounted for by the theory that the various tendencies of the brain reach their working point through a process of slow growth and development, similar to the evolutions of life itself. It therefore, follows that at the age of twenty there may be the commencement of a development which may alter the entire life at thirty; but as that change has already commenced in the brain, so must it affect the nerves and thus the hand. Thus a tendency toward a change of thought or action is indicated years before it takes place.

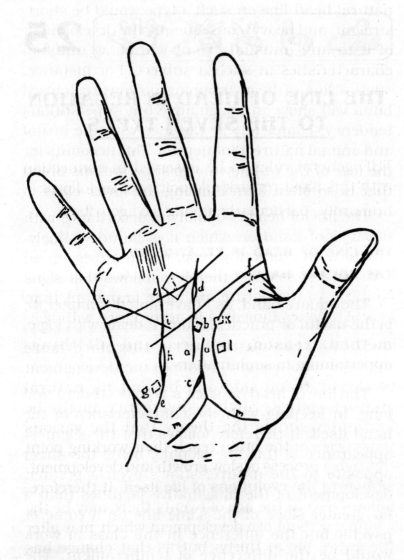

FIG. 21

MODIFICATIONS OF THE PRINCIPAL LINES

Starting with the elementary hand, or the nearest approach to it found in our country, the natural head-line on such a type would be short, straight, and heavy; consequently the development of it to any unusual extent will show unusual characteristics in such a subject. For instance, such a line of head dropping downward toward Luna will show an imaginative but superstitious tendency, completely at variance with the brutal and animal nature it influences. This accounts for the fear of the unknown, the superstitious dread that is so often found among the lower class of humanity, particularly among savage tribes.

THE LINE OF HEAD IN RELATION TO THE SQUARE HAND

The square hand, as I have stated (Chapter 4), is the useful or practical hand; it deals with logic, method, reason, science, and all things appertaining to such matters.

The line of head on such a type is straight and long, in keeping with the characteristics of the hand itself. It therefore follows that the slightest appearance of this line sloping, being the direct opposite to the nature, shows even a greater, development of the imaginative faculties than a far greater slope of the same line on a conic or psychic,but the difference in the class of work would be the difference of temperament. The square hand with the sloping head-line would start with a practical foundation for imaginative work, whereas the other would be purely inspirational and imaginative. This difference is extremely noticeable in the hands of writers, painters, musicians, etc.

THE LINE OF HEAD IN RELATION TO THE SPATULATE HAND

The Spatulate hand (Chapter 5) is the hand of action, invention, independence, and originality. The natural position for the line of head on this type is long, clear, and slightly sloping. When, therefore, on such a hand this sloping is accentuated, the result is that all these characteristics are doubled or strengthened; but when lying straight, the opposite of the type, the subject's practical ideas will keep the others so much in check that the plans of the imagination will not get scope for fulfilment, and, as far as the temperament is concerned, the nature will be restless, irritable, and dissatisfied.

THE LINE OF HEAD IN RELATION TO THE PHILOSOPHIC HAND

The philosophic hand (Chapter 6), is thoughtful, earnest in the pursuit of wisdom, but imaginative and rather eccentric in the application of ideas to everyday life. The natural position for the line of head on this type is long, closely connected with the line of life, set low down on the hand, and sloping. The unnatural type, or the man with the straight line of head on the philosophic hand, the line set high on the hand and straight, is critical, analytical, and cynical; he will pursue wisdom, and particularly the study of his fellow men, only to analyse their faults and failings, to expose their fads, fancies, and foibles; he will stand on the border-land of the mystic, to sneer at the unreal, to laugh in the face of the real; he will fear nothing, neither things spiritual nor things material; he can be imaginative or practical at will; a genius that discredits genius, a philosopher that disarms philosophy—such is the hand of a Carlye.

THE LINE OF HEAD IN RELATION
TO THE CONIC HAND

The conic hand (Chapter 7) belongs to the artistic, impulsive nature, the children of ideas, the lovers of sentiment.

In this type the natural position for the line of head is that which gradually slopes downward to the Mount of Luna, generally to the middle of it. This is the most characteristic, and gives the freedom of Beohemianism to these worshippers of the beautiful; here it is that we find the greatest leaning toward sentiment, romance, and ideality, in opposition to the practial qualities of the square type. These are, indeed, the luxurious children of the Sun, they have a keen appreciation for the things of art, but are often without the power to give expression to their artistic ideas. However, when the line of head is straight, in combination with such a nature, a very remarkable result follows. The subject with such a hand will make every use of his artistic ideas and talents, but in a practical direction; he will intuitively feel what the public demands; he will not care for art so much as for the money it brings; he will conquer the natural love of ease and luxury by strength of common sense and determination; where the man with the sloping head-line would paint one picture he will paint ten—and, furthermore, he will see them. Why? Because through his practical business sense he will know what the public wants, and as is the demand, so will be the supply.

THE LINE OF HEAD IN RELATION TO THE PSYCHIC HAND

The natural position for the line of head on this hand is extremely sloping, giving all the visionary, dreamy qualities in accordance with this type. It is one of the rarest things to find a straight line of head on such a hand, but when found it is generally on the right hand, the left being still very sloping. Such a formation denotes that by the pressure of circumstances the entire nature has undergone a change and has become more practical. This type, even with the straight line of head, can never be very material or business-like, but in matters of art the subject will have a very good chance, as the would have more opportunity to exercise his talents, yet even in art it would require the greatest tact and strongest encouragement to induce him to turn his talents to practical use.

By such illustrations the student will understand how to make every other modification in accordance with the type of hand. The modifications of the head-line are more important than any other marks that the hand possesses.

26

INSANITY AS SHOWN BY THE LINE OF HEAD

IT must be born in mind that any point that is beyond the normal is abnormal. When, therefore, the line of head sinks to an abnormal point on the Mount of Luna, the imagination of the subject is abnormal and unnatural. This will be more important in the elementary, square, spatulate, and philosophic, than in relation to the conic or psychic types. When the line of head, even on a child's hand, reaches this unnatural point, it may grow up to manhood or womanhood with perfect clearness and sanity of ideas, but mental shock or strain can throw the brain off its balance, and insanity may result.

The same development of the line of head, with an unusually high Mount of Saturn, will denote a mordidly imaginative nature from te very start (Plate XIV). Such a subject is gloomy, morose, and melancholy, and this tendency, even without cause, generally increases until the subject completely loses his mental balance.

Temporary insanity is shown by a narrow island in the centre of a sloping line of hed, but this mark generally indicates some brain-illness or temporary aberration.

The hand of the congenital idiot is remarkable for its very small, badly-developed thumb, and for a line of head sloping and made up of broad lines filled with a series of islands, like a chain.

I have further illustrated these remarks in Chapter 46, on various phases of insanity as shown by the hand.

MURDEROUS PROPENSITIES AS SHOWN BY THE LINE OF HEAD

The mere act of murder, such as one man killing another in the heat of passion, or in self-defence, is not shown by the hand except as a past event, and then only when it has deeply affectd a very sensitive nature; but if propensities for crime exist, the age at which they will reach their active or working point in the nature is decidedly shown, as I will proceed to demonstrate.

I have explained in the foregoing remarks that, when the line of head is abnormal in one direction, abnormal characteristics are the result, such as insanity, morbidness. and extreme melarncholy, which under certain conditions lead to self-murder. These, however, are abnormal characteristics denoted by the falling line. We will now consider the abnormalities indicated by the rising line of head.

It will be remembered that I have previously stated that the line of head divides the hand into two hemispheres—that of mind and that of matter;

and that if it be high on the hand, then the world of matter has greater scope, and the subject is more brutal and animal in his desires. This has been amply proved by the hands of those who have lived a life of crime, particularly if they have been murderous in their propensities (Plate XIII).

In such cases the line of head leaves its proper place on the hand and rises and takes possession of the line of heart, and sometimes even passes beyond it. Whether such people murder one or twenty is not the question. The point is that they have abnormal tendencies for crime; they stop at nothing in the accomplishment of their purpose, and under the slightest provocation or temptation they will gratify these strange and terrible propensities.

27

THE LINE OF HEART

... Keep still, my heart,
Nor ask for peace, when care may suit thee best,
Nor ask for love, nor joy, nor even rest,
But be content to love, whate'er betide,
And maybe love will bring thee to Love's side.

CHEIRO.

THE line of heart is naturally an important line in the study of the hand. Love, or the attraction of the sexes from natural causes, plays one of the most prominent parts in the drama of life, and as in the nature so in the hand. The line of heart, otherwise called the mensal (Fig. 13), is that line which runs across the upper portion of the hand at the base of the Mounts of Jupiter, Saturn, the Sun, and Mercury.

The line of heart should be deep, clear, and well coloured. It may rise from three important positions, as follows: the middle of the Mount of Jupiter, between the first and second fingers, and from the centre of the Mount of Saturn.

When it rises from the centre of Jupiter (Fig. 20, *d-d*), it gives the highest type of love—the pride and the worship of the heart's ideal. A man with such a formation is firm, strong, and reliable in his affections: he is as well ambitious that the woman of his choice shall be great, noble, and famous—such a man would never marry beneath his station, and will have far less love-affairs than the man with the line from Saturn.

Next we will consider the line rising from the Mount of Jupiter, even from the finger itself (Fig. 20, e-e). This denotes the excess of all the foregoing qualities: it gives the blind enthusiast, the man so carried away by his pride that he can see no faults, no failings in that being whom he so devotedly worships. Alas! such people are the sufferers in the world of affection: when their idols fall, as idols will sometimes, the shock to their pride is so great that they rarely if ever recover from its effects; but the shock, it must be remarked, is more to their own pride than to the mere fact that the idol they worshipped had feet of clay. Poor worshipper! when wilt thou see that, as with men, women are not perfect; they are but human, and being human they are more fitting than if they were divine. Why, then, place them so high that thay are the more likely to fall? Their place is by they side, the companion of thy humanity, the sister part of all thy faults.

The line rising between the first and second fingers gives a calm but deeper nature in matters of love (Fig. 20, f-f). Such individuals seem to rest between the ideality given by Jupiter and the passionate ardour given by Saturn. They are quieter and more subdued in their passions.

With the line of heart rising from Saturn, the

subject will have more passion in his attachments, and will be more or less selfish in satisfying his affections; in home life he is never so expressive or demonstrative as are those with the line from Jupiter. The excess of this is the same kind of line rising very high on the Mount, often from the very finger of Saturn. Such a subject is far more passionate and sensual than any of the others. It is generally admitted that very sensual people are very selfish—in this case they are extremely so.

When the line of heart is itself in excess, namely, lying right across the hand from side to side, an excess of affection is the result, and a terrible tendency toward jealousy; this is still more accentuated by a very long line of heart rising to the outside of the hand and reaching the base of the first finger.

When the line of heart is much fretted by a crowd of little lines rising into it, it tells of inconstancy, flirtations, a series of *amourettes*, but no lasting affection (Fig. 20).

A line of heart from Saturn, chained and broad, gives an utter contempt for the subject's opposite sex.

When the line of heart is bright red, it denotes great violence of passion.

When pale and broad, the subject is *blase* and indifferent.

When low down on the hand and thus close to

the line of head, the heart will always interfere with the affairs of the head.

When, however, it lies high on the hand, and the space is narrowed by the line of head being too close, the reverse is the case, and the head will so completely rule the affections that it gives a hard, cold nature, envious and uncharitable.

Breaks in the line tell of disappointment in affection—under Saturn, brought about by fatality; under the Sun, through pride; and under Mercury, through folly and caprice.

When the line of heart commences with a small fork on the Mount of Jupiter (Fig. 16, *j-j*), it is an unfailing sign of a true, honest nature and enthusiasm in love.

A very remarkable point is to notive whether the line of heart commences high or low on the hand. The first is the best, because it shows the happiest nature.

The line lying so low that it droops down toward the line of head is a sure sign of unhappiness in affections during the early portion of the life.

When the line of heart forks, with one branch resting on Jupiter, the other between the first and second fingers, it is a sign of a happy, tranquil nature good fortune, and happiness in affection; but when the fork is so wide that one branch rests on Jupiter, the other on Saturn, it then denotes a very uncertain disposition, and one that is not inclined to make the marital relations happy, through its erratic temperament in affection.

When the line is quite bare of branches and thin, it tells of coldness of heart and want of affection.

When bare and thin toward the percussion or side of the hand, it denotes sterility.

Fine lines rising up to the line of heart from the line of head, denote those who influence our thoughts in affairs of the heart, and by being crossed or uncrossed denote if the affection has brought trouble or has been smooth and fortunate.

When the lines of heart, head, and life are very much joined together, it is an evil sign; in all matters of affection such a subject would stick at nothing to obtain his or her desires.

A subject with no line of heart, or with very little, has not power of felling very deep affection. Such a person can, however, be very sensual, particularly if the hand is soft. On a hard hand such a mark will affect the subject less—he may not be sensual, but he will never feel very deep affection.

When, however, the line has been there, but has faded out, it is a sign that the subject has had such terrible disappointments in affection that he has become cold, heartless, and indifferent.

28

THE LINE OF FATE

.... And what is fate?
A perfect law that shapes all things for good;
And thus, that men may have a just reward
For doing what is right, not caring should
No earthly crown be theirs, but in accord
With what is true, and high, and great.
And in the end-the par! as to the whole
So shall all be; in the success of all
So shall all share; for the All-conscious Soul
Notes e'en the sparrow's feeble fall.
..........And such is fate.

CHEIRO.

THE line of fate (Fig. 13), otherwise called the line of destiny, or the Saturnian, is the centre upright line on the palm of the hand.

In the consideration of this line the type of hand plays an important part; for instance, the line of fate, even in the most successful hands, is less marked on the elementary, the square, and the spatulate, than on the philosophic, the conic, or the psychic. These upright lines are more in keeping with the latter hands, and are therefore less important on them; consequently if one sees, as one often will, an apparently very strong line of fate on a conic hand, one must remember that it has not half the importance of a similar line on a square type as far as worldly success is concerned. This point, I am sorry to say, has been completely overlooked by other writers, though it is one of the most significant in this study. It is useless simply to give a map of the hand without clearly explaining this point. The dewildered student sees this long line of fate marked as a sign of great fortune and success, and naturally concludes that a small line on the square hand means nothing, and that a long one on the conic or psychic means success, fame, and fortune, whereas it has not one quarter the importance of the small line shown on the square. I wish to emphasise this as so many students throw up Palmistry in despair through not having this point explained at the start.

The strange and mysterious thing to note is that the possessors of the philosophic, conic, and psychic hands which bear these heavily marked lines are more or less believers in fate, whereas the possessors of the square an spatulate rarely, if ever, believe in fate at all.

Before the student goes farther I would recommend him, once and for all, to settle this doctrine of fate, either for or against.

The line of fate, properly speaking, relates to all wordly affairs, to our success or failure, to the people who influence our career, whether such influences be beneficial or otherwise, to the barriers and obstacles in our way, and to the ultimate result of our career.

The line of fate may rise from the line of life, the wrist, the Mount of Luna, the line of head, or even the line of heart.

If the fate-line rise from the line of life and from that point on is strong, success and riches will be won by personal merit; but if the line be marked low down near the wrist and tied down, as it were, by the side of the life-line, it tells that the early portion of the subject's life will be sacrificed to the wishes of parents or relatives (Fig. 20, *g-g*).

When the line of fate rises from the wrist and proceeds straight up the hand to its destination on the Mount of Saturn, it is a sign of extreme good fortune and success:

Rising from the Mount of Luna, fate and success will be more or less dependent on the fancy and caprice of other people. This is very often found in the case of public favourites.

If the line of fate be straight and a branch run in and join it from the Mount of Luna, it is somewhat similar in its meaning in signifies that the strong influence of some other person, out of fancy, or caprice, will assist the subject in his or her career. On a women's hand, if this ray-line from Luna travel on afterward by the side of the line of fate, it denotes a wealthy marriage or influence which accompanies and assists her (Fig. 20, *h-h*).

If the line of fate in its course to the Mount of Saturn send offshoots to any other Mount, it denotes that the qualities of that particular Mount will dominate the life.

If the line of fate itself should go to any Mount or portion of the hand other than the Mount of Saturn, it foretells great success in that particular direction, according to the characteristics of the Mount.

If the line of fate ascend to the centre of the Mount of Jupiter, unusual distinction and power will come into the subject's life. It also relates to character. Such people are born to climb up higher than their fellows through their enormous energy, ambition, and determination.

If the line of fate should at any point throw a branch in that direction, namely, toward Jupiter, it shows more than usual success at that particular stage of life.

If the line of fate terminate by crossing its own mount and reaching Jupiter, success will be so great in the end that it will go far toward satisfying even the ambition of such a subject.

When the line runs beyond the palm, cutting into the finger of Saturn, it is not a good sign, as everything will go too far. For instance, if such an individual be a leader, his subjects will some day go beyond his wishes and power, and will most probably turn and attack their commander.

When the line of fate is abruptly stopped by the line of heart, success will be ruined through the affections; when, however, it joins the line of heart and they together ascend Jupiter, the subject will have his or her highest ambition gratified through the affections (Fig. 19, h-h).

When stopped by the line of head, it foretells that success will be thwarted by some stupidity, or blunder of the head.

If the line of fate does not rise until late in the Plain of Mars, it denotes a very difficult, hard, and troubled life; but if it goes on well up the hand, all difficulties will be surmounted, and once over the first half of the life all the rest will be smooth. Such success comes from the subject's own evergy, perseverance, and determination.

If the line of fate rise from the line of head, and that line be well marked, then success will be won late in life, after a hard struggle and through the subject's talents.

When it rises from the line of heart extremely late in life, after a difficult struggle success will be won.

When the line rises with one branch from the base of Luna, the other from Venus, the subject's destiny will sway between imagination on the one hand and love and passion on the other (Fig. 21, m-m).

When broken and irregular, the career will be uncertain; the ups and downs of success and failure full of light and shadow.

When there is a break in the line, it is a sure sign of misfortune and loss; but if the second portion of the line begin before the other leaves off, it denotes a complete change in life, and if very decided it will mean a change more in accordance with the subject's own wishes in the way of position and success (Fig. 22, a-a).

A double or sister fate-line is an excellent sign. It denotes two distinct careers which the subject will follow. This is much more important if they go to different Mounts.

A square on the line of fate protects the subject from loss through money, business, or financial matters. A square touching the line in the Plain of Mars (Fig. 21, b), foretells danger from accident in relation to home life if on the side of the fate-line next the line of life; from accident in travel if on the side of the fate-line next the Mount of Luna.

A cross is a sign of truble and follows the same rules as the square, but an island in the line of fate is a mark of misfortune, loss, and adversity (Fig. 21, d). It is sometimes marked with the line of influence from Luna, and in such a case means loss and misfortune caused by the influence, be it marriage or otherwise, which affects the life at that date (Fig. 21, c).

People without any sign of a line off fate are often vey successful, but they lead more a vegetable kind of existence. They eat, drink, and sleep, but I do not think we can really call them happy, for

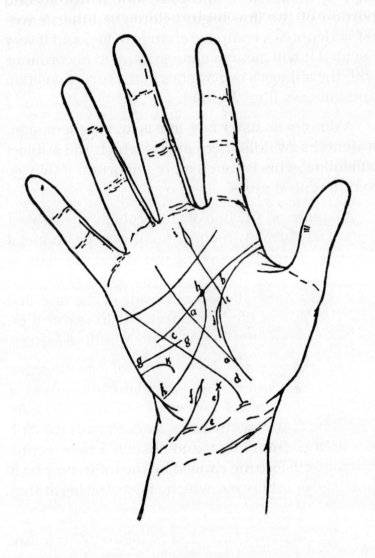

FIG. 22

MODIFICATIONS OF THE PRINCIPAL LINES

181

they cannot feel acutely, and to feel happiness we must also feel the reverse. Sunshine and shadow, smiles and tears comprise the sum total of our lives.

29

THE LINE OF SUN

And there are some who have success in wealth,
And some in war, and some again in peace,
And some who, gaining their success in health,
See other things decrease.
Man can't have all-The sun consumes itself
By burning in its lap more feeble stars.
And those who crave the Hindu idol's part
Oft crush their children' neath their gilded cars.

CHEIRO.

THE line of Sun (Fig. 13), otherwise called the line of Apollo, the line of brilliancy, or the line of success, must, like the line of fate, be considered with the type of hand on which it lies; for instance, it will be more heavily marked on the philosophic, conic, and spatulate, The same rule given in reference to the line of fate therefore applies to this.

I prefer in my work to call this the line of sun, as this name is more expressive and more clear in meaning. It increases the success given by a good line of fate, and gives fame and distinction to the life when it is in accordance with the work and career given by the other lines of the hand; otherwise it merely relates to a temperament that is keenly alive to the artistic, but unless the rest of the hand bears this out, the subject will have the appreciation of art without the power of expression.

The line of Sun may rise from the line of life, the Mount of Luna, the Plain of Mars, the line of head, or the line of heart.

Rising from the ine of life, with the rest of the hand artistic, it denotes that the life will be devoted to the worship of the beautiful. With the other lines good, it promises success in artistic pursuits.

Rising from the line of fate, it increases the success promised by the line of fate, and gives more distinction from whatever date it is marked—from that time things will greatly improve.

It is far more accurate and less misleading to class this line as relating to briliancy or success— as its name implies than to call it the line of Apollo or of art. It depends upon the talent shown by the line of head, and the class of hand itself, to determine in what way the success is shown, whether in art or in riches.

From the Mount of Luna it promises success and distinction, largely dependent upon the fancies and the help of others. In this case it is never a certain sign of success, being so influenced by the fortunes of those with whom we come in contact (Fig. 21, e-e).

With a sloping line of head, however, it is more inclined to denote success in poetry, literature, and things of the purely imaginative order.

Rising upon the Plain of Mars, it promises sunshine after tears, success after difficulty.

Rising from the line of head, there is no caprice of other people in connection with success, the talents of the subject alone being its factor, but not until the second half of life is reached.

Rising from the line of heart it merely denotes a great taste for art and artistic things, and looking at it from the purely practical standpoint it denotes more distinction and influence in the world at that last date in life.

If the third finger be nearly equal in length to the second, the finger of Saturn, a very long line of sun with such a formation makes the subject inclined to gamble with everything—the talents, the riches, and even the chances of life.

The chief peculiarity of this line is that it generally gives, when well marked, a great tendency toward sensitivenss, but when combined with an exceptionally straight line of head it denotes the love of attaining riches, social position, and power.

Many lines on the Mount of Sun show an extremely artistic nature, but multiplicity of ideas will interfere with all success. Sach subjects never have sufficient patience to win either fame or renown (Fig. 21).

A star on this line is perhaps the very finest

sign that can be found. Brilliant and lasting success is in such cases a certainty.

A square on the line of sun is a sign of preservation against the attacks of enemies in reference to one's name and position (Fig. 21, g).

An island on this line means loss of position and name for the length of time that the island lasts, and generally such will occur through scandal (Fig. 21, h),

On a hollow hand the line of Sun loses all power.

The complete absence of the line of sun on otherwise talented and artistic hand indicates that such people, though they may work hard, will find the recognition of the world difficult to gain. Such individuals, no matter how they may deserve honour and fame, will rarely achieve it.

30

THE LINE OF HEALTH, OR THE HEPATICA

Some flowers are bruised that they may be more sweet,
And some lie broken 'neath the rush of feet;
And some are worn awhile, then tossed aside;
Some grace the dead, while others deck the bride.
And so in life I' ve seen the saddest face,
The broken flower, give forth the sweetest grace.

CHEIRO.

THERE has been considerable discussion among writers as to the point where this line rises. My theory, and one which I have proved by watching the growth of this line on the hands of children and young people, is that it rises at the base, or on the face of the Mount of Mercury, and as it grows down the hand and into the line of life, so does it foreshadow the growth of the illness or germ of disease which at the time of its coming in contact with the line of life will reach its climax.

The hepatica (Fig. 13) should lie straight down the hand—the straighter the better.

It is an excellent sign to be without this line, Such absence denotes an extremely robust, healthy constitution. Its presence on the hand in any form indicates some delicate point to be guarded against.

When crossing the hand and touching the line of life at any point, it tells that there is some delicacy at work, undermining the health and constitution (Fig. 17, *k-k*).

When rising form the line of heart at the Mount of Mercury and running into or through the line of life, it foretells some weakness of the heart. If very pale in colour, and broad, it will be bad circulation.

If red in colour, particularly when it leaves the line of heart, with small, flat nails, it gives an indication of heart trouble.

When very red in small spots, it denotes a tendency in the system toward fever.

When twisted and irregular, biliousness and liver complaints.

When formed in little straight pieces, bad digestion (Fig. 19, *i-i*).

In little islands, with long, filbert nails, trouble to lungs and chest (Fig. 20, *i-i*).

The same mark, with the same kind of nail, but broad, throat trouble. (See 'Nails,' Chapter 14).

When heavily marked, joining the line of heart and head, and not found elsewhere, it threatens mental disturbance.

A straight line of hepatica lying down the hand may not give robust health, but it is a good mark because it gives a more wiry kind of health than one crossing the hand.

It will thus be seen that though the student can depend very largely upon the indications afforded him by the hepatica, yet he must look for other illnesses, and for confirmation of illnesses, to other portions of the hand, as, for instance, to the chained life-line for naturally delicate health, to the line of head for head troubles, and to the nails, which must always be noted in conjunction with the study of the hepatica.

THE VIA LASCIVA AND THE LINE OF INTUITION

THE *Via Lasciva*, otherwise called the sister health-line (Fig. 13), is not often found, and is generally confounded with the hepatica. It should run off the palm into the wrist. In such a position it gives action and force to the passions, but if running across the hand into the Mount of Venus it shortens the natural length of life by its excesses (Fig. 17, *l-l*).

THE LINE OF INTUITION

The line of intuition (Fig. 12) is more often found on the philosophic, the conic, and the psychic, than on any other of the seven types. Its position on the hand is almost that of a semicircle from the face of the Mount of Mercury to that of the Mount of Luna. It sometimes runs through or with the hepatica, but can be found clear and distinct even when the hepatica is marked. It denotes a purely impressionable nature, a person keenly sensitive to all surroundings and influences, an intuitional feeling of presentiment for others, strange vivid dreams and warnings which science has never been able to account for by that much-used word, 'coincidence.' It is found more on psychic hands than on any others.

THE GIRDLE OF VENUS, THE RING OF SATURN, AND THE THREE BRACELETS

THE Girdle of Venus (Fig. 13) is that broken or unbroken kind of semicircle rising between the first and second fingers and finishing between the third and fourth.

I must here state that I have never found this sign to indicate the sensuality so generally ascribed to it, except when found on a broad, thick hand. Its real domain is usually on such hands as the conic and psychic. A little study will prove that this mark is as a rule associated with highly sensitive intellectual natures, but natures changeable in moods, easily offended, and touchy over little things. It denotes a highly strung, nervous temperament, and when unbroken it certainly gives a most unhappy tendency toward hysteria and despondency.

People possessing this mark are capable of rising to the highest pitch of enthusiasm over anything that engages their fancy, but they are rarely twice in the same mood—one moment in the height of spirits, the next miserable and despondent.

When the girdle goes over the side of the hand and by so doing comes in contact with the line of marriage (Fig. 16, *k-k*), the happiness of the marriage will be marred through the peculiarities. of the temperament. Such subjects are peculiarly exacting, and hard to live with, If on a man's hand, that man would want as many virtues in a wife as there are stars in the universe.

THE RING OF SATURN

The Ring of Saturn (Fig. 12) is a mark very seldom found, and is not a good sign to have on the hand. I have closely watched people possessing it, and I have never yet observed that they were in any way successful. It seems to cut off the Mount of Fate in such a peculiar way that such people never gain any point that they may work for or desire. Their temperament has a great deal—it may have everything—to do with this, as I always find these people full of big ideas and plans, but with such want of continuity of purpose that they always give up half-way. (See also Plate XIV).

THE THREE BRACELETS

The bracelets (Fig. 13), I do not consider of much importance in reading the lines, or in the study of the hand itself. There is however, one strange and peculiar point with regard to them, and one that I have noticed contains a great deal of truth. I had been taught in my early life, always to observe principally the position of the first bracelet, the one nearest the hand, and that when I saw it high on the wrist, almost rising into the palm, particularly when it rose in the shape of an arch (Fig. 16, m-m). I was always to warn my consultant of weakness in relation to the internal organs of the body—as, for instance, in the bearing of children. Afterwards in my life, when I took up this study in a more practical way, I found there was a great deal of truth in what I at first thought a superstition. In later years, by watching case after case, by going through hospitals, and from what my many consultants have told me in reference to their ailments, I have become convinced that this point deserves being recorded, and consequently I now give it for what it may be worth.

Another significance attached to the bracelets is that, if well and clearly defined, they mean strong health and a robust constitution, and this again, it is interesting to notice, bears out in a manner the point I have called attention to.

33

THE LINE OF MARRIAGE

What matter if the words be said,
The licence paid-they are not wed;
Unless love link each heart to heart,
'Twere better keep those lives apart.

CHEIRO.

OF the many books that have been written on cheiromancy, I am sorry to say that almost all have ignored or have barely noticed this naturally interesting and important point. I will therefore endeavour to give as many details as possible in connection with this side of the study.

What is known as the line or lines of marriage, as the case may be, is that mark or marks on the Mount of Mercury as shown by Fig. 13. It must be first stated, and stated clearly, that the hand does not recognise the mere fact of a ceremony, be it civil or religious—it merely registers the influence of different people over our lives, what kind of influence they have had, the effect produced, and all that is in accordance with such influence. Now, marriage being so important an event in one's life, it follows that, if events can be foretold by the hand, marriage should certainly be marked, even years in advance, and I have always found that such is the case in respect to all important influences; and it is also natural that *affaires de coeur, liaisons,* and so on, can thus be singled out and divided from what is known as marriage, except when the *liaison* is just as important and the influence on the life just as strong. Why there should be a time set apart in one's life to marry, or not to marry, as the case may be, can only be answered by referring to the other mysteries that surround us. If anyone can explain why a permanent magnet brought into an ordinary room has the power to magnetise every other bit of iron in the room, what that power to magnetise every other bit of iron in the room, what that power is, and what the connection is, then he may be able to answer the question; but until all the secret laws and forces of nature are known, we can take no other standpoint than to accept these strange anomalies without having the power to answer the cry of the curious, the perpetual parrot-like 'Why?' of the doubting. The only theory I advance is that, as the press of the finger on the telegraph keyboard in New York at the same moments affects the keyboard in London, so by the medium of the ether, which is more subtle than electricity, are all persons unconsciously in touch with and in communion with one another.

In studying this point of the subject, I wish to impress upon the student that what are known as the lines of marriage must be balanced by marks on other portions of the hand, as I have shown by the influences by the side of the line of fate (Chapter 28), and by the lines of influence by the side of the line of life (Chapter 22).

We will now proceed with the marks in connection with these lines of marriage on the Mount of Mercury.

The lines or lines of marriage may rise on the side of the hand or be only marked across the front of the Mont of Mercury.

Only the long lines relate to marriages (Fig. 18, g); the short ones to deep affection or marriage contemplated (Fig. 18, h). On the line of life or fate, if it be marriage, we will find it corroborated and information given as to the change in life, position, and so on. From the position of the marriage-line on the Mount of Mercury a very fair idea of the age at the time of marriage may also be obtained.

When the important line is found lying close to the line of heart, the union will be early, about fourteen to twenty-one; near the centre of the Mount, about twenty-one or twenty-eight; three-quarters up the Mount, twenty-eight to thirty-five; and so on. But the line of fate on the line of life will be more accurate, by giving almost the exact date of the change of influence.

A wealthy union is shown by a strong, well-marked line from the side of the line of fate next Luna (Fig. 20, h-h), running up and joining the line of fate, when the marriage-line on Mercury is also well marked.

When, however, the line of influence rises first straight on the Mount of Luna and then runs up

196

and into the fate-line, the marriage will be more the capricious fancy than real affection.

When the line of influence is stronger than the subject's line of fate, then the person the subject marries will have greater power and more individuality than the subject.

The happiest mark of marriage on the line of fate is when the influence-line lies close to the fate-line and runs evenly with it (Fig. 20, *l-l*).

The line of marriage on the Mount of Mercury should be straight, without breaks, crosses, or irregularities of any kind.

When it curves or drops downward toward the line of heart, it foretells that the person with whom the subject is married is liable to die first (Fig. 20, *j*)

When the line curves upward, the possessor is not likely to marry at any time.

When the line of marriage is distinct, but with fine hair-lines dropping from it toward the line of heart, if foretells trouble brought on by the illness and bad health of the person the subject marries.

When the line droops with a small cross over the curve, the person the subject is married to may die by accident or sudden death; but when there is a long, gradual curve, gradual ill-health will cause the end.

When the line has an island in the centre or at any portion, it denotes some very great trouble in married life, and a separation while the island lasts.

When the line divides at the end into a dropping fork sloping toward the centre of the hand, it tells of divorce or a Judical separation (Fig. 19, *j*), This is all the more certain if a fine line cross from it to the Plain of Mars (Fig. 19, *k-k*).

When the line is full of little islands and drooping lines, the subject should be warned not to marry. Such a mark is a sign of the greatest unhappiness.

When full of little islands and forked, it is again a sign of unhappiness in marriage.

When the line breaks in two, it denotes a sudden break in the married life.

When the line of marriage sends an offshoot on to the Mount of Sun and into the line of Sun, it tells that its possessor will marry someone of distinction, and generally a person in some way famous.

When, on the contrary, it goes down toward and cuts the line of sun, the person on whose hand it appears will lose position through marriage (Fig. 21, *i-i*).

When a deep line from the top of the Mount grows downward and cuts the line of marriage, there will be a great obstacle and opposition to such marriage (Fig. 18, *i*).

When there is a fine line running parallel with and almost touching the marriage-line, it tells of some deep affection after marriage on the side of the person on whose hand it appears.

CHILDREN

....So oft to bear,
Thro' early hours, thro' later years,
The story of a mother's tears
Or of a father's drunken care.
Ah me! how hard
To bear that load, that heavy cross.
To stagger on, and, stumbling, find
All life but death, all death but loss,
With eyes alone to virtue blind!

CHEIRO.

TO tell accurately the number of children one has had, or is likely to have, seems a very wonderful thing to do, but it is not one bit more wonderful than the details given by the main lines. To do this, however, requires more careful study than is usually given to the pursuit of cheiromancy.

Owing to the accuracy with which I have been credited on this point, I have been largely requested, in writing this book, to give as many details as permissible. I shall endeavour to do so in as clear a way as possible, knowing well the difficulties that lie in the way of a lucid explanation of such a point.

In the first place, a thorough knowledge of all portions of the hand that can touch on this must be acquired. For instance, a person with a very poor development of the Mount of Venus is not so likely at any time to have children as the person with the Mount full and large.

The lines relating to children are the fine upright lines from the end of the line of marriage. Sometimes these are so fine that it requires a microscope to make them out clearly, but in such a case it will be found that all the lines of the hand are also faint. By the position of these lines, by the portion of the Mount they touch, by their appearance, and so on, one can accurately make out whether such children will play an important part in the life of the subject or otherwise; if they will be delicate or strong, if they will be male or female.

The leading points with regard to these lines are as follows:

Broad lines denote males; fine, narrow lines, females.

When they are clearly marked they denote strong, healthy children; when very faint, if they are wavy lines, they are the reverse.

When the first part of the line is a little island, the child will be very delicate in its early life, but if the line is well marked farther, it will eventually have good health.

When one line is longer and superior to the rest, one child will be more important to the parent than all the others.

The numbers run from the outside of the marriage-line in toward the hand.

On a man's hand they are often just as clear as on a woman's, but in such case the man will be exceptionally fond of children and will have an extremely affectionate nature; as a rule, however, the women's hand shows the marks in a superior way. From these observations I think the student will be able to proceed in his or her pursuit of other minute details which I cannot go into here.

THE STAR

THE STAR ON THE MOUNT OF JUPITER

THE star is a sign of very great importance, wherever it makes its appearance on the hand. I do not at all hold that it is generally a danger, and one from which there is no escape; rather, on the contrary, I consider it, with one or two exceptions, a fortunate sign, and one which naturally should depend upon the portion of the hand, or the line, with which it is connected.

When a star appears on the Mount of Jupiter, it has two distinct meanings, according to its position.

When on the highest point of the Mount, on the face of the hand, it promises great honour, power, and position; ambition gratified, and the ultimate success and triumph of the individual (Fig. 19, *m*).

With a strong fate-, head-, and sun-line, there is almost no step in the ladder of human greatness that the subject will not reach. It is usually found on the hand of a very ambitious man or woman, and in the pursuit of power and position there is probably no mark to equal it.

Its second position on the Mount of Jupiter is when it lies almost off the Mount, very low at its base, cutting the base of the first finger, or resting on the side toward the back of the hand. In this case it is also the sign of a most ambitious person, but with this difference, that he will be brought in contact with extremely distinguished people; but unless the rest of the hand be exceptionally fine, it does not promise distinction or power to the individual himself.

THE STAR ON THE MOUNT OF SATURN

On the centre of the Mount of Saturn it is a sign of some terrible fatality (Fig. 19, n). It again gives distinction, but a distinction to be dreaded. It is decidedly wrong to class this sign with the old idea of the mark of murder. It really means that the subject will have some terribly fatalistic life, but that of a man in every way a child of fate, a plaything of destiny; a man cast for some terrible part in the drama of life—he may be a Judas, or he may be a Saviour, but all his work and life and career will have some dramatic and terrible climax, some unrivalled brilliancy, some position resplendent with the majesty of death—a king for the moment, but corwned with doom.

The second position for the star on Saturn is that almost off the Mount, either at the side or cutting into the fingers. This, like the star on Jupiter, denotes that the subject will be brought into contact with one of those who make history, but in this case with one who gains distinction through some terrible fate.

THE STAR ON THE MOUNT OF THE SUN

The star on the Mount of the sun (Fig. 19, *p*) gives the brilliancy of wealth and position, but, as a rule, without happiness. Such wealth has come too late; the price has probably been too dearly paid in the way of health, or perhaps in peace of mind. Certain it is, however, that, though it gives great riches, it never gives contentment or happiness. When in this case by the side of the Mount, it denotes, like the others, that the subject will be brought in contact with rich and wealthy people, without himself being rich in the world's goods.

When, however, it is connected or formed by the line of sun, it denotes great fame and celebrity, but through talent and work in art. It should not be too high on the hand; a little above the middle of the line is its best position, as in the case of Madame Sarah Bernhardt, an impression of whose hand will be found on Plate IX.

THE STAR ON THE MOUNT OF MERCURY

The star in the centre of the Mount of Mercury (Fig. 19, *q*) denotes brilliancy and success in science, business, or the power of eloquence, according to the type of hand, and, as in the foregoing examples, by the side of the Mount it denotes association with people distinguished in those walks of life.

THE STAR ON THE MOUNT OF MARS

The star on the Mount of Mars under Mercury (Fig. 18, *j*), denotes that through patience, resignation, and fortitude the greatest honours will be gained.

On the opposite side of the hand, the Mount of Mars under Jupiter, great distinction and celebrity will arise from a martial life, or a signal battle or warfare in which the subject will be engaged.

THE STAR ON THE MOUNT OF LUNA

The star on the Mount of Luna (Fig. 18, *k*) is, according to my system, a sign of great celebrity arising from the qualities of the Mount, namely, through the imaginative faculties. I do not hold that it relates to drowning, in accordance with other cheiromants. There is another meaning, however, to this sign, which may have given rise to this idea, and that is that when the line of head ends in a star on this Mount the dreamy imaginative faculties will ruin the balance of the line of head, and the result will be mental instability.

THE STAR ON THE MOUNT OF VENUS

In the centre or highest point of the Mount of Venus (Fig. 18, *l*) the star is once more successful and favourable, but this time in relation to the affections and passions. On a man's hand such a sign indicates extraordinary success in all affairs of love—the same on a woman's hand, No jealousies or opposition will rob them of the spoils of conquest.

When lying by the side of the Mount, the amours of such a subject will be with people distinguished for their success in the arena of love.

THE STAR ON THE FINGERS

The star on the tips of outer phalanges of the fingers gives great good fortune inany thing touched or attempted, and on the first phalange of the thumb success through the subject's strength of will.

The star is one of the most important of the lesser signs to seek for.

In the foregoing remarks it should be borne in mind that the indications denoted by this important lesser sign must naturally be in keeping with the tendencies shown by the general character of the hand. It stands to reason, for instance, that the star could have little power of meaning on a hand containing a weak, undeveloped line of head. In dealing with this, as indeed with every other portion of the study, it must be understood that however clear the directions may be, it is impossible to dispense with the exercise of a certain amount of thought and discretion on the part of the student.

36

THE CROSS

THE cross is the opposite to the star, and is seldom found as a favourable sign. It indicates trouble, disappointment, danger, and sometimes a change in the position of life, but one brought about by trouble. There is, however, one position in which it is a good sign to have it, namely, on the Mount of Jupiter (Fig. 18, *m*). In this position it indicates that at least one great affection will come into the life. This is especially the case when the line of fate rises from the Mount of Luna. A strange feature with this cross on Jupiter is that it denotes roughly about the time in life when the affection will influence the individual. When close to the commencement of the line of life and toward the side of the hand, it will be early; on the summit of the Mount, in middle life; and down at the base, late in life.

On the Mount of Saturn (Fig. 18, *n*), when touching the line of fate, it warns of the danger of violent death by accident; but when by itself in the centre of this mount, it increases the fatalistic tendencies of the life.

On the Mount of the Sun it is a terrible sign of disappointment in the pursuit of fame, art, or riches.

The cross on the Mount of Mercury, as a rule, indicates a dishonest nature, and one inclined to duplicity.

On the Mount of Mars under Mercury it denotes the dangerous opposition of enemies; and on the Mount of Mars under Jupiter force, violence, and even death from quarrels.

A cross on the Mount of the Moon under the line of head denotes a fatal influence of the imagination. The man with such a sign will deceive even himself (Fig. 16, *l*).

On the Mount of Venus, when heavily maked, it indicates some great trial or fatal influence of affection; but when very small and lying close to the line of life, it tells of troubles and quarrels with near relatives.

A cross by the side of the line of fate, and between it and the life-line in the Plain of Mars, denotes opposition in one's career by relatives, and means a change in the destiny; but lying on the other side of the hand next to Luna it relates to a disappointment in a journey.

Above and touching the line of head, it foretells some wound or accident to the head.

By the side of the line of sun, disappointment in position.

Running into the line of fate, disappointment in money; and over the line of heart, the death of some loved one.

37

THE SQUARE

THE square (Fig. 15) is one of the most interesting of the lesser signs. It is usually called 'the mark of preservation,' because it shows that the subject is protected at that particular point from whatever danger menaced.

When the line of fate runs through a well-formed square, it denotes one of the greatest crises in the subject's life in a wordly sense, connected with financial disaster or loss, but if the line goes right on through the square all danger will be averted. Even when the line of fate breaks in the centre, the square is still a sign of protection from very serious loss.

When outside the line, but only touching it, and directly under the Mount of Saturn, it denotes preservation from accident.

When the line of head runs through a well-formed square, it is a sign of strength and preservation to the brain itself, and tells of some terrible strain of work or of anxiety at that particular moment.

When rising above the line of head under Saturn, it foretells a preservation from some danger to the head.

When the line of heart runs through a square, it denotes some heavy trouble brought on by the affections. When under Saturn, some fatality to the object of one's affection (Fig. 21, *j*).

When the life-line passes through a square, it denotes a protection from death, even if the line be broken at that point (Fig. 21, *k*).

A square on the Mount of Venus inside the line of life denotes preservation from trouble on by the passions (Fig. 21, *l*). When resting in the centre of the Mount of Venus, it tells that the subject will fall into all kinds of danger through passion, but will always manage to escape.

When, however, lying outside the line of life and touching it from the Plain of Mars, a square on such a place means imprisonment or seclusion from the world.

When on the mounts the square denotes a protection from any excess arising through the qualities of the Mount:

On Jupiter, from the ambition of the subject.

On Saturn, from the fatality that shadows the life.

On the Sun, from the desire for fame.

On Mercury, form the restless, mercurial temperament.

On Mars, from danger through enemies.

On Luna, from an excess of imagination, or from the evil effects of some other line as, for instance, a line of travel.

211

38

THE ISLAND, THE CIRCLE, THE SPOT

THE island is not a fortunate sign, but it only relates to the line or portion of the hand on which it is found. It is interesting to notice that it frequently relates to hereditary evils; as, for instance, heavily marked on the line of heart it denotes heart weakness.

When as one distinct mark in the centre of the line of head, it denotes an hereditary weakness in relation to mentality.

When on the line of life, it denotes illness and delicacy at that particular point.

When on the line of fate, some heavy loss in worldly matters.

When on the line of sun, if foretells loss of position and name, generally through scandal (Fig. 21, *h*).

When on the line of health, if foreshadows a serious illness.

Any line running into or forming an island is a bad indication in relation to the part of the hand on which it is found.

An attendant line on the Mount of Venus

running into an island foretells disgrace and trouble from passion to the man or woman who influences the life (Fig. 18, *p*).

A line forming an island and crossing the hand from the Mount of Venus to the line of marriage foretells that an evil influence at that particular point will cross the life and bring disgrace to the marriage (Fig. 18, *r*). If the same kind of line run to the line of heart, some bad influence will bring trouble and disgrace to the affections; when it runs to the line of head, some influence will direct the talents and intentions into some disgraceful channel; and when it runs into and bars the line of fate, some evil influence will be a barrier to the success of the subject at the date at which the lines join each other.

An island on any of the mounts injures the qualities of the mount on which it is found.

On the Mount of Jupiter it weakens the pride and ambition.

On Saturn it brings misfortune to the subject.

On the Mount of the Sun it weakens the talent for art.

On Mercury it makes a person too changeable to succeed, particularly in anything in relation to business or science.

On Mars it shows a weak spirit and cowardice.

On Luna, weakness in working out the power

of the imagination.

On Venus, a person easily led and influenced by the sport of fancy and passion (Fig. 20, *k*).

THE CIRCLE

If found on the Mount of the Sun, the circle is a favourable mark. This is the only position in which it is fortunate. On any other mount it tells against the success of the subject.

On the Mount of Luna it denotes danger from drowning.

When touching any important line, it indicates that at that particular point the subject will not be able to clear himself from misfortune—in other words, he will, as it were, go round and round in a circle without being able to break through and get free.

THE SPOT

A spot is generally the sign of temporary illness.

A bright-red spot on the line of head indicates a shock or injury from some blow or fall.

A black or blue spot denotes a nervous illness.

A bright-red spot on the line of health is usually taken to mean fever, and on the line of life some illness of the nature of fever.

THE GRILLE, THE TRIANGLE, 'LACROIX MYSTIQUE,' THE RING OF SOLOMON

THE grille (Fig. 15) is very often seen, and generally upon the Mounts of the hand. It indicates obstacles against the success of that particular Mount, and especially means that those obstacles are brought on by the tendencies of the subject in accordance with that portion of the hand in which it is found.

On the Mount of Jupiter it denotes egotism, pride, and the dominative spirit.

On the Mount of Saturn it foretells misfortune, a melancholy nature, and a morbid tendency.

On the Mount of the Sun it tells of vanity, folly, and a desire for celebrity.

On the Mount of Mercury it denotes an unstable and rather unprincipled person.

On the Mount of Luna it foretells restlessness, discontent, and disquietude.

On the Mount of Venus, caprice in passion.

THE TRIANGLE

The triangle (Fig. 15) is a curious sign, and is

often found clear and distinct, and not formed by the chance crossing of lines.

When distinct in shape on the Mount of Jupiter, it promises more than usual success in the management of people, in the handling of men, and even in the organisation of everyday affairs.

On the Mount of Saturn it gives a talent and inclination for mystical work, for the delving into the occult, for the study of human magnetism, and so forth.

On the Mount of the Sun it denotes a practical application of art and a calm demeanour toward success and fame. Success will never spoil such people.

On the Mount of the Mars, it gives science in warfare, great calmness in any crisis, and presence of mind in danger.

On the Mount of Luna it tells of a scientific method in following out the ideas of the imagination.

On the Mount of Venus, calmness and calculation in love, the power of restraint and control over self.

The tripod or spear-head (Fig. 15) is an excellent sign of success on any Mount on which it is found.

'LA CROIX MYSTIQUE'

This strange mark has usually for its domain

the centre of the quadrangle (Fig. 19, *r*), but it may be found at either its upper or lower extremities. It may be formed by the line of fate and a line from the head to the heart, or it may lie as a distinct mark without connection with any other main line.

It denotes mysticism, occultism, and superstition.

These three qualities are widely apart in themselves, although often confounded, and the position this mark takes on the hand is therefore very important.

When high up on the hand toward Jupiter, it will give the belief in mysticism for one's own life, but not the desire to follow it farther than where it relates to self. Such people want their fortunes told, actuated more by curiosity to know how their own ambitions will turn out than by the deeper interest that the study involves for its own sake.

When the 'Croix Mystique' is more closely connected with the line of heart than with that of head, it gives a superstitious nature, and this even more so when it is marked over the centre of the head-line, when that line takes a sharp curve downward. It must be remembered that the length of the line of head has much to do with this. The very short line with the cross over it will be a thousand times more superstitious than the long one. The long one will be the greatest for occultism and particularly so if the 'Croix Mystique' is an independent formation on the line of head.

When it touches the fate-line, or is formed by
it, the love of the mystic will influence the entire
career.

THE RING OF SOLOMON

The Ring of Solomon (Fig. 12) is a sign that
also denotes the love of the occult, but in this case
it shows more the power of the master, the adept,
than the mere love of the mystic denoted by 'Le
Croix Mystique.'

218

40

HANDS COVERED WITH LINES— THE COLOUR OF THE PALM

WHEN the entire hand is covered with a multitude of fine lines like a net spreading over its surface, it tells that the nature is intensely nervous and worried by little thoughts and troubles that would be of no importance whatever to others.

This is particularly so if the palm be soft—such people imagine all sorts of things in the way of ailments and troubles; but if the palm of the hand and firm, it denotes an energetic, excitable nature, but one that is far more successful for other people than for self.

SMOOTH HANDS

Very smooth hands with few lines belong to people calm in temperament and even in disposition. They seldom if ever worry; they rarely lose temper, but when they do they know the reason why. This is again modified by the palm being hard or soft. When firm, it is a greater sign of control and calmness than when soft. In the latter case it is not so much a matter of control as of indifference: the subject will not take sufficient interest to lose temper—that would be too much of an exertion.

THE SKIN

When the palm of the hand is covered naturally with a very fine light skin, the subject will retain the buoyancy and temperament of youth much longer than the person with a coarse skin. This is, of course, much affected by work, but I am speaking of cases where little labour or manual work is done; yet even where there is manual work this can still be observed by the ridges of the skin. It has been proved that even as regards this point no two hands are ever alike; consequently, while work may thicken the cuticle, its individuality remains the same.

THE COLOUR OF THE PALM

The colour of the palm is far more important than the colour of the outside of the hands. This at first sight appears strange but a little observation will prove its truth.

The palm of the hand is under the immediate control and action of the nerves and of the nerve-fluid. According to scientists, there are more nerves in the hand than in any other portion of the body, and, again, more in the palm than in any other portion of the hand.

It will be found that almost every palm has a distinct colour and can be classed as follows:

When pale or almost white in colour, the subject will take very little interest in anything outside of himself—in other words, he will be selfish, egotistical, and unsympathetic.

When the palm is yellowish in colour, the subject will be morbid, melancholy, and morose.

When a delicate pink the nature is sanguine, hopeful, and bright; and when very red, robust in health and spirits, passionate, and quick-tempered.

221

41

THE GREAT TRIANGLE AND THE QUADRANGLE

WHAT is called the great triangle, or the Triangle of Mars, is formed by the lines of life, head, and the hepatica (Fig. 22).

When, as is very frequently the case, the line of health is altogether absent, its place must be filled by an imaginary line to form the base of the triangle, or (as is often found) the line of Sun forms the base (Fig. 22, *a-a*). This latter is by far the greatest sign of power and success, although the subject will not be so broad-minded and liberal as when the base of the triangle is formed by the line of health.

The shape and positions of the great triangle must be considered by themselves, although it contains the upper, the middle, and the lower angle, which three points will be dealt with later.

When the triangle is well formed by the lines of head, life, and health, it should be broad and enclose the entire Plain of Mars. In such case it denotes breadth of views, liberality and generosity of spirit; such a person will be inclined to sacrifice himself to further the interests of the whole, not the unit.

If, on the contrary, it is formed by three small, wavy, uncertain lines, it denotes timidity of spirit, meanness, and cowardice. Such a man would always go with the majority, even against his principles.

When in the second formation of the triangle it has for its base the line of Sun, the subject will then have narrow ideas but great individuality and strong resolution. Such a sign, from the very qualities it exhibits, contains within itself the seeds of worldly success.

THE UPPER ANGLE

The upper angle (Fig. 22, *b*) is formed by the lines of head and life. This angle should be clear, well pointed, and even. Such will indicate refinement of thought and mind, and delicacy toward others.

When very obtuse, it denotes a dull matter-of-fact intellect with little delicacy and feeling and a very small appreciation of art or of artistic things or people.

When extremely wide and obtuse, it gives a blunt, hasty temper, a person who will continually offend people. It also denotes impatience and want of application in study.

THE MIDDLE ANGLE

The middle angle is formed by the line of head

and that of health (Fig. 22, c). If clear and well defined, it denotes quickness of intellect, vivacity, and good health.

When very acute, it denotes a painfully nervous temperament and bad health.

When very obtuse, dullness of intelligence and a matter-of-fact method of working.

THE LOWER ANGLE

The lower angle (Fig. 22, d). when very acute and made by the hepatica, denotes feebleness, and littleness of spirit, when obtuse, it denotes a strong nature.

When made by the line of Sun and very acute, it gives individuality, but a narrow view of things; when obtuse, it gives a broader and more generous mind.

THE QUADRANGLE

The quadrangle, as its name implies, is that quadrangular space between the lines of head and heart (Fig. 22).

It should be even in shape, wide at both ends, but not narrow at the centre. Its interior should be smooth and not crossed with many lines, whether from the head or from the heart. When marked in this way, it indicates evenness of mind. power of intellect anf loyalty in friendship or affection.

224

This space represents within itself the man's disposition toward his fellows, When excessively narrow, it shows narrow ideas. smallness of thought, and bigotry, but more in regard to religion and morals, whereas the triangle denotes conservatism as regards work and occupation. With religious people this is a remarkable sign, the hand of the bigot always having this space extremely narrow.

On the other hand, the space must not be too wide. When it is, the subject's views of religion and morals will be too broad for his own good.

When this space narrows so much in the centre that it has the appearance of a waist, it denotes prejudice and injustice. Again, the two ends should be fairly equally balanced. When much wider under the Mount of the Sun than Saturn, the person is careless about his name, position, or reputation. The opposite of this is shown when the space is narrow. It is in such a case a sign of intense anxiety as to the opinion of other people—what the world thinks, and what one must do to keep up one's reputation.

When excessively wide under Saturn or Jupiter and narrowcr at the other end, it denotes that the subject will change from the generosity of his views and broadness of mind to become narrow and prejudiced.

When the quadrangle is abnormally wide in its entire length, it denotes want of order in the brain, carelessness of thought and ideas, an unconventional nature, and one imprudent in every way.

When the quadrangle is smooth and free from little lines, it denotes a calm temperament.

When very full of little lines and crosses, the nature is restless and irritable.

A star in any portion of the quadrangle is an excellent sign, particularly if it be under some favourable Mount.

Under Jupiter it promises pride and power.

Under Saturn, success in worldly matters.

Under the Mount of the Sun, success in fame and position through art: and between the Sun and Mercury, success in science and research.

TRAVEL, VOYAGES, AND ACCIDENTS

THERS are two distinct ways of telling travels and voyages, One is from the heavy lines on the face of the Mount of Luna; the other, from the little hair-lines that leave the line of life but travel on with if (Fig. 22, *j*). This indication is similar to that of the line of life dividing in the hand; if one branch goes around Venus, the other proceeding to the base to the Mount of Luna, it foretells that the subject will make some great change from his native land to another. It therefore follows that the journeys told by the change in the line of life are far more important than the lines on Luna, which relate more to the minor changes or travels of the subject. It is sometimes found that long lines extend from the *rascette*, or first bracelet (Fig. 22), and rise into the Mount of Luna. These are similar to the travel-lines on Luna, but much more important. When the line of fate shows a considerable and beneficial change at the same point, then these lines are prosperous and fortunate. When, however, the line of fate does not show any advantage gained at the same point, the subject will not improve, to any great extent, in worldly matters by the change.

when such a journey-line ends with a small cross, the journey will end in disappointment (Fig. 22, *e-e*).

When the travel-line ends in a square, it denotes danger from the journey, but the subject will be protected.

When the line ends with an island, no matter how small, the journey will result in loss (Fig. 22. *f*).

On the Mount of Luna the ascendant lines from the *rascette* are the most beneficial.

When the line crosses the hand and enters the Mount of Jupiter, great position and power will be gained by it, and the journey will also be extremely long.

When the travel-line runs to the Mount of Saturn, some fatality will govern the entire journey.

When it runs to the Mount of the Sun, it is most favourable, and promises riches and fame.

When it reaches the Mount of Mercury, sudden and unexpected wealth will arise from it.

When the horizontal lines on Luna cross the face of the Mount and reach the line of fate, the journeys will be longer and more important than those indicated by the short, heavy lines also on the Mount, though they may not relate to a change of country (Fig. 22, *g-g*).

When they enter the line of fate and ascend with it, they denote travels that will materially benefit the subject.

When the end of any of these horizontal lines droop or curve downward toward the wrist, the journey will be unfortunate (Fig. 22, k). When thry rise upard, no matter how short, it will be successful.

When one of these lines crosses another, such a journey will be repeated, but for some important reason.

Any square on such a line will show danger, but protection from accident or misfortune.

If the travel-line runs into the line of head and causes a spot, island, or break, it foretells some danger to the head, or some malady arising from such a journey (Fig. 22, h-h).

ACCIDENTS

I have alluded to accidents considerably in my treatment of the line of travel and in relation to travel, but disasters are more marked on the line of life and line of head than at any other point.

In the first place, the accident marked to the line of life denotes a more immediate danger as follows:

When, from an island on Saturn, a line falls downward and enters the life-line, serious, if not fatal, danger is indicated (Fig. 22, i-i).

When such a line ends by a small cross, either on the line of life or without it, it tells that the subject will have some narow escape from serious accident.

When the same mark occurs lower down, at the base of the Mount of Saturn, the accident will result more from animals than from other causes.

Any straight line from Saturn to the life-line means danger of some kind, but not so serious as from a line possessing the island either on Saturn or lower down.

To the line of head exactly the same rules apply, with this difference, that the danger will be direct to the head itself, but, unless the accident-line cut or break the head-line, it denotes, as it were, that the person has time to foresee the dangers that approach, and such a mark indicates a fright and shock to the brain, but no serious results unless the line is injured or broken.

43

TIME—THE SYSTEM OF SEVEN

IN my own work I use a system as regards time and dates which I have never found mentioned elsewhere. It is one which I consider exceptionally accurate, and I therefore recommend it to the student for his or her consideration. It is the system of seven, and I advance it as being taught by nature in all her mysterious dealings with life.

In the first place, we find from a medical and scientific standpoint the seven a most important point of calculation. We find that the entire system undergoes a complete change every seven years; that there are seven stages of the prenatal existence, that the brain takes seven forms before it takes upon itself 'the unique character of the human brain'; and so forth. Again, we find that in all ages the number seven has played a most important part in the history of the world; as, for instance, the seven races of humanity, the seven wonders of the world, the seven altars to the seven gods of the seven planets, the seven days of the week, the seven colours, the seven minerals, the supposition of the seven senses, the three parts of the body each containing seven sections, and the seven divisions of the world. Again, in the Bible seven is the most important number; but it is superfluous to give further details. The point that bears most largely on this subject is that of the entire system undergoing a change every seven years. My own observation leads me also to advance (simply for the consideration of the student) the theory that the alternate sevens are somewhat alike in their relation to the functional changes of the body. For example, a child very delicate on passing the age of seven is also likely to be delicate on passing the age of twenty-one, whereas a child healthy and strong at the age of seven will again be healthy and strong at the age of twenty-one, no matter how delicate he or he may be through the intermediate years. This is an interesting point in predictions relating to health, and one which I have found not only interesting but extremely reliable. Every line on the hand can be divided into sections giving dates with more or less accuracy. The most important lines, however, and those usually consulted in reference to dates, are those of life and fate. In Fig. 23 it will be noticed that I have divided the line of fate into three great divisions, namely, twenty-one, thirty-five, and forty-nine, and if the student will keep this in mind he will more easily fill in the subdivisions on the human hand itself. The point, however, which I cannot impress too strongly, is that the student must notice the class or type of hand before proceeding or attempting to make the smallest calculation. It stands to reason that there must be the greatest difference between the dates given by the palm of the square or spatulate hand and that of the psychic. If the student will bear this in

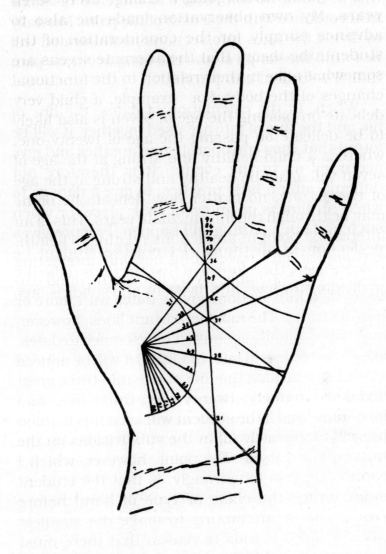

FIG. 23

TIME - THE SYSTEM OF SEVEN

233

and that of the psychic. If the student will bear this in mind, he will reduce or increase his scale in accordance with the length of the palm. Mentally to divide the lines into sections as illustrated will be found the simplest and the most accurate plan that the student can pursue.

When, in the calculation of dates, the line of life and the line of fate are used together, it will be found that they corroborate one another and give accuracy as to the events. It is therefore not difficult, after a little practice, to give a date as to when an illness or an event took place, or when such and such a thing will happen. Practice gives perfection in all things; let not the student be discouraged, therefore, if at first the finds difficulty in dividing the lines into divisions and subdivisions.

44

A FEW WORDS ON SUICIDE

I WILL now deal with a few illustrative types to help the student in the congregation of lines, signs, and formations that go to form each individual character. *It is seldom, if ever, that one distinct mark or peculiarity has the power to ruin or blight any one nature, An evil or dangerous sign as regards character merely shows the particular tendency in this or that direction.* It takes a variety of wheels to make a watch: so does it take a variety of characteristics to make a criminal or a saint.

The hand which may show suicidal tendencies is generally long, with a sloping line of head, and a developed Mount of Luna, particularly toward its base. The line of head is also very much connected with the line of life, and so increases the excessively sensitive nature of the subject. In such a case the individual would not naturally be morbid or even show the inclination for suicide, but the nature is so sensitive and so imaginative that any trouble, grief, or scandal is intensified a thousandfold, and to kill or injure self gives the peculiar satisfaction of self-martyrdom to such a type, as exemplified by Plate XIV.

The same indications being found in connection with a well-developed Mount of Saturn, will give the thoroughly sensitive morbid nature: an individual who will determinedly come to the conclusion that life under any circumstances is not worth living—so the slightest provocation by trouble or disappointment causes him quietly and resignedly to fly to that last resource which he has cherished and thought of for so long.

The excessively drooping line of head (Plate XIV) on a pointed or conic hand denotes the same result, but only through the sudden impulse that is characteristic of the nature. To such a person a shock or trouble is all-sufficient to impart the impulse to the excitable disposition, and before there is time to think, the deed is done.

The opposite of this excitability is shown in the case of the subject's committing suicide when the line of head is not abnormally sloping. Such a person, however, will have the line closely connected with the line of life, a depressed Mount of Jupiter, and a very full-developed Saturn. Such a subject will feel the disappointments of life unusually keenly; he will as well have a melancholy and gloomy turn of mind; he will, however, be logical in weighing every side of the question for life and death, and if he arrives at the conclusion that the game is up and the battle over as far as he is concerned, he will, in a most reasonable and sensible manner, according to his standpoint, proceed to put an end to all misfortunes. What such a person will suffer before he arrives at this conclusion it is scarcely possible to estimate. We are all so wrapped up in our own interests and affairs that we hardly see or notice the pale, worn face that has suffered so patiently, the hollow eyes of wakeful nights, the wasted cheeks of hunger, which appear for a moment by our side, and are gone for ever.

45

PROPENSITIES FOR MURDER

MURDER can be divided into a great many different classes. What the hand principally recognises is that of the abnormal tendency toward crime, the class of crime itself being traced by the type of hand in respect to the inclinations of the subject. That some people have a natural predilection toward murder cannot, I think, be doubted. There are born criminals as well as born saints. It depends upon the development of the will, in keeping with the surroundings and circumstances. whether the criminal tendencies will be developed or not. The destructive tendency as exhibited by children does not denote their want of sense, but denotes the innate sense of destruction before it has been curbed by the fear of consequences, by the will, or the surroundings that are brought to bear upon the nature. Some people born into the world have this propensity more developed than others; the slightest flaw in their surroundings being responsible for the after-evolution of the criminal. Again, I do not hold that to be criminal in giving way to passion, to temptation, is to be weak-minded. On the contrary, crime can only be considered in relation to the individual. What is temptation to one is not temptation to another. I do not hold that because of such things crime should go unpunished; on the contrary, crime must be dealt with for the protection of the community. but what I do hold is, that crime should be punished in accordance with the individual and not in accordance with the crime.

It therefore follows that in the study of crime one must place one's self as far as possible in the position of the criminal. (It is astonishing how many different expressions one finds in the face of a picture from different points of view).

As regards the hand, it divides murder into three very distinct classes:

1. The murderer made so by the instinct to kill, as exhibited in the brute creation, through passion, fury, or revenge.

2. The murderer made so by the greed of gain, the nature that will stop at nothing in order to gratify its covetous tendency.

3. The utterly heartless disposition which feeds on the sufferings of others, the nature that will even live on friendly terms with the victim—the one that will, as it were, deal out death in drops of honey, the person who cannot be touched by the longings for life exhibited by the sufferer, and who, though keenly alive to the danger, feels in that danger a sense of delight, and, with utter lack of moral consciousness, takes more pleasure in such work than in the gain it brings.

The first class is very ordinary. The man or woman becomes a murderer by circumstances. Such an individual may be thoroughly good natured and kind-hearted, but some provocation excites the blind fury of the animal nature, and when the deed is done, such a one is generally crushed and broken by remorse.

In such cases the hand shows no bad sign more than ungovernable temper and brute passion. It is, in fact, the elementary hand, or a near approach to it. The line of head is short, thick, and red, the nails short and red, and the hand heavy and coarse. The most remarkable characteristic, however, will be the thumb. The thumb will be set very low on the hand; it will be short and thick in the second phalange, and the first phalange will be what is called 'the clubbed thumb' (Fig. 8) very short, broad, and square: this is found almost without exception in such types, If in such cases the Mount of Venus is also abnormally large, sexual passion will be the destroyer; when not unusually developed, the greatest failing will be that of ungovernable temper.

In the second class none of these points will be abnormal, the most striking peculiarity will be the line of head, which will be heavily marked, but with a decided growth upward (Plate XIII). it will be found in an abnormal position, rising high toward Mercury, or far before it reaches that point it completely leaves its place on the right hand. as the propensities become stronger, it enters the line

240

of heart, takes possession of it, as it were, and thus completely masks all the generous impulses or kind thoughts of the subject. (See previous remarks on the line of head, Chapter 26). The hand is usually hard, the thumb not abnormally thick, but long, very stiff, and contracted inward. The entire formation gives covetous propensities, and an utter want of conscience in the pursuit of gain.

The third class, to the student of human nature, is the most interesting, though it may be the most terrible.

It is the hand of the subtlest nature in regard to crime. There will be nothing abnormal in connection with the hand itself. It will be only be examination of all the characteristics that the treacherous side of this nature will be discovered. The leading features, however, will be a very thin, hard hand, long, the fingers generally slighty curved inward, the thumb long, and with both phalanges well developed, giving both the ability to plan and the strength of will necessary for execution, it will rarely, if ever, be found bent or inclining outward, although such a formation exists at times on the hands of the first-mentioned class.

The line of head may or may not be out of its proper position. It will, however, be set higher than usual across the hand, but will be very long and very thin, denoting the treacherous instincts. The Mount of Venus may be either depressed on the hand, or very high. When depressed, such a subject will commit crime simply for the sake of crime, when high, the crime will be committed more for the sake of satisfying the animal desires.

Such are the hands of the skilled artists in crime. Murder with such persons is reduced to a fine art, in the execution of which they will study every detail. They will rarely, if ever, kell their victim by violence—such a thing would be vulgar in their eyes—poison is the chief instrument that they employ, but so skilfully that the verdict is usually 'Death from natural causes.

46

VARIOUS PHASES OF INSANITY

IT has often been said that all men are mad on some particular point. It is when this madness passes the half-way point of eccentricity that the title 'lunatic' is bestowed upon the individual. As there are many forms of madness, so are there many indications given by the hand. The chief types which we will consider here are the following:

1. Melancholy and religious madness, hallucinations, etc.

2. The development of the crank.

3. The natural madman.

MELANCHOLY AND RELIGIOUS MANIA

In the first case the line of head, on a rather broad hand, descends with a sharp curve low down on the Mount of Luna, very often to the base, denoting the obnormally imaginative temperament of the subject. In addition to this, the Mount of Venus is not well developed, thus decreasing the subject's interest in all human or natural things; and lastly, the Mount of Saturn dominated.

As a rule, such is the hand of the religious maniac. He commences early in life with strong hallucinations from the extraordinary imagination that he possesses, which imagination, if directed into the proper channel, would probably work off its excess and relieve itself, but if opposed, feeds in itself and thus increases. Af first this is shown only occasionally in fits and starts. Its periods then grow longer and longer, until at last its moments of balance are few and far between. This is the morbid or melancholy type of the religious maniac.

THE DEVELOPMENT OF THE CRANK

This type of mania is generally found in conjunction with two very distincy types—the spatulate and the philosophic.

In the first type it is the very sloping line of head on an extremely spatulate formation. At the commencement it merely denotes daring originality, which will show itself in every possible direction. It dissipates its own power by attempting too many things. owing to the multitude of its inventive ideas. Again I say, if the subject could only get into some position in life where he might work off those ideas, all would be well, and he might even give to the world some great invention or discovery which would benefit mankind. But attempt to crush such a man by some occupation entirely foreign to his nature, and you instantly turn all his current of thought to some extraordinary invention which he attempts to work out in secret; one which he dreams will be successful, and whose success will emancipate him from the slavery he is under. The very fact of his having to work in secret, the weakening of his nerve-power by confinement and by intensity of thought, the excitement under which he labours, is the laboratory where, in the end, he turns himself out—mad.

The next type is the philosophic. This is again shown by a sudden curve of the line of head on the Mount of Luna, and with an accentuated philosophic formation. In this case the crank, and eventually the madman, leans toward the extraordinary in the salvation of mankind. He means well, from first to last, he is, however, a fanatic on whatever point, doctrine, or theory he advances. It requires but unfavourable circumstances, non-success, and the indifference of the public to make this subject pass the half-way mark of eccentricity and become quite unbalanced.

If his weak point be religion, his is never that of the melancholy; on the contrary, he is the only person who knows the secret of the kingdom of heaven—all others are lost. It is not that he wishes to be alone when he gets there—it is his feverish anxiety for others which makes him exceptional. For this object he works day and night, he denies himself the enjoyment of life, even food, in the terrible haste to accomplish his desire; the brain becomes more and more off its balance.

THE NATURAL MADMAN

Malformation of the brain is responsible for this

type, which, by a study of the hand, can be divided into two distinct classes—that of the hopeless idiot, and that of the vicious lunatic.

In the first class we generally find a wide, sloping line of head, formed entirely of islands and little hair-lines. This never gives any hope whatever of reason or intelligence, and denotes that the subject has been brought into the world with a brain insufficient—either in quantity or in quality—to given or control the body, and the hopeless idiot is the result.

In the second division of this type the line of head, instead of being a continuous line, is made up of short, wavy branches running in all directions. A number of them rise inside the line of life on Mars, and cross to the other Mars on the opposite side of the hand. With this formation the nails are generally short and red. Such a type denotes the quarrelsome, vicious lunatic more than any other class. In this case it will be noted that there are often sane moments, but such are extremely rare, and with regard to the last two classes I have never known any recovery.

47

MODUS OPERANDI

IN the first place, I would advise the student to seat himself opposite his subject, so that a good light may fall directly on the hands. I would also advise that no person be allowed to stand or sit in close proximity, as unconsciously a third person will distract the attention of both subject and palmist. There is no special time absolutely necessary for the successful reading of hands. In India they advocate the hour of sunrise, but that is merely because of the fact that the circulation of the blood is stronger at the extremities in the early morning, than after the fatigue of the day, consequently the lines are more coloured and distinct. By placing the subject directly opposite, the student is in a better position to examine both hands at the same time. In proceeding with the examination, first notice carefully the type the hands belong to, whether the fingers are in keeping with the palm, or in themselves relate to a distinct class, next carefully examine the left hand, then turn to the right—see what modifications and changes have occurred there, and make the right hand the basis of your reading.

On all important points. such as illness, death, loss of fortune. marriage, and so forth. see what the left promises before coming to the conclusion that this or that event will take place.

Hold whatever hand you are examining firmly in yours; press the line of mark till the blood flows into it—you will see by this means the tendencies of its growth.

Examine every portion of the hand—back front, nails, skin, colour—before speaking. The first point should be the examination of the thumb, see whether it is long, short, or poorly developed, whether the will-phalange is firm or supple, whether it is strong or weak. Then turn your attention to the palm: note whether it is hard, soft, or flabby.

I would next advise you that you remark the fingers—their proportion to the palm, whether long or short, thick or thin; class them as a whole, according to the type they represent, or if they be mixed, class each individual finger. Then notice the nails, for their bearing on temper, disposition and health. Finally, after carefully examining the entire hand, turn your attention to the mounts. see which mount or mounts have the greatest prominence, and then proceed to the lines. There is no fixed rule as to the line to examine first, the best plan, however, is to start with the lines of life and health combined, then proceed to the line of head, the line of destiny, the line of heart, and so on.

Speak honestly, truthfully yet carefully. You can tell the plainest truths, but you need not shock or hurt your consultant by doing so. Be as careful with that complicated piece of humanity before you as you would be in handling a fine and delicate piece of machinery. Above all things, you must be sympathetic, take the deepest possible interest in every person whose hands you read, enter into their lives, their feelings and their natures. Let your entire ambition be to do good, to be of some benefit to the person who consults you. If this be the foundation of your work, it will never tire or distress you. on the ontrary, it will sustain you. If you meet friends, be thankful fos their friendliness, if you meet enemies, be not argumentative for the sake of argument. Think of your work first, of self last.

Above all things, be not impatient in the pursuit of this knowledge, you will not learn a language in a day, neither must you expect to learn cheiromancy in a day, neither must you expect to learn cheiromancy in an hour. Be not dismayed if you find it more difficult than you have imagined. Consider it earnestly—not in the light of an amusement, but as a work entailing depth of thought, patience of research, and one worthy of the highest talents that you can give. If we study it aright, we hold within our hands the keys of the mysteries of life. In it are hereditary laws, the sins of the fathers, the karma of the past, the effect of the cause, the balance of things that have been, the shadow of things to be.

Let us be careful, then that this knowledge be

used aright. Let us be earnest in work, humble if success may crown work. Let us examine self before we examine others. If we see crime let us consider the temptation of the criminal. If we see faults let us remember we are not perfect.

Let us be careful lest in the pursuit of knowledge we despise what may seem to be beneath us—there is nothing beneath us; there is nothing common, for all fulfil the purpose of humanity. Let us not think there is no truth because we do not know, or that we possess the mysteries of the Sun because we see its light. Let us be humble, that knowledge may raise us; let us be seekers, that we may find.

48

SOME INTERESTING HANDS

THE HAND OF H.H. THE INFANTA EULALIA

THE hand of H.H. the Infanta Eulalia of Spain shown on Plate I, is remarkable, if only for the quantity of lines that appear, most of them contradictory in their meanings, as was the character of the lady, the subject of this sketch.

The Infanta Eulalia was a clever, brilliant woman who could do almost anything and yet did nothing exceptionally well.

As Aunt to Alfonso XIII, ex-King of Spain, she had an exalted position in one of the most distinguished Courts of Europe. She, however, threw overboard her great opportunities, brought descredit on her position by her numerous adventures, made a failure of her marriage and lost the greater part of her fortune.

She could paint extremely well, had considerable talent as a writer and musician, could use a rifle and ride to hounds as few women can and yet for all practical purposes accomplished nothing very remarkable.

I reproduce this hand as an example of the line of Sun, that although appearing well in its early

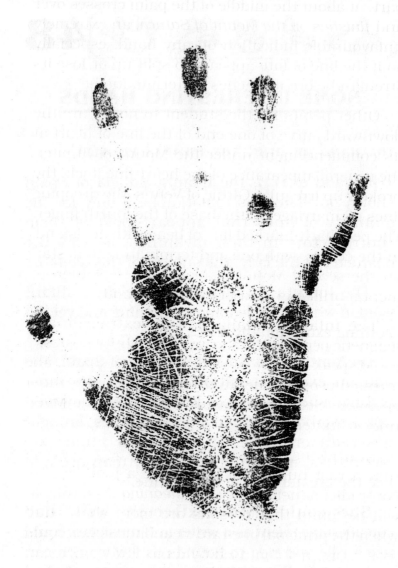

PLATE I
THE HAND OF H.H. THE INFANTA EULALIA

2520

part, at about the middle of the palm crosses over and *finishes on the Mount of Saturn*, an extremely unfavourable indication on any hand, especially so if the line of fate appears to split up or lose its strength before it reaches its termination.

Other points for the student to notice are the downward curve of one end of the line of heart at its commencement under the Mount of Jupiter, the general appearance of the heart-line itself, the broken-up irregular Girdle of Venus, the drooping lines of marriage on the base of the fourth finger. The peculiarly marked line of head with an 'island' in the centre, with one end terminating in a 'star' on the second Mount of Mars, the indication of mental brilliancy, but of an erratic kind.

The Infanta Eulalia had an extraordinary magnetic personality, she was a delightful hostess, could speak fluently every European language, she attrated people to her and yet made innumerable enemies. (See lines crossing from Mount of Mars under Jupiter).

In studying this hand, it is well to bear in mind that a vast number of lines have a tendency to contradict or *neutralise their meaning*. As a rule, it will be found that persons are more successful when the principal lines are clear and distinct and, as it were, not confused by a multitude of minor marks running through them.

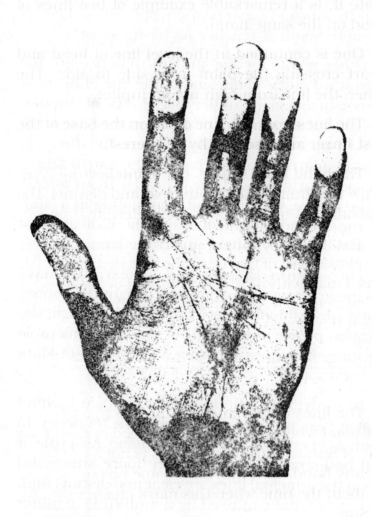

PLATE II

THE RIGHT HAND OF GEN.

SIR REDVERS BULLER.V.C., G.C.B

The right hand of General Sir Redvers Buller, Plate II, is a remarkable example of two lines of head on the same hand.

One is contained in the level line of head and heart crossing the palm from side to side. The other, the line from high up on Jupiter.

The lines from the line of life on the base of the first finger are also worthy of interest.

The hand itself is long, of the intellectual type, while the thumb stands out clear and distinct, the embodiment of will-power and determination.

The fourth or little finger is the one badly developed part of this hand, but Sir Redvers Buller was a man with no great command of language or gift of eloquence, and was unable to defend himself when the moment came when speech would have been a valuable asset. I have written about the indications given by the fourth finger in Chapter 11.

The lines of fate and Sun are also good up to the point where a line may be noticed crossing the line of Sun *toward* Saturn. This is not a good sign on any hand, as it indicates some reverse of fate, at about the time when this mark crosses the line of Sun.

General Sir Redvers Buller had extraordinary power and command over his men when he employed the gift of organisation and authority conferred on him by the line of head coming from Jupiter.

There is, however, something contradictory and even unlucky about persons who have the lines of head and heart running together across the palm. Such people have a kind of 'single track' brain that will not listen to others or take any advice unless it comes from themselves. They may meet with considerable success due to their excessive power of concentration on some one object, until any mark on their line of Sun bends or inclines toward the Mount of Saturn. If such is the case their plans as suddenly turn out wrong and they usually meet with disaster.

Sir redvers Buller was sceptical when I told him that there lay before him another campaign which would bring censure and criticism on him.

This actually occurred when, as Commander-in-Chief in the Boer War, the disaster of 'Spion Kop' and the Modder River brought about his recall and censure by the War Office.

THE HAND OF SIR ARTHUR SULLIVAN, BART

Sir Arthur Sullivan will be remembered for the original and beautiful music he composed for the 'Gilbert and Sullivan Operas.' The reproduction of his right hand on Plate III, shows the line of head separated from that of the life, long and gently curved into the middle of the Mount of Luna. The space between the head-and life-lines denotes the

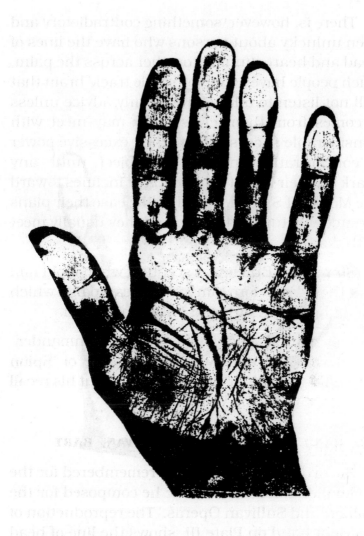

PLATE III

THE RIGHT HAND OF SIR ARTHUR

SULLIVAN, BT.

257

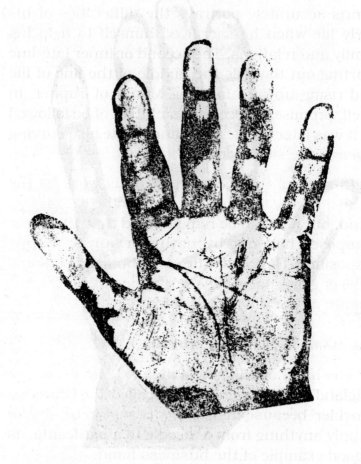

PLATE IV

THE RIGHT HAND OF MR. WILLIAM WHITELEY

dramatic quality of his work, while the curved line of head into the Mount of Luna indicates his great powers of imagination and originality.

The line of fate so closely tied to the Mount of Venus accurately portrays the difficulties of his early life when he sacrificed himself to help his family and relations. The second or inner fate-line starting out towards the middle of the line of life and rising upward into the Mount of Jupiter, in itself, promises successful ambition of be followed as it was later by the main line of fate also curving towards the same mount.

In spite of the recognition of his work by the public, hardly any lines of sun can be see on this hand, but it has to be remembered that this great composer had not by nature a sunny, happy disposition. He cared little or nothing for personal fame or glory, nor did his work bring him any great amout of worldly possession or wealth.

THE HAND OF WILLIAM WHITELEY

The hand of William Whiteley, Plate IV, one of England's great businessmen, called 'the Universal Provider' because his store was said to be able to supply anything from a 'needle to a battleship,' is a good example of the business hand.

It is the square type with fairly long fingers and a very 'level-headed' looking head-line. closely joined to the line of life. There was nothing rash or impulsive in William Whiteley's 'make-up', he was noted for his caution, but at the same time he was always ready for any emergency.

The fate-and sun-lines on this hand are well marked. There is one peculiar line rising from the centre of the line of fate toward the base of the Mount of Jupiter, but which appears to be cut through by a lone from Mars to the Sun. This occurs at the age he had reached when he was shot and killed in his office by his supposed illegitimate son.

When I took the impression of his hand I warned him of danger of a violent death.

Very calmly he asked: 'How far off is that danger'

I replied: 'About thirteen years from now.'

Then thirteen years later he was shot to death at the height of his enormously successful business career.

THE HAND OF THE RRIGHT HON. JOSEPH CHAMBERLAIN, M.P., AND HIS SON, WHO LATER BECAME SIR AUSTEN CHAMBERLAIN

These two right hands, Plates V and VI, are good examples of heredity as shown by hands. It will be noticed that the shape is similar in both father and son, while the lines are very much alike.

I took these impressions in Mr. Chamberlain's private room in the House of Commons. Mr. Chamberlain was keenly interested in my predictions that his son Austen was destined to

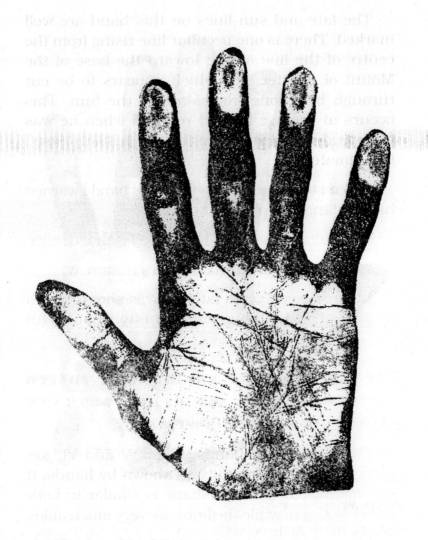

PLATE V

THE HAND OF H.H. THE HAND OF THE RIGHT HON.

JOSEPH CHAMBERLAIN. P.C.

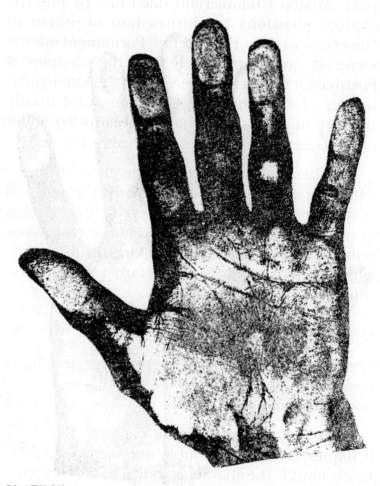

PLATE VI

THE HAND OF RT. HON. SIR

AUSTEN CHAMBERLAIN, K.G

ILLUSTRATIVE OF HEREDITARY TENDENCIES. SEE

HAND OF HIS FATHER OVERLEAF

follow the same political career that he had done.

It is common knowledge that as the years went past, Austen Chamberlain filled one by one the exalted positions his father had occupied in Government life. He entered Parliament at the same age, and successfully filled the positions of Postmaster General, Chancellor of the Exchequer, Leader of the House of Commons and finally received knighthood for his services as President of the Locarno Peace Conference after the war.

Further, he suffered the same class of illness which his distinguished father passed through and at the same periods of his life, even to the serious nervous breakdown that caused him to retire from public life (see health-line attacking the line of life) which caused paralysis to his father in his sixty-third and sixty-fifthy year.

CHEIRO'S OWN HAND

In Plate VII, I reproduce an impression of my own hand as an example of what is called 'the double line of head.'

I have stated in previous pages of this book (Chapter 23), that a double line of head' is very rarely found. The character shown by each of these lines of head is in apparent contradiction to the other. For example, the lower line closely joined to the line of life denotes a mentality extremely sensitive, artistic. and imaginative.

The upper line gives the reverse characteristics: namely, rising on the Mount of Jupiter and running nearly straight across the palm, it denotes self-confidence, ambition, power to dominate others and a level-headed, practical way of looking at life.

One can hardly imagine such mentally opposite characteristics in the same person, but the impression given of my own hand is a good illustration of these statements.

On my left hand there is no sign whatever of any upper head-line—there is only the lower line to be seen; and it is a curious fact that the appearance of the upper head-line on my right hand only commenced to be noticeable when I was about thirty years of age.

At this period of my life, circumstances brought me before the world as a lecturer and public speaker. This forced me to make a supreme effort to overcome my extreme sensitiveness as shown by the lower head-line, with the result that the upper line began to develop and in a few years became *the dominant one* on my right hand.

I have also stated that in cases where, the double line of head, is found, persons who possess these lines are inclined to live what are called double lives of one form or another.

In my own particular case this has been remarkably true, fro more than thirty years one section of the public only knew me under my *nom de guerre* as 'Cheiro', while another section only

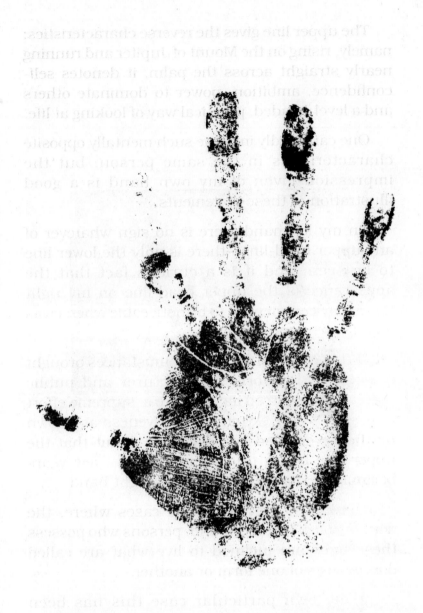

PLATE VII

THE "DOUBLE LINE OF HEAD"

"CHEIRO'S" HAND

PLATE VIII
A BABY'S HAND

knew me under my own name.

I can further state here, that due to the influence of the more sensitive side of my nature, for many years I gave vent to my feelings by writing poetry, both sentimental and religious, while at the same time, the other side was engaged in appearing as a lecturer on the public platform, as War Correspondent, and later, as editor of newspapers in London and Paris.

These 'double lines' of head may be very clearly seen in the impression of my right hand reproduced in this volume.

THE BABY'S HAND TWENTY-FOUR HOURS OLD

The impression of this baby's right hand I took twenty-four hours after its birth. Impression of very young children's hands are very hard to take as the flesh is so soft and pliable and the little ones will not keep still.

In this case, Plate VIII, I succeeded very well and the lines may be quite clearly seen. I made this impression many years ago and the 'baby' has now grown to be a man. He has done very well in a business career (Probably due to the upper line of head lying so straight across the hand)

THE HAND OF MADAME SARAH BERNHARDT

The most remarkable point about this imprint (Plate IX) is the lines of fate and Sun rising so early in life from almost the wrist and running *parallel to one another to the advanced years of the life.*

The 'great Sarah' commenced her dramatic career at the age of sixteen. In spite of her remarkable talents she had many difficulties to contend with, up to the period when on her hand the two lines of fate may be seen coming together about her twenty-sixth year. From this date on her fame and renown became world-wide.

The line of head is clear as if drawn by a rule, while the open space between it and the line of life denotes her impulsiveness and dramatic ability which I called attention to in Chapter 23.

It will be noticed the remarkable number of small lines that appear to be shot out of the line of life in an upward direction. These indicate what may be termed 'spurts of energy', at these moments.

These are not good signs if a heavily-marked line of health is seen attacking the life-line from the Mount of Mercury. In Madame Bernhardt's case there is hardly any health-line, it appears to stop, or fade out, after her early years. As is well known, the great actress had a wonderfully strong constitution once she passed her middle years, which continued to the last period of her life.

Madame Bernhardt was born in Paris, October 22, 1845. She died in Paris, March 26, 1923, in her seventy-eighth year.

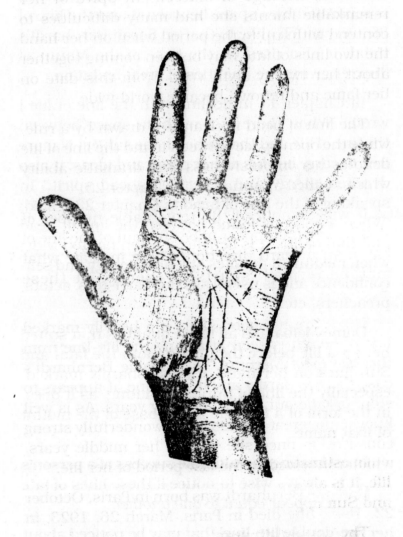

PLATE IX

THE HAND OF MADAME SARAH BERNHARDT

THE RIGHT HAND OF DAME MELBA, G.B.E., THE FAMOUS AUSTRALIAN PRIMA DONNA

It will be noticed that the line of head (Plate X) is separated by a space between it and the line of life, very much alike to that on Sarah Bernhardt's hand, it also rises on the base of the Mount of Jupiter giving the qualities of great ambition.

In Chapter 11 in dealing with the line of life I wrote: 'When there is a medium space between the line of life and that of head, the subject is more free to carry out his or her plans and ideas; it also denotes energy and a very go-ahead spirit.' In speaking of the line of head in Chapter 23, I said: 'When a space is found between the line of head and that of life, it is beneficial when not too wide; when medium it denotes splendid energy and self-confidence and is useful sign for barristers, actors, preachers, etc.,

Dame Melba had all those qualities that suited her for a life before the public. Both the fate- and Sun-lines on her hand are also sharply marked, especially the line of Sun culminating, as it does, in the form of a triangle at the base of the mount of that name.

In estimating the ultimate success of a person's life, it is always wise to notice if these lines of fate and Sun *appear equal to one another.*

The 'double life-line' that may be noticed about the middle of the hand gave Dame Melba enormous vitality and by running outward into a line of travel toward Luna, promised the almost continual run of long voyage from one side of the world to the other which was so much a part of this remarkable woman's career.

Dame Melba consulted me in New York when she wrote in my Visitor's Book:

Cheiro you are *wonderful*—what more can I say?

NELLIE MELBA

THE HAND OF LORD LEIGHTON, P.R.A.

Sir Frederick Leighton, who later became Lord Leighton, had just been elected President of the Royal Academy when he gave me the impression of his hand which appears on Plate XI. His left and right were exactly alike: for some reason of his own he preferred that in my book I should reproduce the left.

For a man's hand, it is almost a perfect example of the 'Conic or Artistic' type, which I have described in Chapter 7, but in Lord Leighton's case, his hands were strong and elastic, which gave him the strength of will to hold in check his natural love of luxury and comfort. His artistic disposition, characteristic of this type, was, however, much in evidence in his beautiful studio and in his home, where he lived more like a Persian prince in a palace than an Englishman.

The line of Sun from the wrist to the third finger is very remarkable. It promised him the fame and glory which came easily to him from the very commencement of his brilliant career.

Lord Leighton studied hands from the standpoint of his art and in all his pictures emphasised their shape and expression.

THE HAND OF 'MARK TWAIN'

The right hand of 'Mark Twain,' Plate XII, does not come out as clear as one would like. It was made by means of smoked paper, a process I employed in the earlier days of my career. I later substituted a process I will describe later on in these pages.

The most remarkable things to notice in the impression of the right hand of this celebrated American humorist is that the line of head lies almost *level across the palm*. This characteristic is found on the hands of persons who develop the faculty of 'seeing both sides' of anything that interests them.

'Mark Twain' had this particular gift in a very marked way and which comes out strongly in all his writings. He was not a 'visionary' by any manner of means. If anything he was an avowed sceptic and had to have facts to support his views or ideas.

When he came to see me I did not know who he was? While I was taking impressions of his hands,

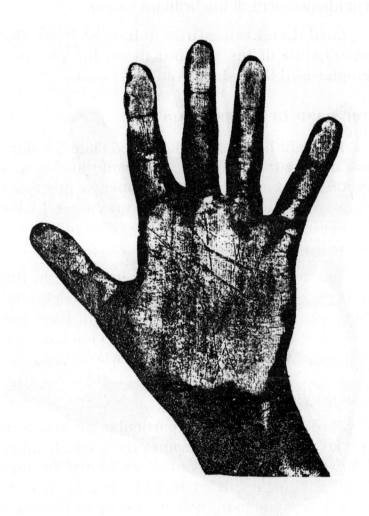

PLATE X

THE RIGHT HAND OF DAME NELLIE MELBA G.B.E.

273

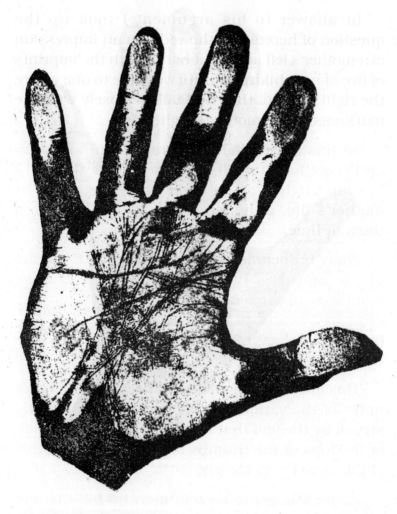

PLATE XI

THE HAND OF LORD LEIGHTON P.R.A

274

he said: The past may leave its mark, I admit, and character may be told down to its finest shades of expression; all that I might believe—but how the future may be even foreshadowed is what I cannot understand.

In answer to his argument I took up the question of heredity. I showed him an impression of a mother's left and right hands with the imprints of five of her children's until we came to one where the right hand of the child tallied closely with the markings of the mother's right hand.

'In this case,' I said, which you can follow up and prove for yourself, every section of this girl's life repeated, even to dates, the events of the mother's life, although twenty years separated them in time.

'Now,' I concluded, 'if one had known the events of the mother's life and seen that the same markings appeared in the hands of the child—then, even say at six years of age, one could have predicted the events which would take place in the fate of the daughter.'

This interested my visitor so deeply that he took notes of the various hands and was particularly struck by the fact that even the circles in the skin of the tops of the thumbs of the mother and this child agreed very closely.

As he was going he told me who he was and added: "The one humorous point in the situation is, that I came here expecting to lose my money by my foolishness, but I have gained a plot for a story which I certainly think should be a 'best seller'."

A short time later he published *Pudd'n Head Wilson*, dealing with thumb-marks, which had an enormous success.

Before he left he wrote in my Visitor's Book the following:

"Cheiro" has exposed my character to me with humiliating accuracy. I ought not to confess this accuracy, still I am moved to do it.

'MARK TWAIN'

THE HAND OF A CONVICTED MURDERER

I obtained the impression of Dr. Meyer's hand (Plate XIII) under the following conditions. On the occasion of my first visit to New York, some reporters representing the *New York World* called and said they wanted to test my powers by having me read imprints of hands without my knowing the names or positions of any of the people. Without demurring, I accepted the test and we at once got to work.

I had described the character and careers of perhaps a dozen of these test cases, when the impressions of a strange-looking pair of hands were put before me. I was struck by the fact that the lines on the left were in every way normal while those on the right were as abnormal as possible. I

276

particularly noticed that on the left hand the line of head lay clear and straight across the centre, whereas on the right it appeared to have twisted out of its place, closing in against the heart-line under-the base of the third finger.

I summed up the impressions before me by stating: Judging from these hands, the owner of them undoubtedly commenced his career in a normal way. He is likely to have been a religious man in his early years.' I thought that it was probable he might have commenced life as Sunday-school tacher and later became interested in science or medicine.

I went on to describe how the man's entire nature slowly and steadily had changed under the continual urge to acquire wealth at any cost, until he was finally prepared even to commit murder for money.

My remarks noted down by the reporters were as follows: 'Whether this man has committed one crime or twenty is not the question, as he enters his forty fourth year he will be found out, arrested, tried, and sentenced to death, It will then be proved, that for years he has used his mentality and whatever profession he has followed to obtain money by crime and has stopped at nothing to achieve his ends. This man in his forty-fourth year will pass through some sensational trial, he will be condemned to die, yet his hands show that he will escape this fate and live on for years—but in prison.'

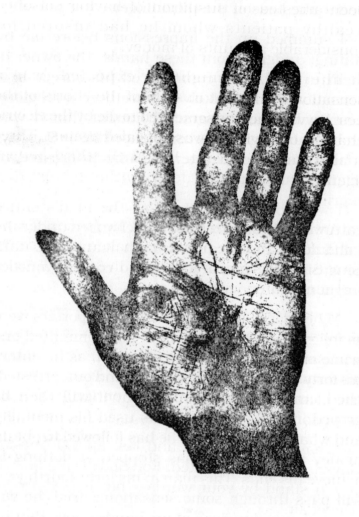

PLATE XII

THE HAND OF MARK TWAIN

278

When the interview with me appeared the following Sunday in the *New York World*, the paper disclosed that the hands I had read were those of a Dr. Meyer from Chicago. He had that very week been arrested on suspicion of having poisoned wealthy patients whom he had insured for considerable amounts of money.

The trial, as might be expected, was a sensational one, but in spite of the efforts of the best lawyers, he was sentenced to die by the electric chair. The conviction was appealed against. Three trials in all took place, but at the third he was again condemned to death without hope of a reprieve.

A week before his execution, he requested that I should go and see him. I was taken to his cell in Sing Sing prison. As long as I live, I shall never forget the interview.

'Cheiro,' gasped the now completely broken man, 'at that interview you gave the reporters, what you said about my early life was true. But you also said that although I should be sentenced to the electric chair, I should live on for years—but in prison.

I have lost my third and last appeal in a few days I am to be executed. For God's sake, tell me if you stand by your words—that I shall escape 'the chair.'

Even if I had not seen his line of life going on clear and distinct well past his forty-fourth year, I

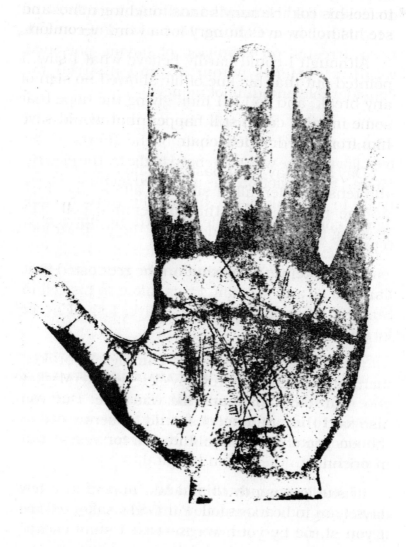

PLATE XIII

THE HAND OF DR. MAYER.

CONVICTED OF MURDER

believe I would have tried to give him hope. To me it was torture to see that poor wretch before me, to feel his cold clammy hands touching mine, and see his hollow eyes hungry for a word of comfort.

Although I could hardly believe what I saw, I pointed out that his line of life showed no sign of any break, and so I left him, giving the hope that some miracle could still happen that would save him from the dreaded 'chair.'

Day after day went past, with no news to relive the tension. Mentally I suffered almost as much as the poor man in the condemned cell. The evening papers, full of details of the preparations for the execution fixed for the next morning were eagerly bought up. I bought one and read every line.

Midnight came. Suddenly boys rushed through the streets screaming Special Edition. I read across the front page, "MEYER ESCAPES THE CHAIR SUPREME COURT FINDS FLAW IN INDICTMENT." The miracle had happened. The sentence was altered to imprisonment for life. Meyer lived for fifteen years. When the end did come, the died peacefully in the prison hospital.

If students study this hand, they will see how closely its indications follow the descriptions I have given of the line of head showing the tendencies for premeditated murder in early pages of this book. Students must not confuse this rising line of head *against the heart-line* with the one straight

281

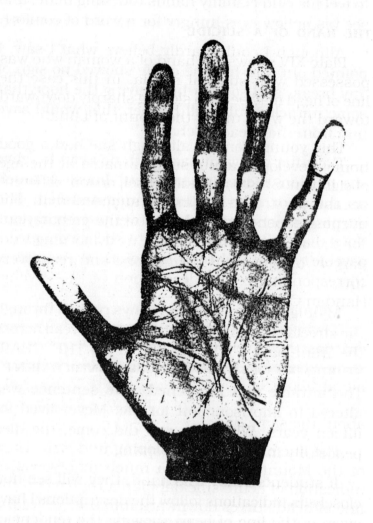

PLATE XIV

THE HAND OF A SUICIDE

282

line of head and heart combined, which will be seen in further impressions given later.

THE HAND OF A SUICIDE

Plate XIV shows the hand of a woman who was possessed with suicidal mania. In this case the line of head may be seen sloping sharply downward toward the wrist under the Mount of Luna.

This young woman, although she had a good home, developed acute sucidal mania at the age of eighteen. She tried to kill herself on four different occasions until she finally succeeded in her purpose as she entered her twenty-eighth year: Note that her hand belongs to the long *narrow* psychic type with 'philosophic' joints to the fingers, corresponding to my description of the Psychic Hand in Chapter 8.

It is interesting to bear in mind that this young girl has the Circle of Saturn at the base of the second finger with a line from it cutting the line of life at about her age of twenty-eight and on the line of Sun the commencement of an 'island' at about the same date.

The line of head when sloping under the base of the Mount of Luna is a much more positive indication of acute suicidal mania than when the line of head curves downward into the face of the Mount of Luna. In the latter case the subject has a naturally despondent nature which only requires some added blow of fate or disappointment, which the highly imaginative disposition exaggerates (sloping head-line on Luna), to bring about the fatal act.

49

HOW TO MAKE CLEAR IMPRESSIONS OF HANDS

PRINTERS' ink, especially the kind employed by the police for fingerprints in all cities, is the best means I have found for making good impressions of hands.

Readers can purchase this ink at any establishment where they sell printers, materials.

At the same place, get a small gelatine roller, which is generally fitted in a metal frame with a wooden handle.

Next, get a few quires of white coated paper about the size of an ordinary sheet of typewriting paper. I specify *coated or glazed* paper, as it takes the best imprints. When you have obtained these requisites, go to any hardware store and get a rubber mat about a quarter to a half inch thick, what is called a 'kneeling mat' will do very well. These are necessary to make a springy cushion, so that the fine lines come out clearly.

Place a sheet of the coated white paper on the upper surface of the rubber mat. Smooth out a small portion of the printers' ink by running the gelatine roller over it on a piece of glass.

When all is ready, run the gelatine roller over the subject's left and right hands, press them firmly down on the sheet of paper, turn the hand *over on the back* and with the flat part of the thumb press the paper lightly into the hollow of the palm and wrist, peel off the sheet of paper, starting from the fingers, and you will find you have obtained a clear impression of all the lines of the hand.

You may at first find some difficulty with persons who have a dry, acid skin, which may make the imprints in many cases look 'spotted.' This can be got over by first washing the hands yu are going to treat with warm water, drying them thoroughly and sprinkling with a light dusting of some powder like talc. If you have not got talc, a little chalk will do as well.

There are many ways of removing the printers' ink from the hands. The simplest and best is to get a small tin of the powder sold at all motor supply stores for cleaning oil and grease off hands, rub this on the hands in hot water and the ink will come off easily.

PART TWO
NUMEROLOGY

50

THE SIGNIFICANCE OF NUMBERS

THE ancient Hindu searchers after Nature's laws, it must be remembered, were in former years masters of all such studies, but in transmitting their knowledge to their descendants, they so endeavoured to hide their secrets from the common people that in most cases the key to the problem became lost, and the truth that had been discovered became buried in·the dust of superstition and charlatanism, to be reformed, let us hope, when some similar cycle of thought in its own appointed time will again claim attention to this side of nature.

This ancient people, together with the Chaldeans and Egyptians, were the absolute masters of the occult or hidden meaning of numbers, in their application to time and in their relation to human life.

When examining such questions, we must not forget that it was the Hindus who discovered what is known as the precession of the Equinoxes, and in their calculation such an occurrence takes place every 25,827 years; our modern science after labours of hundreds of years has simply proved them to be correct:

How, or by what means they were able to arrive at such a calculation. has never been discovered—

observations lasting over such a period of time are hardly admissible, and calculation without instruments is also scarcely conceivable, and so science has only been able, first to accept their statement, and later to acknowledge its accuracy.

Their judgment, together with that of the Chaldeans, as to the length of what is now known as the cycle of years of the planets, has been handed down to us from the most remote ages, and also by our modern appliances has been proved correct, so when one comes to a study such as this, as to the value of the numbers 1 to 9, which, as the seven harmonies of music are the bases of all music that has ever been conceived, these above-stated numbers are the basis of *all our numbers and calculations,* it is then only logical to accept the decisions of those great students of long past ages and at least examine their deductions with a mind free from bias and prejudice.

It is impossible here to give in detail all the reasonings and examples the exist for a belief in the occult side of numbers, but it may interest my readers if I give a few illustrations of why the number 7 has for ages been regarded as *the number of mystery relating to the spiritual side of things,* and why the number 9 has in its turn come to be regarded as the *finality or end of the series on which all our materialistic calculations are built,* but the most casual observer can only admit that beyond the number 9 all ordinary numbers become but a mere repetition of the first 9. A simple illustration of this will readily suffice. The number 10, as the zero is not a number, becomes a repetition of the number 1. The number 11 added together as the ancient occultists laid down in their law of *natural addition*, namely adding together from left to right, repeats the number 2, 12 repeats 3, 13 repeats 4, and so on up to 19, which in its turn becomes 1 plus 9 equals 10, and so again the repetition of 1. 20 represents, 2, and so on to infinity. The occult symbolism of what are called compound numbers, that is, those numbers from 10 onwards, I will explain later.

In this way it will be seen that in all our *materialistic* systems of numbers, the numbers 1 to 9 are the base on which we are compelled to build, just as in the same way the seven great or primary harmonies in music are the bases of all music, and again as the seven primary colours are the bases of all our combinations of colours. In passing, it may be remarked that all through the Bible and other sacred books, the 'seven,' whenever mentioned, always stands in relation to the spiritual or *mysterious God force*, and has a curious significance in this sense whenever employed.

For a few instances of this, take the seven days (or cycles) of the creation as referred to in Genesis:

The seven heavens, so often referred to.

The seven thrones.

The seven seals.

The seven churches.

The seven days' march round the walls of

Jericho, when, on 'the seventh day,' the walls fell, *before that mysterious, God force* symbolised in the number of seven. It is also remarkable that there are exactly seven generations from David to the birth of Christ. In Revelation we read of the seven spirits of God sent forth into all the earth.' Ezekiel speaks of 'The seven angels of the Lord that go to and from through the whole earth,' which is believed to be a reference to the magnetic influences of the seven creative planets which radiate through the earth.

Again, we have the seven Spirits referred to in the Egyptian religion:

The seven Devas of the Hindus' Bible:

The seven Amschaspands of Persian faith.

The seven Angels of the Chaldeans.

The seven Sephiroth of the Hebrew Cabala.

The seven Archangels of Revelation, etc., etc.

Let us now take another view of this strange number. If we were to examine every class of occult teaching from the Hindu, Chinese, Egyptian, Greek, Hebrew, or modern school, whichever one may choose, in every case — and without a single exception — we shall find that the quality of the number 7 stands for the expression of that mysterious God force in Nature before referred to.

In the most ancient rules of occult philosophy we find the rule laid down that the number 7 *is the only number capable of dividing `the number of Eternity,'* and continuing in itself as long as the number representing Eternity lasts, and yet, *at every addition of itself producing the number 9,* or

290

in other words, it produces the basic numbers on which all materialistic calculations are built and on which all human beings depend and the whole edifice of human thought finds expression.

EXAMPLE

The number 1 is the first number. It represnts the First Cause, Creator, God or Spirit, call it as you like. A Circle or the zero, 0', has always been taken as the symbol of endlessness—otherwise Eternity. Place the 1 and the figure zero by its side, and you get the significant symbol of eternity such as 1 plus 0, the 10, and then, places as many of these emblems of eternity side by side as you like, and you get such a figure as 1,000,000. Divide by the mystic number 7 and you get the number 142857.

$$7)1,000,000$$
$$142857$$

Add as many zeros as you like, and keep on dividing by the 7, and you yourself may go on through all eternity and you can only get repetitions of the same 142857, which from time immemorial has been called the 'sacred number.' Now add this number wherever you find it by natural addition, it will give you the figure 27, and as you have seen by the rule of natural addition described on a preceding page, you keep adding till only one number remains, to arrive at what is known as 'the root of the number.' You: add again 27 by natural addition, and 2 plus 7 equals 9, or in other words, you get the full range of the first series of numbers on which all *materialistic or human calcultions can be built.*

Now, let us return to the symbolism of seven for a moment. You know, of course, that Buddha is always represented as sitting in the centre of a Lotus. Let us examine, then, the secret of such a selection. It is not perhaps generally known that the 7 is reproduced in many strange ways in Nature herself, and that flowers that have *not been crossed* by intermingling with other flowers have their outside petals in the number of seven, but as flowers are so easily crossed with other varieties, and it is so difficult to find a pure type, Buddha took the Lotus, which never becomes crossed or loses its individuality, as the emblem of the religion he taught, because, first, its seven foundation petals are always in evidence, and further, the religion he taught was that the creative Spirit was the foundation and origin of all things, and thus again bore silent but unmistakable testimony to the creative action of the seven planets from which all religions have had their origin.

Long before man made his creeds, or civilisations their laws, the influence of these seven planets had become known on the earth. Out of the dark night of antiquity their light became law and as far as we can penetrate, even to the very confines of prehistoric days, in all races, in all countries, we find the influence of the seven planets through all and in all.

DAYS OF THE WEEK

The seven days of the week have been the outcome of the influence of the seven creative planets and gave the names of the days of week, in every land or clime. Take any nation you may choose, this fact remains the same, and is so expressed in almost every language, Chinese, Assyrian, Hindu, Egyptian, Hebrew, Greek, Latin, French, German, or English. In modern languages Monday or Moonsday in English becomes Montag in German or Lundi (Lune) in French, Lunes in Spanish, and so on until one comes to Saturday or Saturn's day, the day on which God ordered the Hebrews that no work should be done, and giving them this command He said, `It is a sign between Me and the children of Israel for ever.'[1] And Saturday, year by year, in our modern civilisation is becoming more and more a day of rest.

In connection with this thought, it is worthy of remark that Saturn, the last planet in the series of the seven creative planets of our solar system, in all religions, Hebrew or otherwise, represents 'cessation,' or rest from labour in another sense. In this strange example one can see the connection between the seven days of the week and the seven creative planets, and it throws a new light on the

---

1 Wherever the Jews went they obeyed this command, even causing their Roman conquerors and other pagan nations to follow their example. Josephus wrote: `There is not a city of the Grecians, nor any of the barbarians, nor any nation whatsoever, whither our custom of resting on the seventh day hath not come.'
The seventh day of the Jews is Saturday, called the Sabbath from the Hebrew word Sabbath - to rest.

verse, 'God made the sun, moon, and stars and appointed them *for sings and for seasons and for days and for years.'* Even Mr. Maunder, the eminent author of so many works on astronomy, calls attention to this strange division of the week into seven days when he says in his *Astronomy of the Bible*: 'the period of seven days does not fit precisely into either months or seasons of the year. It is not a division of time *that man would naturally adopt,* it runs across all natural division of time,' but this author, not seeing or perhaps knowing the great hidden truth contained in the number 7, worried only over the point, that it was not a division of time *which man would naturally adopt.'* But as everything on the earth and above the earth has its meaning, and especially its secret or soul meaning, its place, position, and number, in the order of things,' which is the highest form of design, *every day of the week, every hour of the day, and every minute of the hour, has both its meaning and number.*

It is invariably conceded by every class of scientist that the regularity, order, and system of the wonderful machinery of the heavens is beyond all comparison.

We know today that the heavenly bodies move through their orbits with such precision that in millions of years they do not vary one minute of time. We know that they exercise an influence on this earth which is felt by the veriest atoms in the earth, though what this force is, or with what incredible speed it acts, may forever remain a mystery. It was in dealing with this mysterious law that the ancient philosophers by study, experiments, concentration of mind, and perhaps intuition, arrived at the fixation of certain laws governing life, which may be as accurate as their discovery that the precession of the Equinoxes takes place once in every 25,827 years.'

It is from these wonderful students of Nature that we have received the first idea as to the divisions of the Zodiac into twelve periods of 30 degrees, and further, that each period produces a definite and well-known influence on the earth and on human beings born in any of its twelve periods. They further subdivided these 30-degree periods into division of three periods of 10 degrees each, in which the planets are also found to have an influence, and they pursued their investigations until they worked out a system demonstrating that each day had its own particular meanings due to vibrations in the ether, which keeps the earth in instaneous report with its entire solar system, and lastly, that as the sun enters a new degree of the Zodiac in mid-winter at about rate of every 2½ to 3 minutes, and in summer at the rate of 3 to 4¾ minutes, that its magnetic influence varied the effect of the vibrations or ether waves of each planet, and so enabled these students of Nature to carry their system in this way down to almost the smallest fraction of time.[1]

In examining this subject, let us take for an example any remarkable piece of mechanism we may have seen, such as a clock. We have noticed how wheel fits into wheel and how the entire mechanism is put into motion as the ray or tooth

[1] This applies, of course, to the motion of the Sun through the symbolic or cabbalistic Zodiac used in the East.

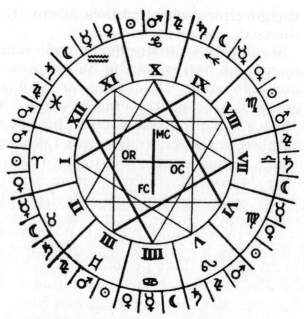

Map showing the twelve Divisions of the Zodiac, each division
subdivided into three parts of 10 degrees.

SIGNS OF THE ZODIAC

SIGNS OF THE SEVEN PLANETS

I.	Aries, the Ram	☉	The Sun
II.	Taurus, the Bull	♀	Venus
III.	Gemini, the Twins	☿	Mercury
IV.	Cancer, the Crab	☾	Moon
V.	Leo, the Lion	♄	Saturn
VI.	Virgo, the Virgin	♃	Jupiter
VII.	Libra, the Balance	♂	Mars
VIII.	Scorpio, the Scorpion		
IX.	Sagittarius, the Archer		
X.	Capricorn, the Goat		
XI.	Aquarius, the Water-Bearer		
XII.	Pisces, the Fishes		

This map represents the Sun's entry into Aries in the Vernal
Equinox on March 21-23 of every year. The letters at the points of
the central cross stand for: OR-Oriental or Eastern; MC-Mid-
Heaven; OC-Occidental or Western; FC-Lower Heaven.

FIG. 24

of the governing wheel presses against the tooth of the next, and so on.

Keeping this illustration in your mind for a moment, let us regard the 360 degrees of the Zodiac into which the sun appears to pass, from degree to degree on an average of every 4 minutes as the teeth of one of our wheels. This 360 degrees multiplied by the 4 minutes gives 1,440 minutes, and this, divided by 60, to bring it to hours, gives us the 24-hour day, which becomes in its turn another spoke in the great wheel of time, and consequently, by the advance of the Sun, must bring us to the commencement of another day *under new and distinct influences, and so on until the year itself is completed.*

Now as science proves that it takes the Sun 30 days to pass from one division of the Zodiac into another, again we have the illustration of another wheel, as it were, but a still slower one, being put into motion, and consequently with the change in the heavenly mechanism another set of influences are brought to bear upon the earth, and so on until the twelve months of the year have in their turn experienced the influence of the Sun in the twelve divisions of the Zodiac.

Let us now return for a moment to the part played by the seven creative planets. No-one today, I believe, can plead ignorance of the effect of one of these planets, namely the Moon, on the earth itself and on the people who inhabit the earth. We all know, or at least have heard, about the effect of the moon on the brain of people mentally unbalanced. We know how it causes tides to rise and fall along our shores, but still perhaps we do not realise that even in the deepest ocean its pull or attraction is so great that it causes hundreds of thousands of tons of dead weight of water to be drawn up by it to such a height as 70 feet in the Bay of Fundy and in the Bristol Channel.

Scientists, like Darwin in England, Flammarion in France, and others in Germany, made the starting discovery that there are actually tides *in the solid earth itself*, which are affected by the attraction of the moon. *What then of the effect of the moon on the brain itself, which contains the most subtle essence and is one of the greatest mysteries known in life?*

Granted that this be admitted, what then of the part played on human nature by the rest of the planets, which are in each individual case far larger than the Moon ?

The following table showing the dimensions of each of the planets will illustrate better than any words I may use this side of the argument:

Diameter of Mercury	2,000 miles
the Moon	2,100
Venus	7,510
the Earth	7,913
Mars	4,920
Jupiter	88,390
Saturn	71,900
Uranus	33,000
Neptune	36,000
the Sun	860,000

I ask, is it logical, with such a demonstration before one, to admit that effect of the Moon and to deny any effect to the other planets that are in fact so much larger than it?

Let us now return to the important side of the question as regards the rules set forth in ths book. You will very natually ask, how and when were such numbers arrived at that represent the mechanical action or influence of the celestial system on the people of this earth? I could write an entire volume on this side of the question alone, but in the following necessarily condensed pages you will find the general law explained which may be sufficient to elucidate the system contained in the following chapters.

In the first place, the secret or occult significance of numbers was revealed to man so far back in the world's history that the exact place of their discovery has never been recorded, but it suffices to state that if one back in one's investigations to the most distant period in the history of any race who made themselves in any degree responsible for such studies, even there one would find that these numbers representing the qualities of the solar system and the basis of all our later forms of calculation existed.

In working out the idea contained in these pages, I have carefully investigated every important form of occultism bearing on this question, but whether it has been Hindu. Egyptian, Chaldean, or Greek, the symbols of these numbers have

299

always appeared the same, and their relation to months, days, hours, and people representing certain numbers, has been more or less alike.

What is called the secondary numbers' as illustrated on subsequent pages I myself have brought into a practical form. but they have in every case been built up from long investigation and experience extending over many years. Although we may never be able to find out the exact time in past ages when the influence of these numbers was discovered, that is no reason why we should not accept what has been given us by those ancient students. There are many other things we are forced to accept in life from being conscious of their truth, even when we are not able to get back to their birth or beginnings.

The origin of life we know not, but we are none the less conscious that life exists. The balance, poise, and hidden laws governing our own solar system have also never been explained, together with a thousand other things in our everyday life. The very origin of numbers is itself a mystery; yet we are forced to employ them, and as Balzac says, `without them, the whole edifice of our civilisation would fall to pieces.'

In the Book of the Wisdom of Solomon, now included in the Apocrypha, Solomon says:

For God Himself gave me an unerring knowledge of the things that are, to know the constitution of the world, the beginning and the end and middle of times, the alterations of the solstices, the changes of seasons and the positions of the planets, the nature of living creatures and the thoughts of men, all things that are either secret or manifest I learned, for He that is the artificer of all things taught me this wisdom.

I ask, could anything be more forcible or convincing than such a statement, particularly when it is remembered that the true Seal of Solomon was none other than the seven-pointed star which contained the nine numbers which constitute the base of all our calculations, and which is the root of the system of numbers as applied to human life?

Even in our chemistry we have given a number and symbol to all the elements:

Water is	1010 its symbol is H_2O
Hydrogen	212 its symbol is H
Oxygen	1030 its symbol is O
Nitrogen	1969 its symbol is N
Carbon	1050 its symbol is C
and so on.	

All occult studies point to the fact that the ancient students had a foundation for ascribing to every human being *his number in the universe*, and if we admit, as we do, that there is a moment for birth and a moment for death, so also in the links of years. days, and hours, that make up the chain of life, it is not illogical to assume that *every link of life has also both its number and place*. I claim that by such a study man may become more perfect by his fitting in with the laws, system. and order of things to which he owes his being.

There is evidence that those ancient students were conversant with the fact that there were two more distant planets that Saturn in our solar system, for they assigned beyond the seven creative planets' the orbits for two more heavenly bodies, and they described them as governing the thoughts *on the mental side of Nature* and not the physical, and their description of them is in exact accordance with our present-day knowledge of the effect of the recently discovered planets of Uranus and Neptune on human life.

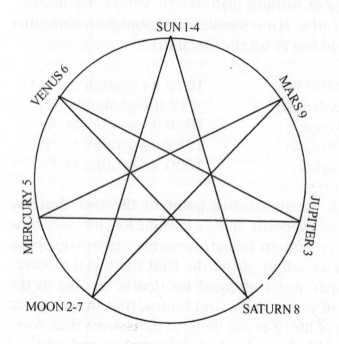

FIG. 25.
THE SEVEN-POINTED SEAL OF SOLOMON:
EXPLANATION

The Sun, with the numbers 1 hyphen 4, represents the combination of the Sun and the planet Uranus (the male quality of Creation being the Sun with the feminine Uranus *of the mental or spiritual plane)*. The Moon, with the numbers 2 hyphen 7, represents the Moon and Neptune, the Moon being feminine on the material or earth plane with Neptune (masculine) *on the mental or spiritual plane*. The meaning of the lines of the star being: That Life starts from the Sun—proceeds to the Moon, from that to Mars, from Mars to Mercury, Mercury to Jupiter, Jupiter to Venus, Venus to Saturn, and from Saturn (symbol of death) it returns to the Sun — or God from whence it came— to begin all over again in another cycle, *and so on through eternity.*

51

THE PLANETARY NUMBERS OF THE MONTHS

ALTHOUGH later in these pages the reader will find how the single and compound numbers have each their particular meaning in connection with human life, it is well at this stage to understand how and why the months have received their particular numbers.

The true solar year commences with the Sun's entrance into the Vernal or Spring Equinox on the 21st to the 23rd day of March of every year, and appears to pass through each Sign of the Zodiac of 30 degrees each, one after the other, taking slightly under 365¼ days in so doing, making our year popularly accepted as 365 days.

The Earth, revolving once upon its own axis each 24 hours, causes the whole of the 13 Signs of the Zodiac in their turn to pass over each portion of the Earth once each 24 hours. The Moon revolves round the earth in a lunar month of 28 days. This wounderful mechanism, if I may call it so, is exactly like the hour-hand, minute-hand, and second-hand of a clock.

What is called the first sign of the Zodiac is the 'period of the number 9' or the Zodiacal *Sign of ARIES*, from the 21st March to the 19th April. It is ruled by the Planet Mars in its *positive* aspect, and has the 9 for its number.

The 'period of the number 6' is the Zodiacal *Sign of TAURUS* from the 20th April to the 20th May. It is ruled by the Planet Venus in its *positive* aspect, and has the 6 for its number.

The 'period of the number 5' is the Zodiacal *Sign of GEMINI*, from the 21st May to the 20th June. It is ruled by the Planet Mercury in its *positive* aspect, and has the 5 for its number.

The 'period of the 2 and 7' is the Zodiacal *Sign of CANCER*, From the 21st June to the 20th July. It is ruled by the Moon in its *positive* aspect, and has the double figure of 2-7 for its number.

The 'period of the 1 and 4' is the Zodiacal *Sign of LEO*, from the 21st July to the 20th August. It is ruled by the Sun in its *positive aspect*, and has the double figures of 1—4 for its number.

The 2nd 'period of the number 5' is the Zodiacal *Sign of VIRGO* from the 21st August to the 20th September. It is ruled by the Planet Mercury in its *negative* aspect, and has the 5 for its number.

The 2nd 'period of the number 6' is the Zodiacal *Sign of LIBRA* from 21st September to the 20th October. It is ruled by the Planet Venus in its *negative* aspect, and has the 6 for its number.

The 2nd 'period of the number 9' is the Zodiacal *Sign of SCORPIO* from the 21st October to the 20th November. It is ruled by the Planet Mars in its *negative* aspect, and has the 9 for its number.

The 'period of the number 3' is the Zodiacal *sign of SAGITTARIUS*, from the 21st November to 20th December. It is ruled by the Planet Jupiter in its *positive* aspect, and has the 3 for its number.

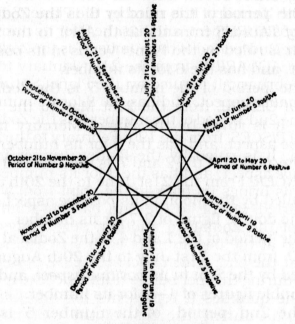

Period of Number 1-4 Positive
August 21 to September 20

July 21 to August 20
Period of Number 1-4 Positive

June 21 to July 20
Period of Numbers 2-7 Positive

September 21 to October 20
Period of Number 6 Negative

May 21 to June 20
Period of Number 5 Positive

October 21 to November 20
Period of Number 9 Negative

April 20 to May 20
Period of Number 6 Positive

November 21 to December 20
Period of Number 3 Positive

March 21 to April 19
Period of Number 9 Positive

December 21 to January 20
Period of Number 8 Negative

January 21 to February 19
Period of Number 8 Positive

February 19 to March 20
Period of Number 3 Negative

THE FIRE TRIANGLE
1st "House," March 21 to April 19.
2nd "House," July 21 to August 20.
3rd "House," November 21 to December 20.
THE AIR TRIANGLE
1st "House," May 21 to June 20.
2nd "House," September 21 to
October 20.
3rd "House," January 21 to February 19.
THE WATER TRIANGLE
1st "House," June 21 to July 20.
2nd "House," October 21 to
November 20.
3rd "House," February 19 to
March 20.
THE EARTH TRIANGLE
1st "House," April 20 to May 20.
2nd "House," August 21 to September 20.
3rd "House," December 21 to January 20.

FIG. 26

THE FOUR DIVISIONS OF THE ZODIAC FIRE, WATER, AIR,

EARTH

306

The 'period of the number 8' is the Zodiacal *Sign of CAPRICORN*, from the 21st December to the 20th January. It is ruled by the Planet Saturn in its *positive* aspect, and has the 8 for its number.

The 2nd 'period of the number 8' is the Zodiacal *Sign of AQUARIUS*, from the 21st January to the 21st February. It is ruled by the Planet Saturn in its *negative* aspect, and has the 8 for its number.

The 2nd 'period of the number 3' is the Zodiacal *Sign of PISCES*, from the 19th February to the 20th March. It is ruled by the Planet Jupiter in its *negative* aspect, and has the 3 for its number.

This brings us back to the point from which we started. Owing to the Sun passing from one Sign of the Zodiac to another, seven days are allowed at the beginning of each sign and seven days at the end, which is called the 'Cusp of the Sign'; during this period the number of the month and the qualities it represents *are not quite so strong* as during the rest of the period, and partakes to a certain extent *of the qualities of the Sign which is passing away* with those of the one *that is coming into action.*

It will be observed that the Planets have a Positive and Negative quality in accordance with the period of the Zodiac they rule; the Positive giving the more physical and forceful qualities, the Negative the mental.

For example, the symbol of the 9 *positive* in the Sign of Aries is: A man in armour with his visor closed and a naked sword in his hand.

The 9 *negative* in the Sign of Scorpio is represented by a man also in armour, but with the visor up showing his face, and the sword in its sheath, giving the picture of the mental warrior rather than the physical.

307

The Sun and the Moon are the only two Planets having what is called 'double numbers,' because the Sun and Uranus are interrelated one to another, so the number of the Sun is written as 1-4.

The Moon being interrelated with Neptune is written as 2-7.

A curious thing, and one well worth noting, is that there appears to a sympathy and attraction between the numbers 1-4 and 2-7, and it will be found that persons born under any of the 1-4 numbers, such as the 1st, 4th, 10th, 13th, 19th, 22nd, 28th, and 31st, are sympathetic and get on well with people born under the numbers 2-7, such as the 2nd, 7th, 11th, 16th, 20th, 25th, and 29th and more especially so if either of these two sets of people is born in the 'House of the Moon,' namely between the 20th June and July 21st-27th, or in the 'House of the Sun,' between the 21st July and August 20th-27th.[1]

[1] NOTE.- I have added the seven days of the 'Cusp' to each of these periods.

THE NUMBERS GIVEN TO THE DAYS OF THE WEEK ARE AS FOLLOWS:

Sunday	1-4	Thursday	3
Monday	2-7	Friday	6
Tuesday	9	Saturday	8
Wednesday	5		

These numbers correspond to the Planets as follows:

Sun	1	Venus	6
Moon	2	Neptune	7
Jupiter	3	Saturn	8
Uranus	4	Mars	9
Mercury	5		

 **52**

THE NUMBERS 1 TO 9, CALLED THE SINGLE NUMBERS; HOW THEY INFLUENCE MEN AND WOMEN, TOGETHER WITH THEIR HIDDEN MEANING, AND THE CHARACTER OF PERSONS INDICATED BY THEM

THERE is no getting away from the fact that there are only nine Planets in our Solar System, also that *there are only nine numbers by which all our calculations on this earth are made.* Beyond these nine numbers all the rest are repetitions, as 10 is a 1 with a zero added, an 11 is 1 plus 1, a 2; a 12 is 1 plus 2, a 3; and so on; every number, no matter how high, can be reduced to a single figure by what is called 'natural addition' from *left to right.* The final single number that remains is called the 'spirit or soul number' of all the previous numbers added together.

In this first part of this study there are only nine numbers to be considered, and one has but to master the occult meaning of each of these nine numbers as they occur in the Birth dates of men and women to find a Key to secrets of human nature that open a source of amazing interest.

I will endeavour to write as simply as possible that all who read may clearly understand what these numbers mean, even in the most everyday actions of life.

Without going into any elaborate desription of why this or that influence has been given to any particular number, I will without more preamble go straight to the subject, and show how each person may find what their number may be and how they may utilise this information.

The nine numbers we have got to study are: 1, 2, 3, 4, 5, 6, 7, 8 and 9. These numbers were given to the Planets that control our system in the most distant ages of civilisation, and have been used and adopted by all students of occultism, Chaldean, Hindu, Egyptain, or Hebrew.

The secret underlying the whole of this idea is that of the mysterious law of vibration. The day of Birth giving a Key number that is related to the Planet bearing the same number, this representing a vibration that lasts all through life, and which may, or may not, be in accord with the 'Name number,' which I will explain later, and with the vibrations of individuals with whom we are brought into contact.

First we must consider each number in relation to the Planet it—if I may use a simple expression—represents.

53

THE NUMBER 1

THE number 1 stands in this symbolism for the Sun. It is the beginning -that by which all the rest of the nine numbers were created. The basis of all numbers is *one* - the basis of all life is *one*. This number represents all that is creative, individual, and positive. Without going into further details, a person born under the Birth number of 1, or any of its series, has the underlying principles of being in his or her work creative, inventive, strongly individual, definite in his or her views, and in consequence more or less obstinate and determined in all they as individuals undertake. This relates to all men and women born under the number I, such as on the 1st, 10th, 19th, or 28th of any month (the addition of all these numbers making a 1), but more especially so if they happen to be born between the 21st July and the 28th August, which is the period of the Zodiac called the 'House of the Sun,' or from the 21st March to the 28th April, when the Sun enters the Vernal Equinox and is considered elevated or all-powerful during this period. It is for this reason, which you will observe has a logical basis, that people born under the number 1 in *these particular periods* must have the qualities that I have given to all number 1 people *in a distinctly more marked degree.*

Number 1 people are ambitious; they dislike restraint, they always rise in whatever their profession or occupation may be. They desire to become the heads of whatever their businesses are, and as departmental chiefs they keep their authority and make themselves respected and 'looked up to' by their subordinates.

These number 1 people should endeavour to carry out their most important plans and ideas on all days that vibrate to their own number, such as on the 1st, 10th, 19th, or 28th of any month, but especially in thsoe periods I have described before, namely, from the 21st July to the 28th August, and from the 21st March to the 28th April. Outside of their own numbers, number I people get on well with persons born under the 2, 4, and 7, such as those born on the 2nd, 4th, 7th, 11th, 13th, 16th, 20th, 22nd, 25th, 29th and 31st, especially those born in *the strong periods indicated.*

The days of the week most fortunate for numbers 1 persons are Sunday and Monday, and especially so if one of their 'own numbers' should also fall on that day, such as the 1st, 10th, 19th, or 28th, and next to that their intechangeable numbers of 2, 4, 7 such as the 2nd, 4th, 7th, 11th, 13th, 16th, 20th, 22nd, 25th, 29th, or 31st.

The most fortunate colours for persons born under the number 1 are all shades of gold, yellows and bronze to golden brown.

Their 'lucky' jewels are the topaz, amber, yellow diamond, and all stones of these colours.

If possible, they should wear a piece of amber next their flesh.

FAMOUS PEOPLE BORN UNDER THE NUMBER 1

	Born		Represents a
Alexander the Great		1st July	1
James I	28th June	,,	1
Charles I	19th Nov.	,,	1
George I	28th May	,,	1
George II	10th Oct.	,,	1
Duke of Wellington	1st May	,,	1
General Gordon	28th Jan.	,,	1
President Garfield	19th Nov.	,,	1
General' Booth	10th April	,,	1
Field-Marshal			
Earl Haig	19th June	,,	1
Queen Alexandra	1st Dec.	,,	1
Field-Marshal			
Lord French	28th Sept.	,,	1
David Livingstone	19th Mar.	,,	1
Lord Charles			
Beresford	10th Feb.	,,	1
Annie Beasant	1st Oct.	,,	1
President Wilson	28th Dec.	,,	1
President Monroe	28th April	,,	1
President Hoover	10th Aug.	,,	1
Orville Wright	19th Aug.	,,	1
Sven Hedin	19th Feb.	,,	1
Chopin	1st Mar.	,,	1
William Dean Howells	1st Mar.	,,	1
Bismarck	1st April	,,	1
Sir Edwin Arnold	10th June	,,	1
Sir Robert Ball	1st July	,,	1
John Calvin	10th July	,,	1
Mary Anderson	28th July	,,	1

313

Alexandre Dumas	28th July	"	1
Oliver Wendell Holmes	28th Aug.	"	1
President Adams	19th Oct.	"	1
Cheiro'	1st Nov.	"	1
Delcass'e	1st Nov.	"	1
William Hogarth	10th Nov.	"	1
Captain Cook	28th Oct.	"	1
Danton	28th Oct.	"	1
Goethe	28th Aug.	"	1
Oliver Goldsmith	10th Nov.	"	1
Ferdinand de Lesseps	19th Nov.	"	1
Thomas More	28th May	"	1
Nansen	10th Oct.	"	1
Sir Charles Napier	10th Aug.	"	1
Charles Stewart Parnell	28th June	"	1
Adelina Patti	10th Feb.	"	1
Edgar Allan Poe	19th Jan.	"	1
Lord Russell of Killowen	10th Nov.	"	1
Sir H. M. Stanely	28th Jan.	"	1
Brigham Young	1st June	"	1
Brigitte Bardot	28th Sept.	"	1
Twiggy	19th Sept.	"	1
Richard Burton	19th Nov.	"	1
Charles Laughton	1st Nov.	"	1

54

THE NUMBER 2

THE number 2 stands in symbolism for the Moon. It has the feminine attributes of the Sun, and, for this reason alone, although number 1 and number 2 people are decidedly opposite in their characters, their vibrations are harmonious and they make good combinations.

Number 2 persons are gentle by nature, imaginative, artistic, and romantic. Like the number 1 people, they are also inventive, but they are not as forceful in carrying out their ideas. Their qualities are more *on the mental* than the physical plane and they are seldom as strong physically as those born under the number 1.

Number 2 people are all those who are born on the 2nd, 11th, 20th, or 29th in any month, but their characteristics are the more marked if they are born between the 20th June and the 27th July, this period being what is called the 'House of the Moon'. I have added the seven days of the 'Cusp' to the 20th July.

Number 2 persons and number 1 vibrate together, and in a lesser degree with number 7 people, such as those born on the 7th, 16th or 25th in any month.

Number 2 persons should endeavour to carry out their chief plans and ideas on days whose numbers vibrate with their own, such as on the 2nd, 11th, 20th, or 29th of any month, but more especially during the period of the 20th June to the 27th July.

The days of the week more (fortunate or 'lucky' for them are Sunday, Monday, and Friday (the reason Friday is favourble in this case is that it is governed by Venus), and especially so if, like the number 1 people, one of their own numbers should fall on either of these days, such as the 2nd, 11th, 20th, or 29th and next to these their interchangeable numbers of 1, 4, 7 such as the Ist, 4th, 7th, 10th, 13th, 16th, 19th, 22nd, 25th, 28th, or 31st.

The chief faults they should guard against are—being restless and unsettled, lack of continuity in their plans and ideas, and lack of self-confidence. They are also inclined to be oversensitive, and too easily get despondent and melancholy if they are not in happy surroundings.

For 'lucky' colours they should wear all shades of green, from the darkest to the lightest, also cream and white, but as far as possible they should avoid all dark colours, especially black, purple, and dark red.

Their 'lucky' stones and jewels are pearls, moonstones, pale green stones, and they should carry a piece of jade always with them, and, if possible, next their skin.

FAMOUS PEOPLE BORN UNDER THE NUMBER 2

Thomas Chatterton, the Boy Poet	Born 20th Nov.	Represents a 2	
Swedenborg	29th Jan.	"	2
Marie Antionette, Queen of France	2nd Nov.	"	2
Gladstone	29th Dec.	"	2
Queen Elizabeth of Rumania	29th Dec.	"	2
Sadi Camot, President of France	11th Aug.	"	2
General Boulanger	29th April	"	2
Napoleon III	20th April	"	2
King Victor Emmanuel III	11th Nov.	"	2
Edison	11th Feb.	"	2
David Garrick	20th Feb.	"	2
Lord Curzon of Kedleston	11th Jan.	"	2
Ibsen	20th Mar.	"	2
William Lecky	20th Mar.	"	2
Charles II	29th May	"	2
Sir Edward Elgar	2nd June	"	2
Thomas Hardy	2nd June	"	2
Gluck	2nd July	"	2
President Adams	11th July	"	2
President Harding	2nd Nov.	"	2
President Poincare	20th Aug.	"	2
Paul Bourget	2nd Sept.	"	2
Henry George	2nd Sept.	"	2
Amelia E. Barr	29th Mar.	"	2
Max O'Rell	2nd Mar.	"	2

Eugene Field	2nd Sept.	"	2
Henry George	2nd Sept.	"	2
Joseph Jefferson	20th Feb.	"	2
Pope Leo XIII	2nd Mar.	"	2
Alfred de Musset	11th Nov.	"	2
Pope Pius X	2nd June	"	2
Bob Hope	29th May	"	2
Sophia Loren	20th Sept.	"	2
Bing Crosby	2nd May	"	2
Harold Wilson	11th Mar.	"	2

55

THE NUMBER 3

THE number 3 stands in symbolism for the Planet Jupiter, a Planet which plays a most important role both in Astrology and in all systems of Numerology.

It is the beginning of what may be termed one of the main lines of force that runs right through all the numbers from 3 to 9.

It has a special relation to every third in the series, such as 3, 6, 9, and all their additions. These numbers added together in any direction produce a 9 as their final digit, and the 3, 6, 9 people are all sympathetic to one another.

Persons having a 3 for their Birth number are all those who are born on the 3rd, 12th, 21st or 30th in any month, but the number 3 has still more significance if they should be born in what is called the 'period of the 3', from the 19th February to March 20th—27th, or from the 21st November to December 20th—27th.

Number 3 people, like the number 1 individuals, are decidedly ambitious; they are never satisfied by being in subordinate positions; their aim is to rise in the world, to have control and authority over others. They are excellent in the execution of commands; they love order and discipline in all things; they readily obey orders themselves, but they also insist on having their orders obeyed.

Number 3 people often rise to the very highest positions in any business, profession, or sphere in which they may be found. They often excel in positions of authority in the army and navy, in government, and in life generally; and especially in all posts of trust and responsibility, as they are extremely conscientious in carrying out their duties.

Their faults are that they are inclined to be dictatorial, to 'lay down the law' and to insist on carrying out their own ideas. For this reason, although they are not quarrelsome, they succeed in making many enemies.

Number 3 people are singularly proud; they dislike being under an obligation to others; they are also exceptionally independent, and chafe under the least restraint.

Number 3 people should endeavour to carry out their plans and aims on all days that vibrate to their own number, such as on the 3rd, 12th, 21st, and 30th of any month, but more especially when these dates fall in the period of the 3', such as from the 19th February to March 20th—27th, and from the 21st November to December 20th—27th.

The days of the week more 'lucky' for them are Thursday, Friday, and Tuesday; Thursday being the most important. These days are especially good if a number making a 3 should fall on it, such as the 3rd, 12th, 21st or 30th, and next in order their interchangeable numbers of 6 and 9 such as the 6th, 9th, 15th, 18th, 24th, 27th.

Number 3 people are more in harmony with those born under their own number or under the 6 and 9, such as all those who are born on a

3RD, 12TH, 21ST, 30TH

6TH, 15TH, 24TH

9TH, 18TH, 27TH

For 'lucky' colours they should wear some shade of mauve, violet, or purple, or some touch of these colours should always be with them; also in the rooms in which they live. All shades of blue, crimson, and rose are also favourbale to them, but more as secondary colours.

Their 'lucky' stone is the amethyst. They should always have one on their persons, and, if possible, wear it next their skin.

FAMOUS PEOPLE BORN UNDER THE NUMBER 3

King George V	Born 3rd June	Represents a	3
Emperor Frederick of Germany	21st Nov.	"	3
Gambetta of Italy	30th Oct.	"	3
Lord Russell	12th Aug.	"	3
Abraham Lincoln, President	12th Feb.	"	3
Winston Churchill, M.P.	30th Nov.	"	3
Field-Marshal Lord Roberts, V.C.	30th Sept.	"	3
Rudyard Kipling	30th Dec.	"	3
Sir Arthur Sullivan	12th May	"	3

Sir Charles Hawtrey	21st Sept.	"	3
Lord Beaconsfield	21st Dec.	"	3
Darwin	12th Feb.	"	3
George Pullmam	3rd Mar.	"	3
Bishop Heber	21st April	"	3
Sir Alfred Austin	30th May	"	3
Richard Cobden	3rd June	"	3
The Earl of Aberdeen	3rd Aug.	"	3
King Haakon	3rd Aug.	"	3
George IV	12th Aug.	"	3
The First Lord Oxford and Asquith	12th Sept.	"	3
William Cullen Bryant	3rd Nov.	"	3
Mrs. Craigie	3rd Nov.	"	3
Pope Benedict	21st Nov.	"	3
Mark Twain'	30th Nov.	"	3
President Felix Faure	30th Jan.	"	3
Mendelssohn	3rd Feb.	"	3
Cardinal Newman	21st Feb.	"	3
Dean Swift	30th Nov.	"	3
Voltaire	21st Nov.	"	3
Ramsay MacDonald	12th Oct.	"	3
Joseph Stalin	21st Dec.	"	3
Frank Sinatra	12th Dec.	"	3
John Osborne	12th Dec.	"	3
Henry Moore	30th July	"	3

56

THE NUMBER 4

THE number 4 stands in its symbolism for Planet Uranus. It is considered related to the Sun. number 1, and in occultism is written as 4—1

Number 4 people have a distinct character of their own. They appear to view everything from an opposite angle to everyone else. In an argument they will always take the opposite side, and although not meaning to be quarrelsome, yet they bring about opposition and make a great number of secret enemies who constantly work against them.

They seem naturally to take a different view of anything that is presented to their minds. They instinctively rebel against rules and regulations, and if they can have their way they reverse the order of things, even in communities and governments. They often rebel against constitutional authority and set sup new rules and regulations either in domestic or public life. They are inclined to be attracted to social questions and reforms of all kinds and are very positive and unconventional in their views and opinions.

Number 4 people are all those who are born on the 4th, 13th, 22nd, and 31st in any month; their individuality is still more pronounced if they are bom in the Zodiacal period of the Sun and

Moon, namely, between the 21st June and July 20th—27th (Moon period) and from the 21st July to end of August (Sun period).

Number 4 people do not make friends easily. They seem more attracted to persons born under the 1, 2, 7 and 8 numbers.

They are seldom as successful in worldly or material matters as people born under the other numbers, and as a rule they are more or less indifferent as to the accumulation of wealth. If they do acquire money or have it given to them they generally surprise people by the way they employ it or the use they put it to.

They should endeavour to carry out their plans and ideas on all days that have their number 4, such as the 4th, 13th, 22nd, and 31st of any month, but especially so if these dates come in their strong period, from the 21st June to July 20th—27th, or from the 22nd July to the end of August.

The days of the week more fortunate or 'lucky' for them are Saturday, Sunday, and Monday, especially so if their 'own number' should fall on one of these days, such as the 4th, 13th, 22nd, or 31st, and next in order their interchangeable numbers of 1, 2, 7 such as the 1st, 2nd, 7th, 10th, 11th, 16th, 19th, 20th, 25th, 28th, or 29th.

Their chief faults are that they are most highly strung and sensitive, very easily wounded in their feelings, inclined to feel lonely and isolated, and are likely to become despondent and melancholy unless they have achieved success. As a rule they make few real friends, but to the few they have, they are most devoted and loyal, but are always inclined to take the part of 'the under-dog' in any argument or any cause they espouse.

For 'lucky' colours, they should wear what are called 'half-shades,' 'half-tones,' or 'electric colours.' 'Electric blues' and greys seem to suit them best of all.

Their 'lucky' stone is the sapphire, light or dark, and if possible they should wear this stone next their skin.

FAMOUS PEOPLE BORN UNDER THE NUMBER 4

The Earl of Stafford	Born 13th April	Represents a	4
George Washington	22nd Feb.	"	4
Lord Byron	22nd Jan.	"	4
George Eliot	22nd Nov.	"	4
Lord Baden-Powell of Gilweil	22nd Feb.	"	4
The Queen of Holland	31st Aug.	"	4
Sarah Bernhardt	22nd Oct.	"	4
Thomas Carlyle	4th Dec.	"	4
Faraday	22nd Oct.	"	4
Lord Leighton	4th Dec.	"	4
Prince Charlie	31st Dec.	"	4
Sir Francis Bacon	22nd Jan.	"	4
James Russell Lowell	22nd Feb.	"	4
Haydn	30th April	"	4
Thomas Huxley	4th May	"	4

Alphonse Daudet	13th May	"	4
Sir Arthur Conan Doyle	22nd May	"	4
George III	4th June	"	4
Julian Hawthorne	22nd June	"	4
Rider Haggard.	22nd June	"	4
General Goettals	22nd June	"	4
Nathaniel Hawthorne	4th July	"	4
Emma Eames	13th Aug.	"	4
Archbishop Corrigan	13th Aug.	"	4
Ex-Sultan Abdul Hamid	22nd Sept.	"	4
Saint Augustine	13th Nov.	"	4
Heinrich Heine	13th Dec.	"	4
Immanuel Kant	22nd April	"	4
Sir Isaac Pitman	4th Jan.	"	4
Pope Pius IX	13th May	"	4
Russell Sage	4th Aug.	"	4
Schubert	31st Jan.	"	4
Sir Arthur Sullivan	13th May	"	4
Richard Wagner	22nd May	"	4
Sir Hamilton Harty	4th Dec.	"	4
Laurence Olivier	22nd May	"	4
Maria Callas	4th Dec.	"	4
Charles de Gaulle	22nd Nov.	"	4
Yehudi Menuhin	22nd April	"	4

57

THE NUMBER 5

THE number 5 stands in symbolism for the Planet Mercury, and is versatile and mercurial in all its characteristics.

Number 5 people are all those who are born on the 5th, 14th, and 23rd in any month, but their characteristics are still more marked if they are born in what is called the 'period of the 5', which is from the 21st May to June 20th—27th, and from the 21st August to September 20th—27th.

Number 5 people *make friends easily* and get on with persons born under *almost any other number*, but their best friends are those who are born under their own number, such as the 5th, 14th, and 23rd of any month.

Number 5 people are mentally very highly strung. They live on their nerves and appear to crave excitement.

They are quick in thought and decisions, and impulsive in their actions. They detest any plodding kind of work and seem naturally to drift into all methods of making money quickly. They have a keen sense of making money by inventions and new ideas. They are born speculators, prone to Stock Exchange transactions, and generally are willing and ready to run risks in all they undertake.

They have the most wonderful elasticity of character. They rebound quickly from the heaviest blow; nothing seems to affect them for very long;

like their symbol, quicksilver, which Mercury represents, the blows of Fate leave no indentations on their character. If they are by nature good they remain so; if bad, not all the preaching in the world will make the slightest effect on them.

Number 5 people should endeavour to carry out their plans and aims on all day that fall under their 'own number,' such as the 5th, 14th, or 23rd of any month, but more especially when these dates fall in the 'period of the 5,' namely from the 21st May to June 20th—27th, or from the 21st August to September 20th—27th.

The days of the week more fortunate or 'lucky' for them are Wednesday and Friday, especially if their 'own number' falls on one of these days.

Their greatest drawback is that they exhaust their nervous strength to such an extent that they often fall victims to nervous breakdowns of the worst kind, and under any mental tension they easily become irritable and quick-tempered, unable to 'suffer fools gladly.'

Their 'lucky' colours are all shades of light grey, white, and glistening materials, but just as they can make friends with people born under all kinds of numbers, so can they wear all shades of colours, but by far the best for them are light shades, and they should wear dark colours as rarely as possible.

Their 'lucky' stone is the diamond, and all glittering or shimmering things; also ornaments made of platinum or silver, and if possible, they should wear a diamond set in platinum next their skin.

	Born		Represents a 5
St. Louis of France	23rd May.		Represents a 5
Louis XVI	23rd Aug.	"	5
Empress Eugenie	5th May	"	5
H.M. King George VI	14th Dec.	"	5
H.R.H. The Duke of Windsor	23rd June	"	5
Samuel Pepys	23rd Feb.	"	5
Sir Hiram Maxim	5th Feb.	"	5
Lord Lister	3rd April	"	5
T.P. O'Connor, M.P.	5th Oct.	"	5
Jean de Reske	14th Jan.	"	5
Sir Henry Bessemer	14th Mar.	"	5
Humbert I of Italy	14th Mar.	"	5
Shakespeare	23rd April	"	5
Thomas Hood	23rd May	"	5
Chateaubriand	14th Sept.	"	5
Benedict Arnold	14th Jan.	"	5
Bamum	5th July	"	5
Erard	5th April	"	5
Handel	23rd Feb.	"	5
Fahrenheit	14th May	"	5
Josephine, Queen of France	23rd June	"	5
Karl Marx	5th May	"	5
Mesmer	23rd May	"	5
Sir Gilbert Parker	23rde Nov.	"	5
Cardinal Richelieu	5th Sept.	"	5
W.T. Stead	5th Feb.	"	5
Talleyrand	14th Feb.	"	5
Neil Armstrong	5th Aug.	"	5
Dwight Eisenhower	14th Oct.	"	5
Albert Einstein	14th Mar.	"	5

58

THE NUMBER 6

THE number 6 stands in symbolism for the Planet Venus. Persons having a 6 as their Birth number are all those who are born on the 6th, 15th, or 24th, of any month, but they are more especially influenced by this number if they are born in what is called the 'House of the 6th,' which is from the 20th April to May 20th-27th, and from the 21st September to October 20th-27th.

As a rule all number 6 people are extremely magnetic; they attract others to them, and they are loved and often worshipped by those under them.

They are very determined in carrying out their plans, and may, in fact, be deemed obstinate and unyielding, except when they themselves become deeply attached: in such a case they become devoted slaves to those they love.

Although number 6 people are considered influenced by the Planet Venus, yet as a rule theirs is more the 'mother love' than the sensual, They lean to the romantic and ideal in all matters of the affections. In some ways they take very strongly after the supposed qualities of Venus, in that they love beautiful things, they make most artistic homes, are fond of rich colours, also paintings, statuary, and music.

If rich they are most generous to art and artists, they love to entertain their friends and make everyone about them, but the one thing they cannot stand is discord and jealousy.

When roused by anger they will brook no opposition, and will fight to the death for whatever person or cause they espouse, or out of their sense of duty.

The number 6 people have got the power of making more friends than any other class, with the exception of the number 5, but especially so with all persons born under the vibration of the 3, the 6, the 9, or all their series.

Their most important days in the week are Tuesdays, Thursdays, and Fridays, and especially so if a number of 3, 6 or 9, such as the 3rd, 6th, 9th, 12th, 18th, 21st, 24th, 27th, or 30th, should fall on one of those days.

Number 6 people should endeavour to carry out their plans and aims on all dates that fall under their 'own number.' such as the 6th, 15th, or 24th, of any month, but more especially when these dates fall in the 'period of the 6 ' namely, between the 20th April and May 20th-27th, or from the 21st September to October 20th-27th.

Their 'lucky' colours are all shades of blue, from the lightest to the darkest, also all shades of rose or pink, but they should avoid wearing black or dark purple.

Their 'lucky' stone is especially the turquoise, and, as far as possible, they should wear one, or a piece of turquoise matrix, next their skin.

Emeralds, are also 'lucky' for the number 6 people.

FAMOUS PEOPLE BORN UNDER THE NUMBER 6

Queen Victoria	Born 24th May	Represents a 6
Napoleon I	15th Aug.	" 6
Frederick the Great	24th Jan.	" 6
Duke of		
Marlborough	24th May	" 6
Emperor Maximilian		
of Mexico	6th July	" 6
Henry VI	6th Dec.	" 6
Oliver Cromwell	24th April	" 6
Cecil Rhodes	6th July	" 6
Joan of Arc	6th Jan.	" 6
Admiral lord		
Jellicoe	6th Dec.	" 6
President Taft	15th Sept.	" 6
Sir Walter Scott	6th Dec.	" 6
Sir Henry Irving	6th Feb.	" 6
Joseph Choate	24th Jan.	" 6
Susan B. Anthony	15th Feb.	" 6
Michael Angelo	6th Mar.	" 6
Elizabeth		
Browning	6th Mar.	" 6
Henry Ward		
Beecher	24th June	" 6
President Diaz	15th Sept.	" 6
Sir William		
Herschel	15th Nov.	" 6
Grace Darling	24th Nov.	" 6
Warren Hastings	6th Dec.	" 6
King George I	24th Dec.	" 6

John Knox	24th Nov.	"	6
Moliere	15th Jan.	"	6
Max Muller	6th Dec.	"	6
Daniel O' Connell	6th Aug.	"	6
Count de Paris	24th Aug.	"	6
Admiral Peary	6th May	"	6
Sir Arthur Pinero	24th May	"	6
Rembrandt	15th July	"	6
Alfred Tennyson	6th Aug.	"	6
George Westinghouse	6th Oct.	"	6
P.G.Wodehouse	15th Oct.	"	6
Gamal Nasser	15th Jan.	"	6
Alexander Fleming	6th Aug.	"	6

59

THE NUMBER 7

THE number 7 stands in symbolism for the Planet Neptune, and represents all persons born under the 7, namely those who are born on the 7th, 16th, or 25th of any month, but more especially influences such persons if they were born from the 21st June to July 20th-27th, the period of the Zodiac called the 'House of the Moon'. The Planet Neptune has always been considered as associated with the Moon, and, as the part of the Zodiac I have mentioned is also called the First House of Water, the connection of Neptune whose very name is always assoicated with Water is then logical and easily understood.

Now, as the number of the Moon is always given as a 2, this explains why it is that the number 7 people have as their secondary number the 2, and get on well and make friends easily with all those born under the Moon numbers, namely, the 2nd, 11th, 20th, and 29th, of any month, especially so if they are also born in the 'House of the Moon,' from the 21st of June to the end of July.

People born under the number 7, namely, on the 7th, 16th, or 25th of any month, are very independent, original, and have strongly marked individuality.

At heart they love change and travel, being

restless in their natures. If they have the means of gratifying their desires they visit foreign countries and become keenly interested in the affairs of far-off lands. They devour books on travel and have a wide universal knowledge of the world at large.

They often make extremely good writers, painters, or poets, but in everything they do, they sooner or later show a peculiar philosophical outlook on life that tinges all their work.

As a class they care little about the material things of life; they often become rich by their original ideas or methods of business, but if they do they are just as likely to make large donations from their wealth to charities or institutions, The women of this number generally marry well, as they are always anxious about the future, and feel that they need some rock to rest on lest the waters of Fate sweep them away.

They number 7 people have good ideas about business, or rather their plans are good if they will only carry them out. They have usually a keen desire to travel and read a great deal about far-oft countries. If they can they will become interested in matters concerning the sea, and in trade or business they often become merchants, exporters, and importers, dealing with foreign countries, and owners or captains of ships if they can get the chance.

Number 7 people have very peculiar ideas about religion. They dislike to follow the beaten track; they create a religion of their own, but one that appeals to the imagination and based on the mysterious.

These people usually have remarkable dreams and a great leaning to occultism; they have the gift of intuition, clairvoyance, and a peculiar quieting magnetism of their own that has great influence over others.

Number 7 people should endeavour to carry out their plans and aims on all days that fall under their 'own number,' such as the 7th, 16th, or 25th of any month, but more especially when these dates fall in the 'period of the 7,' namely, from the 21st June to July 20th-27th — and less strongly from that date to the end of August.

The days of the week more fortunate or 'lucky' for them are the same as for the number 2 people, namely, Sunday and Monday, especially if their 'own number' falls on one of these days, or their interchangeable numbers of 1, 2, 4, such as the 1st, 2nd, 4th, 10th, 11th, 13th, 19th, 20th, 22nd, 28th, 29th, or 31st.

Their 'lucky' colours are all shades of green, pale shades, also white and yellow, and they should avoid all heavy dark colours as much as possible.

Their 'lucky' stones are moonstones, 'cat's-eyes', and pearls, and if possible, they should wear a moonstone or a piece of moss against next their skin.

FAMOUS PEOPLE BORN UNDER THE NUMBER 7

Queen Elizabeth 1	Born 7th Sept.	Represents a	7
Louis XIV	16th Sept.	"	7
Empress Charlotte of Mexico	7th June	"	7
Lord Rosebery	7th May	"	7
Lord Balfour	25th July	"	7
Admiral Earl Beatty	16th Jan.	"	7
Bonar Law, M.P.	16th Sept.	"	7
Charles Dickens	7th Feb.	"	7
Sir Joshua Reynolds	16th July	"	7
Oscar Wilde	16th Oct.	"	7
Ernst Haeckel	16th Feb.	"	7
Camile Flammarion	25th Feb.	"	7
Prince Imperial	16th Mar.	"	7
Sir John Franklin	16th April	"	7
Robert Browning	7th May	"	7
Ralph Waldo Emerson	25th June	"	7
Dean Farrar	7th Aug.	"	7
Bret Harte	25th Aug.	"	7
Philip D. Armour	16th May	"	7
Andrew Carnegie	25th Nov.	"	7
Sir Isaac Newton	25th Dec.	"	7
Rousseau	16th April	"	7
Sardou	7th Sept.	"	7
De Witt Talmage	7th Jan.	"	7
William Wordsworth	7th April	"	7
Noel Coward	16th Dec.	"	7
David Frost	7th April	"	7
Pablo Picasso	25th Oct.	"	7
Billy Graham	7th Nov.	"	7

60

THE NUMBER 8

THE number 8 stands in symbolism for the Planet Saturn. This number influences all persons born on the 8th, 17th, or 26th in any month, but still more so if their birthday comes between the 21st December and the 26th January, which period is called the House of Saturn (Positive), and from the 26th January to February 19th-26th, the period called the House of Saturn (Negative).

These people are invariable much misunderstood in their lives, and perhaps for this reason they feel intensely lonely at heart.

They have deep and very intense natures, great strength of individuality; they generally play some important role on life's stage, but usually one which is fatalistic, or as the instrument of Fate for others.

If at all religious they go to extremes and are fanatics in their zeal, In any cause they take up, they attempt to carry it through in spite of all arguments or opposition, and in doing so they generally make bitter and relentless enemies.

They often appear cold and undemonstrative, though in reality they have warm hearts towards the oppressed of all classes; but they hide their feelings and allow people to think just what they please.

These number 8 people are either successes

or great failures; there appears to be no happy medium in their case.

If ambitious, they generally aim for public life or government responsibility of some kind, and often hold very high positions involving great sacrifice on their part.

It is not, however, from a worldly standpoint, a fortunate number to be born under, and such person often are called on to face the very greatest sorrows, losses, and humiliations.

The 'lucky' colours for poeple born under the 8 are all shades of dark grey, black, dark blue, and purple. If number 8 persons were to dress in light colours they would look awkward, and as if there were something wrong with them.

The number 8 being a Saturn number, Saturday is therefore their most important day, but on account of the number 4 having influence on a Sunday and in secondary way on a Monday, the number 8 people will find Saturday, Sunday, and Monday their most important days.

Number 8 people should endeavour to carry out their plans and aims on all days that fall under their 'own number,' such as the 8th, 17th, or 26th in any month, but more especially so when these dates fall in the 'period of the 8,' namely, from the 21st December to January 20th-27th, and from that date to February 19th-26th; also if these dates fall on a Saturday, Sunday, or Monday, or their interchangeable number, which is 4, such as the 4th, 13th, 22nd, or 31st.

Their 'lucky' stones are the amethyst and the

dark toned sapphire, also the black pearl or the black diamond and if possible they should wear one of these next their skin.

The number 8 is a difficult number to explain. It represents two worlds, the material and the spiritual. It is in fact, if one regards it, like two circles just touching together.

It is composed of two equal numbers: 4 and 4.

From the earliest ages it has been associated with the symbol of an irrevocable Fate, both in connection with the lives of individuals or nations. In Astrology it stands for Saturn, which is also called the Planet of Fate.

One side of the nature of this number represents upheaval, revolution, anarchy, waywardness, and eccentricities of all kinds.

The other side represents philosophic thought, a strong leaning towards occult studies, religious devotion, concentration of purpose, zeal for any cause espoused, and a fatalistic outlook colouring all actions.

All persons who have the number 8 clearly associated with their lives feel that they are distinct and different from their fellows. At heart they are lonely, they are misunderstood, and they seldom reap the reward for the good they may do while they are living. After their death they are often extolled, their works praised, and lasting tributes offered to their memory.

Those on the lower plane generally come into conflict with human justice and have some tragic ending to their lives. Those on the higher plane carry their misunderstood motives ans lay bare the tragedy of their souls before Divine Justice.

To distinguish in which of these two classes a number 8 person falls, one must find by the comparison of their 'fadic' numbers if they are completely dominated by the recurrence of 8 in the principal events of their lives, or if some other equally powerful number such as the 1, 3, or 6 series does not more or less balance the sequel of events registered under the 8 and all its series.

If the latter is the case. one may be sure that by the long series of reincarnations they have passed through, they have paid the price in some former state, and are now passing towards the higher, where Divine Justice will give them their reward.

If, on the contrary, we find that the person is completely dominated by the number 8, always recurring in important events, or if instead of 8 the nearly equally fatalistic number of 4 is continually recurring, we may then be sure that we are in the presence of one of those strange playthings of Fate with the possibilities that tragedy may be interwoven in their Destiny.

In the more ordinary tragedies of everyday life, we can find an illuminating example in the life and execution of Crippen whose principal actions were singularly influenced by the terrible combination of the 8 and the 4.

Looking back over his career, and especially the events which led up to his paying that terrible forfeit at the hands of the law, one will find these numbers associated in the most dramatic way with this man's life, as illustrated by the following facts:

The figures of the year he was born in (1862), if added together, produce an 8 (17 equals 1 plus 7 equals 8). He was born on the 26th January, or 2 plus 6 equals 8.

His wife was not seen alive after dinner with him on the 31st January, which is a 4, and the month of January is itself called the House of Saturn, whose number is an 8.

He made his statement to Inspector Drew (which was later to be used as overwhelming evidence against him) on the 8th July.

The human remains were found in the cellar on 13th July, which again makes the number 4.

To try to escape he chose the name `Robinson,' which has, strange to say, 8 letters in it.

He was recognised on board the *Montrose* on the 22nd July, which again equals a 4.

The name of the ship he chose to leave Europe by (the *Montrose*) has 8 letters, and the ship that brought him back to his doom, the *Megantic*, was also composed of 8 letters.

He was arrested, as this ship reached Canada, on the morning of the 31st July, which again equals 4.

His trial finished on Saturday, 22nd October, which is again the 4, and October being the month of the detriment of Saturn' gives again the 8.

The occult number by which Saturday is designated is an 8.

His execution was fixed for the 8th November.

His appeal was heard and refused on Saturday, 5th November. The 5 added to the 8, which Saturday is a symbol of, again makes the figure 13, which number again equals a 4.

When his appeal failed, the date of execution was changed to the 23rd November. The addition of 2-3 makes a 5, and the division of the Zodiac which represents this portion of November is designated as 3; and this 3, if added to the date (the 23rd), makes the figure 26, which by addition (2 plus 6) again equals 8. Or if the 3 were added to the number of 23 we would get 26 or the 8.

The symbol of the number 8, I may also mention, from time immemorial, in occult studies, is called the 'symbol of human justice'.

Lastly, *when Crippen's 'Key numbers,' the 4 and 8, came together, it was the fatal year of his life.* He was 48 *years old when executed.*

It is not my province to judge or condemn this unfortunate being. Crippen, in any case, suffered as few men have been called upon to suffer; but I may add that the combination of such numbers as 4 and 8 as the 'Key numbers' in any life, indicate an individual terribly under the influence of Fate, and one especially unfortunate through his or her affections.

I have followed out many cases of people having similar 'Key numbers,' and in every case they seem sooner or later to come into conflict with what the 8 represents, namely, the symbol of human justice.' They are generally condemned, even in ordinary social life, by the weight of circumstantial evidence, and they usually die with their secret, appealing, as it were, from the sentence of 'human justice,' which, as a rule, has been against them, to that of the Divine Justice in the world beyond.

The occult symbol of 8 has from time immemorial been represented by the figure of Justice with a Sword pointing upwards and a Balance or Scales in the left hand.

There are many very curious things in history as regards this number. The Greeks called it the number of Justice on account of its equal divisions of equally even numbers.

The Jews practised circumcision on the 8th day after birth. At their Feast of Dedication they kept 8 candles burning, and this Feast lasted 8 days.

Eight prophets were descedned from Rahab.

There were 8 sects of Pharisees.

Noah was the 8th direct descent from Adam.

The strange number of three eights (888) is considered by students of Occultism to be the number of Jesus Christ in His aspect as the Redeemer of the world. Curiously enough, the addition of 888 makes 24 and 2 plus 4 gives the 6 which is the number of Venus, the representative of Love.

This number 888 given to Christ is in direct opposition to 666 which Revelation says 'is the number of the Beast or the number of Man . The numbers 666 if added together gives 18 (1 plus 8 equals 9). This 9 is the number of Mars, the symbol of War, destruction, and force, which is decidedly the opposition of the 6 with the symbol of Love.

REMARKABLE PEOPLE BORN UNDER THE 8

Mary I of England	Born 17th Feb.	Represents an	8
King Albert of Belgium	8th April	"	8
Queen Mary	26th May	"	8
Alfonso XIII of Spain	17th May	"	8
Joseph Chamberlain	8th July	"	8
George Bernard Shaw	26th July	"	8
David Lloyd George	17th Jan.	"	8
Prince Albert	26th Aug.	"	8
Admiral Dewey	26th Dec.	"	8
Bernadotte, King of Sweden	26th Jan.	"	8
Colonel Cody	26th Fab.	"	8
Wilkie Collins	8th Jan.	"	8
Louis Conde of France	8th Sept.	"	8
Sir Humphry Davy	17th Dec.	"	8
Gounod	17th June	"	8
Jenner	17th May	"	8
La Fontaine	8th July	"	8
Mary, Queen of Scots	8th Dec.	"	8
Sir John Millais	8th June	"	8
General von Moltke	26th Oct.	"	8
Pierpont-Morgan	17th April	"	8

345

Richard I	8th Sept.	"	8
J.D. Rockefeller	8th July	"	8
Jules Verne	8th Feb.	"	8
John Wesley	17th June	"	8
Christian Barnard	8th Oct.	'	8
Elizabeth Taylor	17th Feb.	"	8
Rudolf Nureyev	17th Mar.	"	8
Compton Mackenzie	17th Jan.	"	8

61

THE NUMBER 9

THE number 9 stand in symbolism for the Planet Mars. This number influences all persons born on the 9th, 18th, and 27th of any month, but still more so if their birthday falls in the period between the 21st March and April 19th-26th (called the House of Mars Positive) or in the period between the 21st October and November 20th-27th (called the House of Mars Negative).

Number 9 persons are fighters in all they attempt in life. They usually have difficult times in their early years, but generally they are, in the end, successful by their grit, strong will, and determination.

In character, they are hasty in temper, impulsive, independent, and desire to be their own masters.

When the number 9 is noticed to be more than usually dominant in the dates and events of their lives they will be found to make great enemies, to cause strife and opposition wherever they may be, and they are often wounded or killed either in warfare or in the battle of life.

They have great courage and make excellent soldiers or leaders in any cause they espouse.

Their greatest dangers arise from foolhardiness and impulsiveness in word and action. They are also peculiarly prone to accidents from fire and explosions and rarely get through life without injury from such causes. As a general rule they go under many operations by the surgeon's knife.

They usually experience many quarrels and strife in their home life, either with their own relations or with the family they marry into.

They strongly resent criticism, and even when not conceited, they have always a good opinion of themselves, brooking no interference with their plans. They like to be 'looked up to' and recongnised as 'the head of the house'.

They are resourceful and excellent in organisation, but they must have the fullest control; if not, they lose heart and stand aside and let things go to pieces.

For affection and sympathy they will do almost anything, and the men of this number can be made the greatest fools of, if some clever woman gets pulling at their heartstrings.

As a rule they get on with persons whose birth date is one of the series of 3, 6, or 9, such as those born on the 3rd, 6th, 9th, 12th, 15th, 18th, 21st, 24th, 27th, or 30th of any month. All these numbers are in harmonious viration to the number 9 people.

This number 9 has some very curious properties. It is only number in calculation that, multiplied by any number, always reproduces itself, as for example 9 times 2 is 18, and 8 plus 1 becomes again the 9, and so on *wtih every number it is multiplied by.*

It is, perhaps, not uninteresting to notice that.

At the 9th day the ancients buried their dead.

At the 9th hour Christ died on the Cross.

The Romans held a feast in memory of their dead every 9th year.

In some of the Hebrew writings it is taught that God has 9 times descended to this earth:

Ist in the Garden of Eden,

2nd at the confusion of tongues at Babel,

3rd at the destruction of Sodom and Gomorrah,

4th to Moses at Horeb,

5th at Sinai when the Ten Commandments were given,

6th to Balaam,

7th to Elisha,

8th in the Tabernacle,

9th in the Temple at Jerusalem,

and it is taught that at the 10th coming this earth will pass away and a new one will be created.

Both the First and Second Temples of the Jews were destroyed on the 9th day of the Jewish month called Ab. On the 9th day of Ab Jews who follow their religion cannot wear the Talith and Phylacteries until the Sun has set.

There are so many curious things connected with the number 9 that it would not be possible to deal with one-half of them in a book of this description.

This number is supposed to be a fortunate one

to be born under, provided one controls it and is not carried away by the excesses of temper and violence that it also represents.

The 'lucky' colours for persons born under the number 9 are all shades of crimson or red, also all rose tones and pink.

Their most important days in the week are Tuesday, Thursday, and Friday, but more especially Tuesday (called Mars Day).

Number 9 people should endeavour of carry out their plans and aims on all days that fall under their 'own number,' such as the 9th, 18th, or 27th in any month, but more especially when these dates fall in the 'period of the 9', between the 21st March and April 19th-26th, or from the 21st October to November 20th-27th. And when the 9th, 18th, or 27th falls on their 'own day,' as mentioned above, or one of their interchangeable numbers which are the 3 and 6, such as the 3rd, 6th, 12th, 15th, 21st, 24th, and 30th.

Their 'lucky' stones are the ruby, garnet, and bloodstone, and they should wear one of these stones next their skin.

For all purposes of occult calculation the numbers 7 and 9 are considered the most important of all.

The 7 has always been understood to relate to the spiritual plane, acting as the God or creative force on the Earth, and being creative, it is the uplifting 'urge' towards the higher development of the spiritual in humanity.

The 9 on the contrary, being, in the Planetary

World, the representative of the Planet Mars, is the number of physical force in every form, and consequently stands in relation to the material.

When this explantion is carefully considered it throws an illuminating light on that mysterious text in Revelation, Chapter 13, verse 18: 'Here is wisdom. Let him that hath understanding count the number of the beast, for it is the number of man, and his number is 666.'

This strange text has puzzled the theological mind for centuries, yet if you will take the trouble to add 666 together you will get 18, and 1 plus 8 gives you the figure 9, which in turn represents the 9 Planets of our Solar System, the 9 numbers upon which man builds all his calculations, and beyond which he cannot go except by continual repetition of the numbers 1 to 9.

'666' producing its 'spirit number' (as explained in a preceding page) of 9 is therefore, in all truth as Revelation states, 'the number of man'.

The hidden meaning of this number is one of the greatest secrets of occultism, and has been concealed in a thousand ways, just as the cryptic text in Revelation has hidden it for centuries from the minds of theologians.

The number 9 representing man and everything to do with the physical and material plane, is the number of force, energy, destruction, and war in its most dominant quality. In its relation to ordinary life it denotes energy, ambition, leadership, dominion. It represnts iron, the metal from which the weapons of warfare and made, and the Planet Mars which it stands for in Astrology is the Ruler of the Zodiacal Sign Aries which is the Sign of the Zodiac which governs England. This symbolism was evidently well known by Shakespeare when he wrote, 'England, thou seat of Mars.'

The number 9 is an emblem of matter that can never be destroyed, so the number 9 when multiplied by any number always reproduces itself, no matter what the extent of the number is that has been employed.

The Novendiale was a fast in the Roman Catholic Church to avert calamities, and from this came the Roman Catholic system of Neuvanies.

In Freemasonry there is an order of 'Nine Elected Knights,' and in the working of this Order 9 roses, 9 lights, and 9 knocks must be used.

All ancient races encouraged a fear of the number 9, and all its multiples.

The number 9 is considered a fortunate number to be born under, provided the man or woman does not ask for a peaceful or monotonous life, and can control their nature in not making enemies.

The following are a few illustrations of such birthdays :

Kaiser Wilhelm	Born 27th Jan.	Represents a	9
King Edward VII	9th Nov.	"	9
Sir Evelyn Wood, V.C.	9th Feb.	"	9
President Theodore Roosevelt	27th Oct.	"	9
President Grover			

Cleveland	18th Mar.	"	9
Lord Carson	9th Feb.	"	9
Sam Gompers	27th Jan.	"	9
Ernest Renan	27th Feb.	"	9
President Ulysses Grant	27th April	"	9
Sir James Barrie	9th May	"	9
Julia Ward Howe	27th May	"	9
Jay Gould	27th May	"	9
Elizabeth, Empress of Austria	18th Aug.	"	9
Franz Josef, Emperor of Austria	18th Aug.	"	9
Fredrick III of Germany	19th Oct.	"	9
Kepler	27th Dec.	"	9
Louis Kossuth	27th April	"	9
Leopold II, of Belgium	9th April	"	9
Nicholas II, of Russia	18th May	"	9
Paganini	18th Feb.	"	9
Whitelaw Reid	27th Oct.	"	9
George Stephenson	9th June	"	9
Edward Heath	9th July	"	9
Richard Nixon	9th Jan.	"	9
Margot Fonteyn	18th May	"	9
Marlene Dietrich	27th Dec.	"	9
Greta Garbo	18th Sept.	"	9
Peter Sellers	18th Sept.	"	9

62

THE OCCULT SYMBOLISM OF 'COMPOUND' NUMBERS, WITH ILLUSTRATIONS

I AM now going to put before my readers one of the most amazing systems comprised in the occult calculations of names and numbers that it has been my good fortune to eludicate. This system, which has never before been made public on the lines I am going to present, will, I know, be of inestimable value to those who may care to follow the rules I shall give.

I feel sure, from long experience, that the occult philosophy I am now about to pass on will be of the greatest *practical utility* to every man or woman, who wishes for aid in the hard struggle for existence that is, alas, the fate of so many sons and daughters of humanity.

Shakespeare, that Prince of Philosophers, whose thoughts will adorn English literature for all time, laid down the well-known axiom: 'There is a tide in the affairs of men which, taken at the flood, leads on to fortune.' The question has been asked again and again: Is there some means of knowing when the moment has come *to take the tide at the flood*?

My answer to this question is, that the great

Architect of the Universe in His Infinite Wisdom so created all things in such harmony of design that He endowed the human mind with some part of that omnipotent knowledge which is the attribute of the Divine Mind as the Creator of all.

It is this desire for knowledge implanted in the mind of humanity that places mankind above the animal creation, and makes men and women as 'gods' in their desire 'to know.'

We are told that Solomon the King asked to be given Wisdom as the greatest gift that God could give him, and in the ancient Hebrew of the Book of Solomon we can yet read his inspiring words:

I thank Thee, O Great Creator of the Universe, that Thou has taught me the secrets of the Planets, that I myst know the Times and Seasons of Things, the secrets of men's hearts, their thoughts, and the nature of their being. Thou gavest unto me this knowledge which is the foundation of all my Wisdom.

It is these self-same 'Secrets of the Planets' that I have endeavoured to teach in these pages.

I now ask my readers to give their attention and concentration to the following system which I will put as briefly and in as clear language as possible.

To find the exact day in any month of the year whose vibration will be favourable, or in other words 'lucky' to any individual, the simplest rule is to work out by following table the occult number produced by the letters of their name.

This ancient Chaldean and Hebrew alphabet

355

sets out the number or value of each letter. It is the best system I know for this purpose; its origin is lost in antiquity, but it is believed that it was originated by the Chaldeans, who were masters in all magical arts, and by them passed to the Hebrews.

It will be seen that there is no number 9 given in the alphabet following, for the simple reason that those ancient masters of Occultism knew that in the 'Highest Sphere' the number 9 represents the 9-lettered name of God, and for this reason no single letter was ascribed to it.

If, however, the letters in a name should total up an produce the number 9, the meaning of it is that given as I set out in the previous chapter dealing with the number 9, and for the compound numbers of the 9 such as the 18, 27, etc.

A	=	1	G	=	3	N = 5			T	=	4
B	=	2	H	=	5	O = 7			U	=	6
C	=	3	I or J	=	1	P = 8			V	=	6
D	=	4	K	=	2	Q = 1			W	=	6
E	=	5	L	=	3	R = 2			X	=	5
F	=	8	M	=	4	S = 3			Y	=	1
									Z	=	7

The next important question to answer is the following: Are all the Christian and Surnames to be added together to find the last digit or number?

The answer to that is, that it is *the most used* Christian and Surname that must be added together to give the Key number; when the

Surname is more used or more in evidence than the Christian name, then it is taken to given the Key number.

I have only space in a book of this description to give illustrations of a few well-known names. One I will take was always spoken of as Lloyd George—the other, Ex-Prime Minister, was called simply Baldwin.

The names Lloyd George and the Ex-Prime Minister of England, if transcribed into numbers are as follows :

						B	=	**2**
			G	=	**3**	**A**	=	**1**
L	=	**3**	**E**	=	**5**	**L**	=	**3**
L	=	**3**	**O**	=	**7**	**D**	=	**4**
O	=	**7**	**R**	=	**2**	**W**	=	**6**
Y	=	**1**	**G**	=	**3**	**I**	=	**1**
D	=	**4**	**E**	=	**5**	**N**	=	**5**
		------			-------			------
	18 = 9			**25 = 7**			**22 = 4**	

In Lloyd George's case, the word Lloyd alone produces the single number of 9, which, as I have previously explained, is connected with persons who have a hard fight with circumstances in their early lives and who, if they rise to positions of authority in nations, are often the case of wars or (as with Lloyd George) play an active part in them.

The word George in itself produces the single number of 7. This is, as I have also previously explained, a magnetic number, and favourable if used by itself. In this case, however, the two names are never used alone, but always together, as Lloyd

George: now add the two single numbers of each name together 7 plus 9 and you get *the compound number of* 16, the occult symoblism of which is 'a Shattered Citadel' or 'a Lightning-struck Tower.' A full description of the compound numbers will be found later in these pages.

If, however, the word David were added it would produce another 7, and if the name David Lloyd George was employed *in continuous use* instead of Lloyd George, the addition of the 7 for the word David would make the total of the three names the number 23, which, as will be seen in Chapter 63 dealing with the meaning of the compound numbers, is considered a fortunate number.

However, by some hidden law of destiny over which man has no control, he became known and called Lloyd George, and so his name foreshadowed that he would one day in his marevellous career fulfil the symbolism of 'a Shattered Citadel' or 'a Lightning-struck Tower.'

The other Ex-Prime Minister was for some unknown reason never called by his political followers or the general public anything else but Baldwin. This name, as you will notice, totals up to the number 22, and in its single figure to a 4.

The number 4, as I explained in a previous chapter, is not considered a fortunate number; people under it are usually misunderstood. They work hard and strive earnestly to carry out their ideas, but their plans are difficult and usually meet with great opposition.

Taking again these two well-known public leaders for another illustration, I now come to the most curioius side of this study of numerology, namely, that the 'compound' numbers have an *extraordinary meaning of their own,* which throws an added light on the mysterious connection they have in the still deeper side of occultism as applied to people's names.

Taking again the name Lloyd George, we find the first word Lloyd gives the 'compound' number 18. In occult symbolism this number is represented as 'a rayed moon from which blood is dropping like rain; in a field below a wolf and a dog are catching drops of blood in their opened mouths.'

Taking the word George, the 'compound' number is 25. In symbolism this number is classed as 'a number of strength gained by experience and ultimate gain through strife.'

The conclusion therefore is that if Lloyd George had become known in the world as plain George he would have retained to the end the high position he had gained.

Lloyd George was born on January 17th; he was therefore by his birth a number 8 man, which is unfortunately not in harmonious vibration with has name number, and further, by being an 8, increases the fatalistic indications, given by the number of his name—a 16.

The 'compound' number of 22, made by the name Baldwin, in the same occult symbolism of numbers is not at all favourable from a purely worldly sense as a leader of men. The single number of a name, it must be remembered, represents the man or woman *as they apper to be*. The 'double' or 'compound' number represents *the hidden forces that use the man or woman as their instrument*. The symbolism of the number 22 is 'a good man blinded by the folly of others, with a knapsack on his back full of Errors; he offers no defence against a ferocious tiger who is biting him.'

I have, of course, no political leanings in any direction; I merely am your mentor in these studies.

Sketch your world exactly as it goes — without offence — to friend or foes.

and I have only quoted the symbolism given to these numbers since the most ancient times.

SIR AUSTEN CHAMBERLAIN

As Sir Austen Chamberlain was generally spoken of as Austen Chamberlain, his numbers are as follows:

A	=	1	C	=	3
U	=	6	H	=	5
S	=	3	A	=	1
T	=	4	M	=	4
E	=	5	B	=	2
N	=	5	E	=	5
		---	R	=	2
		24 = 6	L	=	3
			A	=	1
			I	=	1
			N	=	5
					----
					32 = 5

Both the single numbers and the compound

360

numbers in this name are singularly fortunate, especially if used separately, as I have explained in a previous chapter; the number 6 is usually found associated with persons who rise to high positions of authority—especially in political life.

The compound number 24 is also favourable, and in occult symbolism it is put down as a number that brings 'the assistance and association of people of high rank, and gain through such association.'

The simple number of 5, as in the name Chamberlain, is, as I said on a previous page, a 'lucky' number, especially for those who lead changeable lives with a large element of risk, change, and speculation involved in their career; while the compound number of 32 is also given in occult symbolism as a magical number and is put down as associated with what is called 'the Paths of Wisdom.'

His title of 'Sir' produces the number 6, again a favourable number, and if we now add the single numbers of all the three together, we get 6 plus 6 plus 5 equals 17, a compound number whose occult symbolism is curiously enough the 8-pointed Star of Venus, a symbol of Peace and Love, which is peculiarly suitable for the career of a man who make superhuman efforts towards bringing peace between nations at Locarno. If, however, he was only known as Austen Chamberlain, the total of these two words produce the number 11, which, as my readers will see farther on, gives warning of 'hidden dangers, trial and treachery from others.

Sir Austen Chamberlain was born on October 16th. Neither the single number of 7 nor the compound are in harmonious vibration with the number of his name, This was not a favourable promise for a successful ending of his career, as is explained later on in these pages.

RAMSAY MACDONALD

We will take the first Labour Prime Minister of England for our next illustration. His numbers are as follows:

R	=	2	M	=	4
A	=	1	A	=	1
M	=	4	C	=	3
S	=	3	D	=	4
A	=	1	O	=	7
Y	=	1	N	=	5
		---	A	=	1
	12	= 3	L	=	3
			D	=	4

			32	=	5

It will be seen that the name Ramsay produces 3 as its simple number and 12 for its compound number.

As I have explained earlier in this book, the single number dentoes the person *as he appears to be* in the eyes of his fellow mortals, while the compound number represents the hidden forces in the background of the career.

In this case, the single number 3 is strong and

362

powerful, and is generally associated with ambitious people who gain positions of authority and who do especially well in government departments.

The occult symbolism of the compound number 12, is however, that of 'the Victim or the Sacrifice.'

The letters of the name MacDonald produce the single number of 5, an excellent number, as I explained before, and the compound number 32 is, as in the case of Sir Austen Chamberlain, also a good number with its symblism of 'the Paths of Wisdom.'

The addition, however, of the two single numbers of the name Ramsay MacDonald, 5 plus 3, produces an 8, a number which, I have explained earlier, represents two world, the material and the spiritual, one side assoicated with philosophic thought, concentration of purpose and zeal for any cause espoused, the other representing upheavals and revolutions.

This combination, taken with the meaning of the compound number that stands for his Christian name giving the symbolism of 'the Victim or the Sacrifice,' foreshadowed very clearly that Ramsay MacDonald, no matter what his great qualities, would in the end be made 'the victim' or 'the sacrifice' of his political party and be associated in his career with upheavals and revolutions.

The addition of the numbers of the two names 12 and 32 produces the compound number of 44, which in the explanation of compound numbers given in Chapter 63 reads: 'This number is full of the gravest warnings for the future. It foreshadows disasters brought about by association with others.' A decidedly ominous indication of the future of the leader of one of England's political parties. Further, as he was born on October 12th, the single number of which is a 3, this is not in harmonious vibration with his Name number, an 8, Consequently one might have expected a great deal of muddle and jumble to be associated with his career.

If this man had really understood the extraordinary meaning there is in a name when transcribed into numbers, he would never have allowed his party or his public to call him by the single word Ramsay. He should never have allowed such familiarity, but insisted on being called, *if he could do it*, by the single word MacDonald with its magical number of 32.

Later on in this book (Chapter 81) will be found examples from the names of Presidents of the United States.

In the following chapter I will explain the symbolism that from the most ancient times has been given to what is called 'compound numbers,' and at the same time I will give the system I have alluded to at the beginning of this chapter, whereby readers will be able to understand how it is that they can know when the 'lucky' day comes, so that they may be able to take hold of any good opportunity which may present itself.

63

THE 'COMPOUND' OR 'SPIRITUAL' NUMBERS FULLY <u>DESCRIBED</u>

IN the preceding chapters I have given the meanings of what are called the principal or 'single, numbers —also called the 'root' numbers— from 1 to 9. I will now proceed with the next step in the curioius study of Numerology, namely, the explanation of the occult symbolism given to what are called the 'double' or 'compound' numbers, and how such knowledge may be made use of in everyday life.

Although this is a much more advanced and more difficult part of the study of numbers, I will endeavour to make it as clear and as easy to understand as I have endeavoured to do with the single numbers in the earlier chapters.

Before launching out into this side of the subject, I must, I feel, give a few words of explanation so as to prepare my readers for what is to follow.

I have already explained that the single numbers denote what the man or woman *appears to be* in the eyes of their fellow mortals, while the double or compound numbers show the hidden influences that play their role behind the scenes as it were, and in some mysterious way often foreshadow the future or the hidden current of destiny of the individual.

When one passes the major or root numbers of 1 to 9, what is called the greater symbolism of numbers commences, and continues until 5 times 9 is reached, or the number 45; at this point the mystical number of 7 is brought into operation and added to the number of 45, producing 52, which stands for the 52 weeks of year. This number of 52, multiplied by 7, gives 364 as the ordinary days of the year in that ancient period of Time when trade unionism had not made its appearance. These ancient and wonderful people, however, used the 365th day of each year as *the one great festival holiday of all,* and *no work of any kind* was allowed to be done by man, woman, child, or beast. This number of 365 is based on the passage of the Sun through the twelve divisions of the Zodiac, which is the origin of the calculation of the year period which is found in every civilisation.

As I said before, the meaning of the single numbers from 1 to 9 represents how the man or woman appears in the eyes of his fellows. they are the numbers of *individuality and personality.*

All numbers from 10 up become in symbolism 'double' or 'compound' numbers; the 12, if we take it for an example, has for its root or fadic number a single number such as the 3, but at the same time the 1 and 2 of which the twelve is composed are 'compound' and have a meaning of their own distinct from the number 3.

How and in what age these 'compound' numbers became illustrated by symbolism, we do not know and never can know. We can only say that they appear to have always existed.

Symbols may be called the Language of Nature. and as such we must take them.

The meanings ascribed to the numbers 1 to 9 belong then to *the physical or material side of things,* and 'compound' numbers from 10 on belong to the more *occult or spiritual side of life.* Distinct symbolism has been given to the 'compound' numbers up to that mysterious number of 52, and this symbolism I will now proceed to give in as clear language as it may be possible to translate them. I have already illustrated in a previous chapter by examples from names such as Lloyd George, Baldwin. Austen Chamberlain, and Ramsay MacDonald, the information one is able to get by knowing the meaning of the 'compound' number and using it in relation to the information given by the single number, but later on it will be my privilege to explain a still more practical application of this knowledge which will enable one actually to pick out what days will be fortunate and what will be unfortunate, which will be, I think, of inestimable value to my readers.

The universally accepted symbolism of the compound numbers in ancient times was given in pictures and may still be found in the Tarot Cards which have been handed down to us from the most distant ages and whose origin is lost in antiquity

10. Symbolised as the 'Wheel of Fortune.' It is

a number of honour, of faith and self-confidence, of rise and fall; one's name will be known for good or evil, according to one's desires; it is a fortunate number in the sense that one's plans are likely to be carried out.

11. This is a ominous number to occultists. It gives warning of hidden dangers, trial, and treachery from others. It has a symbol of 'a Clenched Hand,' and 'a Lion Muzzled,' and of a person who will have great difficulties to contend against.

12. The symbolism of this number is suffering and anxiety of mind. It is also indicated as 'the Sacrifice' or 'the Victim' and generally foreshadows one being sacrificed for the plans or intrigues of others.

13. This is a number indicating change of plans, place, and such-like, and is not unfortunate, as is generally supposed. In some of the ancient writings it is said, ' He who understands the number 13 will be given power and dominion.' It is symbolised by the picture of 'a Skeleton' or 'Death,' with a scythe reaping down men, in a field of new-grown grass where young faces and heads appear cropping up on every side. It is a number of upheaval and destruction. It is a symbol of 'Power' which if wrongly used will wreak destruction upon itself. It is a number of warning of the unknown or unexpected, if it becomes a 'compound' number in one's calculations.

14. This is a number of movement, combination of people and things, and danger from natural forces, such as tempests, water, air, or fire.

This number is fortunate for dealings with money, speculation, and changes in business, but there is always a strong element of risk and danger attached to it, but generally owing to the actions and foolhardiness of others. If this number comes out in calculations of future events the person should be warned to act with caution and prudence.

15.   This is a number of occult significance, of magic and mystery; but a rule it does not represent the higher side of occultism, its meaning being that the persons represented by it will use every art of magic they can to carry out their purpose. If associated with a good or fortunate single number, it can be very lucky and powerful, but if associated with one of the peculiar number, such as a 4 or an 8, the person it represents will not scruple to use any sort of art, or evern 'black magic,' to gain what he or she desires.

It is peculiarly associated with 'good talkers,' often with eloquence, gift of Music and Art and a dramatic personality, combined with a certain voluptuous temperament and strong personal magnetism. For obtaining money, gifts, and favours from others it is a fortunate number.

16.   This number has a most peculiar occult symbolism. It is pictured by a Tower Struck by Lightning from which a man is falling with a Crown on his head.' It is also called 'the Shattered Citadel.'

It gives warning of some strange fatality awaiting one, also danger of accidents and defeat of one's plans. If it appears as a 'compound' number relating to the future, it is a warning sign that should be carefully noted and plans made in advance in the endeavour to avert its fatalistic tendency.

17.   This is a highly spiritual number, and is expressed in symbolism by the 8-pointed Star of Venus, a symbol of 'Peace and Love.' It is also called 'the Star of the Magi' and expresses that the person it represents has risen superior in spirit to the trials and difficulties of his life or his career. It is considered a 'number of immortality' and that the person's name 'lives after him.' It is a fortunate number if it works out in relation to future events, provided it is not associated with the single numbers of fours and eights.

18.   This number has a difficult symbolism to translate. It is pictured as 'a rayed moon from which drops of blood are falling; a wolf and hungry dog are seen below catching the falling drops of blood in thier opened mouths, while still lower a crab is seen hastening to join them.' It is symbolic of materialism striving to destroy the spiritual side of the nature. It generally associates a person with bitter quarrels, even family ones, also with war, social upheavals, revolutions; and in some cases it indicates making money and position through wars or by wars. It is, however, a warning of treachery, deception by others, also danger from the elements, such as storms, danger from water, fires, and explosions. When this 'compound' number appears in working out dates in advance, such a date should be taken with a great amount of care, caution, and circumspection.

19.   This number is regarded as fortunate and extremely favourable. It is symbolised as 'the Sun' and is called 'the Prince of Heaven.' It is a number promising happiness, success, esteem, and honour, and promises success in one's plans for the future.

20.   This number is called 'the Awakening'; also 'the Judgment.' It is symbolised by the figure of a winged angel sounding a trumpet, while from below a man, a woman, and a child are seen rising from a tomb with their hands clasped in prayer.

This number has a peculiar intepretation: the awakening of new purpose, new plans, new ambitions, the call to action, but for some great purpose, cause, or duty. It is not a material number and consequently is a doubtful one as far as wordly success is concerned.

If used in relation to a future event, it denotes delays, hindrances to one's plans, which can only be conquered through the development of the spiritual side of the nature.

21.   This number is symbolised by the picture of 'the Universe,' and it is also called 'the Crown of the Magi.' It is a number of advancement, honours, elevation in life, and general success. It means victory after a long fight, for 'the Crown of the Magi' is only gained after long initiation and tests of determination. It is a fortunate number of promise if it appears in any connection with future events.

22.   This number is symbolised by 'Good Man blinded by the folly of others, with a knapsack on his back full of Errors.' In this picture he appears

to offer no defence against a ferocious tiger which is attacking him. It is a warning number of illusion and delusion, a good person who lives in a fool's paradise; a dreamer of dreams who awakens only when surrounded by danger. It is also a number of false judgement owing to the influence of others.

As a number in connection with future events its warning and meaning should be carefully noted.

23.　This number, is called 'the Royal Star of the Lion.' It is a promise of success, help from superiors and protection from those in high places. In dealing with future events it is a most fortunate number and a promise of success for one's plans.

24.　This number is also fortunate; it promises the assistance and association of those of rank and position with one's plans; it also denotes gain through love and the opposite sex; it is a favourable number when it comes out in relation to future events.

25.　This is a number denoting strength gained through experience, and benefits obtained through observation of people and things. It is not deemed exactly 'lucky,' as its success is given through strife and trials in the earlier life. It is favourable when it appears in regard to the future.

26.　This number is full of the gravest warnings for the future. It foreshadows disasters brought about by association with others; ruin, by bad speculations, by partnerships, unions, and bad advice.

If it comes out in connection with future events one should carefully consider the path one is treading.

27.   This is good number and is symbolised as 'the Sceptre.' It is a promise of authority, power, and command. It indicates that reward will come the productive intellect; that the creative faculties have sown good seeds that will reap a harvest. Persons with this 'compound' number at their back should carry out their own ideas and plans. It is a fortunate number if it appears in any connection with future events.

28.   This number is full of contradictions. It indicates a person of great promise and possibilites who is likely to see all taken away from him unless he carefully provides for the future. It indicates loss through trust in the others, opposition and competition in trade, danger of loss through law, and the likelihood of having to begin life's road over and over again.

It is not fortunate number for the indication of future events.

29.   This number indicates uncertainties, treachery, and deception of others; it foreshadows trials, tribulation, and unexpected dangers, unreliable friends, and grief and deception caused by members of the opposite sex. It gives grave warning if it comes out in anything concerning future events.

30.   This is a number of thoughtful deduction, retrospection, and mental superiority over one's fellows, but, as it seems to belong completely to the mental plane, the persons it represents are likely to put all material things on one side — not because they have to, but because

they wish to do so. For this reason it is neither fortunate nor unfortunate, for either depends on the mental outlook of the person it represents. It can be all powerful, but it is just as often indifferent according to the will or desire of the person.

31.   This number is very similar to the preceding one, except that the person it represents is even more self-contained, lonely, and isolated from his fellows. It is not a fortunate number from a wordly or material standpoint.

32.   This number has a magical power like the single 5, or the 'compound' numbers 14 and 23. It is usually associated with combinations of people or nations. It is a fortunate number if the person it represents holds to his own judgment and opinions; if not, his plans are likely to become wrecked by the stubbornness and stupidity of others. It is a favourable number if it appears in connection with future events.

33.   This number has no potency of its own, and consequently has the same meaning as the 24—which is also a 6—and the next to it in its own series of 'compound' numbers.

34.   Has the same meaning as the number 25, which is the next to it in its own series of 'compound' numbers.

35.   Has the same meaning as the number 26, which is the next to it in its own series of 'compound' numbers.

36.   Has the same meaning as the number 27, which is the next to it in its own series of 'compound' numbers.

37. This number has a distinct potency of its own. It is a number of good and fortunate friendships in love, and in combinations connected with the opposite sex. It is also good for parternships of all kinds. It is a fortunate indication if it appears in connection with future events.

38. Has the same meaning as the number 29, which is the next to it in its own series of 'compound' numbers.

39. Has the same meaning as the number 30, which is the next to it in its own series of 'compound' numbers.

40. Has the same meaning as the number 31, which is next to it in its own series of the 'compound' numbers.

41. Has the same meaning as the number 32, which is next to it in its own series of 'compound' numbers.

42. Has the same meaning as the number 24.

43. This is an unfortunate number. It is symbolised by the signs of revolution, upheaval, strife, failure, and prevention, and is not fortunate number if it comes out in calculations relating to future events.

44. Has the same meaning as 26.

45. Has the same meaning as 27.

46. Has the same meaning as 37.

47. Has the same meaning as 29.

48. Has the same meaning as 30.

49. Has the same meaning as 31.

50. Has the same meaning as 32.

51.   This number has a very powerful potency of its own. It represents the nature of the warrior; it promises sudden advancement in whatever one undertakes; it is especially favourable for those in military or naval life and for leaders in any cause. At the same time it threatens enemies, danger, and the likelihood of assassination.

52.   Has the same meaning as 43.

We have now completed the 52 numbers which represent the 52 weeks of our year, and for all practical purposes there is no necessity to proceed farther. I will now show my readers the method of employing the symbolism of these 'compound' numbers together, with the 'single' numbers whose meaning they have learned earlier in this book.

The rule to follow is: One must add the date one wishes to know about to the total of the compound numbers of one's name, see what number this gives one and read the meaning I have given to the added number. EXAMPLE. I will suppose you wish to know if, say, Monday the 26th April will be a favourable day for you to carry out some plan: let us say, to ask for a rise in your position or in your wages. Take the number given to each letter of your name from the alphabet I have shown you, add to the total 'compound' number or its single digit the number given by the addition of the 26th April, 2 plus 6 an 8, add this 8 to the total of your Name number and Birth number and look up the meaning I have given to the final number produced, and you will find at once whether Monday, the 26th, will be favourable to you or not. If you see that it does not give fortunate number, then add the next day, the 27th, or the next until you come to a date *that is indicated as favourable.* Act on the favourable date thus shown, and you will find that the day thus indicated will be fortunate for you.

Suppose your name to be John Smith born 8th January, work the name out as follows:

J	=	1	S	=	3
O	=	7	M	=	4
H	=	5	I	=	1
N	=	5	T	=	4
		---	H	=	5
		18 = 9			----
					17 = 8

EXAMPLE. You now add the 9 and the 8 together, which gives you the 'compound' number of 17, whose units added together give 8. To this add the 8 produced by similar means from the 26th April, this gives you the number 16, with 7 for the last single number.

Look up the meaning I have given to the compound number 15: you will find it stated 'for obtaining money, gifts, and favours from others, it is a fortunate number.' Therefore the occult influences playing on John Smith, born 8th January, would be favourable on the 26th April for his using that date to ask favours or carrying out his plans. If it had not given favourable indications 'John Smith' should then work out the 27th April, or the next day or the next, until he found a date indicated as fortunate.

The same rule applies for every name and every date of birth.

64

MORE INFORMATION OF HOW TO USE 'SINGLE' AND 'COMPOUND' <u>NUMBERS</u>

FOLLOWING the publication of some articles I published in a leading London paper, I received some thousands of letters asking for further information as to how to make the Birth number and the Name number accord. I have, therefore, worked out the following example.

If possible, make the Birth number and the number given by the Name agree; the vibrations will then all be in harmony, and will give a greater promise of success if the number is a favourable one.

As an illustration, take again the example I gave in the previous chapter, of John Smith:

J	=	**1**		**S**	=	**3**
O	=	**7**		**M**	=	**4**
H	=	**5**		**I**	=	**1**
N	=	**5**		**T**	=	**4**
		---		**H**	=	**5**
	18 = 1 plus 8 = 9					---
					17 = 1 plus 7 = 8	

The single number of John totals a 9, and the single number of Smith equals an 8; the 8 and 9 added together make 17, and 1 plus 7 makes 8.

The number of the entire Name is therefore an 8. If John Smith were born on any day making an 8, such as the 8th, 17th, or 26th of a month, the number of the Name and the number of the Birth *would then be in harmony,* and although the 8 is not such a lucky number to have in an ordinary way, yet in such a case there would be *no clash in the numbers;* and if John Smith, knowing this, used the dates making an 8, such as the 8th, 17th, or 26th, for his important transactions, he would find himself more fortunate.

If, on the contrary, he had another number, say 2, as his Birth number, such as the 2nd, 11th, 20th, or 29th, his Name and his Birth number would *not be in vibration one to the other,* and there would always be a muddle or jumble in his affairs, and he would also not be able to decide which number to act on or what date he should use.

As he cannot alter his Birth number, then the thing to do is to alter the *Name number.* If he added a letter making a 3 to his name, such as a C, a G, an L, or an S, which in the Alphabet I gave in a previous chapter have the number 3, and wrote his name, say, 'John C. Smith,' or 'John G. Smith,' and insisted on being known and called as that, this new Number 3, added to the 17, which John Smith made before, would now give a total of 20, or a single number of 2, and then both the Name number and the Birth number *would be in harmonious vibration together,* and he would also be sure that he would be right in selecting any date that makes a 2, such as the 2nd, 11th, 20th, or 29th of any month, as the most favourable day to make any change or carry out any important plan.

If, however, 'John Smith' was born under an 8, such as the 8th, 17th, or 26th of any month, as the total of the numbers of his name also make an 8, I would then not advise him to add a letter or change the Name number, but to work under the 8, as I explained earlier.

Surely, this is a simple, clear rule, and will help those countless readers who may be puzzled as to how to get their Name number and Birth number to accord.

However, if a person is born under either of those peculiar number such as a 4 or an 8, and if the Name number should also total up to a 4 when one is born under an 8, or to an 8 when one is born under a 4, then for material success it would be better if one added some letter, as I explained in the case of John Smith, so that the total of your number is no longer a 4 or an 8, but one with a more fortunate vibration, making, say, a 1, 3, 6, or 9. Such a change in the majority of cases will produce most fortunate results and set up entirely new vibrations, which will change a lonely, unlucky life into one of happiness and success.

I would also strongly advise all those who have the combination of 4 and 8 when they make the change by altering their name to produce another number, such as a 1,3,6,or 9, to wear the colours and jewels I have set out for these numbers in an earlier chapter in this book dealing with 'single' numbers, and I am absolutely confident that they will never regret having followed my advice.

I also advise that in order to get the best advantage out of one's numbers, that in living in cities and towns a person should select a house to live in whose number also gives the same vibration as the Birth and Name number, If they live in the country they should give a name to their house which produces the same number as the Birth and Name. Especially in the case of a person having an 8 for the Birth number and a 4 for the Name number, or vice versa, they should, under no circumstances, live in a house whose number worked out to the single digit of a 4 or an 8.

65

WHY THE BIRTH NUMBER IS THE <u>MOST IMPORTANT</u>

THE Birth number is the easiest and clearest to use for everyday matters, and for all those who are not advanced students in occult symbolism. It indicates with authority and decision the exact date for action, namely a date which will be *in accord and harmony with the Birth number,* and the rules concerning it are simple and easy to understand.

A person born on, say, the 1st, 10th, 19th, or 28, of any month will be quite safe in picking out any one of these dates as the best date for any important action. As the number 4 is what may be called the feminine or negative side of the 1, he or she can take this numbers as *an associate number,* but on account of the peculiar qualities of this number 1 I do not advise it to be chosen for any *worldly or material offairs.* This number 4 will generally be found by number 1 persons as coming into their lives 'on its own,' if I may be permitted to describe its action as such, but more in the nature of a fatalistic number which has an influence on their lives *outside of their control* and certainly not always connected with the happier side of life. In many instances of number 1 people in my collection, the number 4, such as the 4th, 13th, 22nd, and 31st, has brought on these dates the news of an accident, a death, or a sorrow which has played some important part in their lives. The number 1 people also often find that they seem unconsciously to be drawn to live in houses whose number makes a 4, such as a house in a terrace or street numbered 4, 13, 22, 31, 40, 49, etc., and although such houses may be proved to be associated with important events in the career, yet I have seldom found them associated with happy *material* advantages.

A person whose Birth number is an 8 should certainly never live in a house whose number makes, a 4, 13, 22, 31, 40, etc., and neither should a person whose Birth number makes a 4 live in a house whose number makes an 8, 17, 26, 35, 44, etc., not, at least, if they wish to escape sorrow, misfortune, and strange fatality.

The second best numbers for a person whose Birth number makes a 1 are the interchangeable numbers of the 2—7, and dates these numbers make, such as the 2nd, 7th, 11th, 16th, 20th, 25th, or 29th, and houses under the numbers 2, 7, 11, 16, 20, 25, 29, 34, etc., are generally not unfavourable; but as these numbers are related to change or unsettled conditions, the number 1 person seldom settles down in houses under the 2—7 numbers, or finds conditions brought into his or her life under the dates given by these numbers as relating to *fixed or settled matters*.

Under the law of harmony and vibration, there is no question but that number 1 persons should be associated as much as possible with the same number 2 in all its forms. Persons born under the 3 should employ their number 3, and so on for all the numbers with the exception of those born under the 4 and the 8. In the latter cases I recommend, then *not to increase* the peculiar influence of the 4 and 8 , but to choose more fortunate vibrations.

This is where the power and knowledge of the Name number will apply. A number 4 or a number 8 person who desires to get under more fortunate vibrations, as they cannot alter their Birth number they can at least *change their Name number* and live under it and so beocme equally as fortunate as those whose Birth number is a lucky one.

I will give an example of what I mean.

Suppose a man or woman has been born on, say, the 8th, 17th, or 26th, of January, and the Name number works out, let us say, to a final total of a 1, 3, 5, or 6 (I have purposely taken the strong or positive numbers). Then I most certainly advise the number 8 persons to drop using the 8 in all their transactions and use instead any strong number *the name may give,* such as a 1, 3, 5, or 6, and a number 4 person should do likewise.

You will notice I have not used the 9 in giving this rule, and my reason for not doing so is that the 4, which is the symbol of the Planet Uranus, and the 8, which represents the Planet Saturn, are so antagonistic in their qualities to the 9, the symbol of Mars, that it is better to keep such numbers apart.

This may sound strange to those who have not made any study of occultism, but believe me, the above rule is not laid down at random or by any shadowy guess-work; on the contrary, it has a solid foundation in the science of the Planets, and anyone who has ever studied Astrology will tell you that I am right when I say that any combination of the Planets of Mars (9) and Saturn (8) or Uranus (4) can only foreshadow troubles and disasters of all kinds.

To resume, the reason I advise that the Birth number is the most important as the Key to the main 'fadic' number influencing the life is that in the first place *it is unalterable;* secondly, it is related to the planet's influence at the moment of birth, and thirdly, by some mysterious law of vibration - which, even if we do not understand, we must admit to exist even in such so-called inanimate objects as crystals, molecules, and atoms, the moment of birth decides the note of harmony or vibration, and so has its influence on the actions of our lives from the cradle to the grave.

Further, the Birth number relates to the material side of life, the Name number to the more occult or spiritual side of our existence.

Also the Name number is more difficult to be sure of - *it must be the product of the name we are most known by.* This presents a problem for the average man or woman. Many men are more known by their surnames than by their Christian and surname together, and many women are called by some 'pet' name to the complete extinction of their Christian name. In working out such cases mistakes may easily be made and a number allotted which is not the true one, whereas by going by the Birth number and using it *as the foundation* no mistake can be made.

If, then, it is found that the name *one thinks* is the correct one, and if its numbers gives the same number, or any degree of the same number as the Birth number, then one can be absolutely certain that no mistake is being made, for if both the Name number and the Birth number accord there is nothing one can desire better.

If the Name number does not accord with the Birth number, it can be made to agree by the addition of an initial or an alteration in the Christian name, so that both give the same vibration; and I advise this to be done in every case where the Birth and Name numbers do not agree, except in the case of the numbers 4 and 8 which I have spoken of earlier in this chapter.

Those who are advanced students in occult symbolism can utilise the hidden meaning given by both Christian and surnames to work out the finer shades of destiny, but for all ordinary cases— and I must not lose sight of the fact that I am writing this book for the average man and woman, those who want to help themselves in the easiest possible way, and who have, perhaps, no time for deep and abstruse study to all those, I know I cannot do better than to advise them to follow closely the rules governing the Birth number as set out in these pages.

NOTE. The number on the month of Birth or the year of Birth is not *so personal or so intimate* in regard to close calculations as in the number of the day of Birth.

The number of the month is useful as far as general matters, and the number of the year to the wider courrent of events.

EXAMPLE. A person born, say, on the 6th June, 1866. Write this down in the following order:

6th	=	**6 (Individual or Personal)**
June	=	**5 (General Matters)**
1866 = **21** =		**3 (Current of Destiny)**

The numbers 6, 5, and 3 should be regarded as separate and distinct and not added together.

The year number totalled and added to itself indicates an important year in the Destiny.

Example	**1866**	=	**21**
	21		

	1887		

A further illustration of this is given later in the case of William I of Prussia.

66

SOME ILLUSTRATIONS OF NAMES AND NUMBERS

AS it is impossible in a book of this size to go into every shade of the occult significance of numbers that spring from the foundation of 1 to 9, I must confine myself to giving a few illustrations of how to use the numbers allotted to the letters of the Hebrew alphabet for the purpose of showing how Destiny appears interwoven with numbers and names.

The great Napoleon originally wrote his name as Napoleon Buonaparte. Later on in his life he changed it to Napoleon Bonaparte. This change had a curious significance:

Napoleon equals in numbers a 5
Buonaparte equals in numbers a 5

The number 5, as I showed earlier in these pages, is considered a magical number and was carried by the ancient Greeks as a mascot when they went into battle. The two numbers of 5, if added, producing 10, are equally important and strangely significant in this case.

When Napoleon altered the spelling to Bonaparte, it altered the vibration of this word to an 8, and if you refer to what I said about this number you will find on the lower plane it represents revolution, anarchy, waywardness, conflict with human justice, and on the lower plane a tragic ending to the life. Although a great man, Napoleon was on the lower plane of existence, as can be seen if one looks up how the number 8 (Saturn) and the 9 (Mars) dominated the chief events of his career. As Napoleon Bonaparte the two names total the number 13, which number, in the occult symbolism which accompanies this system of letters and numbers, bears the curious picture of a skeleton with a scythe *mowing men down*, also a symbol of 'Power' which 'if wrongly used will bring destruction upon itself.'

This was so borne out by Napoleon's career that further comment is unnecessary.

Some remarkable illustrations of the significance of names and numbers may be had from examples of ships.

The United States battleship *Maine*, which so mysteriously exploded in Havana Harbour, and in which every man on board was lost, gives for the word 'Maine' the number 16 for its compound number, the symbolism of this number being, as you will have read earlier, 'A Tower Struck by Lightning.' The mystery of the blowing up of this warship has never been solved, but it caused the declaration of war by the United States against Spain.

Another tragic ship disaster was that of the *Waratah* which, after leaving Australia, sank with all her passengers and crew as if she has been swallowed up by the ocean. The number of the word 'Waratah' equals 20, which, as you have read in Chapter 63, is called 'the Judgment.' This number is symbolised by the figure of a winged angel sounding a trumpet, while from below a man, a woman, and a child are seen rising from a tomb with their hands clasped in prayer.

Yet another illustration might be taken from the fate of the *Leinster*, the Holyhead and Kingstown mail-boat that was torpedoed by a German submarine within sight of the Irish coast during the last months of the 1914-1918 War.

The word 'Leinster' gives the compound number of 28, 'a number full of contradictions,' which also indicates 'loss through trust in others.' This boat was carring a large number of soldiers as well as passengers, who certainly trusted their lives to others, in the belief that the boat would be accompanied by some of the destroyers from Kingstown Harbour. For some unexplained reason the order to the destroyers never came—the *Leinster* sailed alone, and in less than an hour met her fate and the loss of several hundred lives.

I know two men who at the last moment avoided going on that boat on that particular night by noticing that the compound numbers of their names made 28, the same number as the *Leinster*, and as they had read that in this system of symbolism it is not a fortunate number, and being struck by the coincidence of the name of the boat making the same number, both men took their luggage off at the last moment, and so escaped.

It is quite natural that under the tension of war people are more inclined to watch for the slightest clue that might give a warning of danger. I know of many instances where men actually saved their lives by following the clue given by this system of numbers. In one case a man resting by the side of his battery was amusing himself asking the birth dates of the men around him. He was startled to find that they were all born under the number 8, he himself being born on the 26th January, a number 8 man in the 'period of the 8.' It had just dawned on him that the day of the month also happened to be an 8, namely the 17th February, and looking up, he counted the number of the battery: *it was also an 8,* Just then German gun opened fire. He counted the shells as they dropped, each one coming nearer and nearer. As the seventh fell he could not resist the dread that overcame him - he rushed out into the open, and as he did so, the eighth shell struck his battery– he was the only one who escaped.

67

EXAMPLES OF HOW NUMBERS RECUR IN LIVES

AMONG my collection on the influence of numbers in connection with events, I have many that are decidedly interesting.

The following appeared in many of the London newspapers :

Sir Alma-Tadema, the famous artist, says his important number is 17. He was 17 when he first met his wife; their first house had that number; it was on August 17th that the work of rebuilding his home began, and on November 17th that he took up his residence there. His second marriage was in 1871, — and here 17 is the result of the figures added together. His house, in the artistic quarter of St. John's Wood, was again a multiple of 17, Sir Alma-Tadema was born on January 8th which would account for the 17th, which gives the single number 8, having such importance in his life.

King Edward VII was born on the 9th November in a month that is called in Astrology 'the second house of Mars' and governed by 9, the number of Mars.

His marriage took place in the year 1863, which numbers added to the other make 9; he was to have been crowned on the 27th of June, which figures together make 9, and he was actually crowned on August 9th.

King Edward often referred to me 'as the man who would not let him live past 69.' On the occasion when I first had the honour of meeting him as Prince of Wales in Lady Arthur Paget's house, he asked me to 'work out his numbers.' I did so and explained the reason his 'fadic' or 'root' numbers were the 6 and the 9.1 then told him that when these two numbers came together would be his fatal year, and further than the event should take place on a day making the number 6 in a month governed by the 6, which would be May. He never forgot my prediction and it is my melancholy privilege to record that the last occasion when I had any conversation with his late Majesty was few weeks before his death He was joining the royal train at Victoria to make his usual journey to the Continent when he noticed me, I happening also to be going abroad. He sent an equerry to call me, and he said smiling broadly:

'Well, "Cheiro," I'm still alive, as you see, but from that warning of yours, as I am now in my 69th year, I must take care' — a reference to the fact that according to the fadic system of numbers his 69th year was for him a dangerous year. He then spoke briefly of his racing wagers, and concluded by emphasising how remarkably my advice had been crowned by success.

Alas, in a few short weeks he returned to Buckingham Palace, and the public heard with consternation of his illness, which proved fatal. On May 6th — in his 69th year, the first time that these 'fadic' numbers came together — my prediction was fulfilled

Incidentally, King Edward mentioned that his 'dear friend,' as he called him, Lord Randolph Churchill, was extremely superstitious in regard to the number 13, and attributed many adverse events to the fact that he was born on the 13th of February, 1849, the total of whose numbers 22 also made a 4.

I explained to King Edward that the idea that 13 was an unfortunate number was not supported by occultism; that it was in fact an important number if persons were born on the 4th, 13th, 22nd, or 31st, and it was simply regarded as ill-omened because in occultism it was looked upon with veneration.

A few years before his death in London in January, 1895, I had a brief interview with this famous statesman, and he reminded me that my theory of numbers had interested him very much. From King Edward he had gathered that I thought that 4 was his fadic number, and I confirmed this. It was also represented with almost all the leading events of his life.

Another remarkable instance of prediction by numbers was in the case of my meeting with the then Sir Charles Russell. I explained to him that his important numbers were the 1 and the 4, with what are called their interchangeable numbers of 2 and 7, and that he would reach the highest position his career could give him on a date that made a 1, such as the 1st, 10th, 19th, or 28th in a month governed by the 2 and 7, such as July, which is governed by those numbers, and in a year whose number added up to the number of 4. He made a careful note of this, and when he wore his robes of Lord Chief Justice of England for the first time he sent to me to come to the Law Courts. After the ceremony of installation was over he came to me in his private room and as a souvenir gave me a signed impression of his hand.

68

THE DREAD OF THE 13 UNFOUNDED

NEARLY all people have an extraordinary dread of the number 13, which, if they only knew the real truth, is not at all the unlucky number they imagine it to be.

The origin of this dread is due primarily to the fact that it was much used in connection with occultism, and was in far-off times regarded as a powerful although a fatalistic number. As I stated before in previous pages, in some of the old writings of famous Adepts it is said, 'He who understands the number 13 hath the Keys of power and dominion.'

The opposition of the early Church to occultism was one of the principal reasons why this number became 'taboo.' It was given out that as 13 sat down to the Last Supper it would be unlucky if 13 were to eat together, and that one of the 13 would die within the year, and so forth.

I must say I could never see the logic of this, for if Christ had not been crucified the Scriptures would not 'have been fulfilled,' in which case Christianity would never have existed.

There was another reason, however, why 13 was dreaded, and this was because the occult symbolism that stood for this number was represented by a mystic picture of 'a skeleton with a scythe in its bony hands reaping down men.'

It was a curious picture that few could understand, and those who did kept their knowledge to themselves in an age when even to speak of such thing was to forfeit one's life by torture or at the stake.

This picture allotted to the number 13, although drawn or painted in many different ways, always contained the same idea: a skeleton reaping in a field, hands and feet springing up among new-grown grass, the crowned head of a man fallen at the point of the scythe, while a female head with flowing hair parted in the centre appeared in the background.

To find the true interpretation of this weird picture one must go back to the meaning attached to the single number 4, of which the 13 makes a second 4 in its compound number.

The single 4, as you have read earlier in these pages, is a strange number in itself. Persons dominated by it are usually misunderstood and lonely in their lives; people who bring about opposition with secret enemies constantly at work against them; they reverse the order of things in communities and governments; they are attracted to social questions and reforms of all kinds; they rebel against authority and set up new dynasties or republics.

The 13 has all these qualities in its higher scale, but even more accentuated. It cuts down all before it, reversing the order of things shown by the hands and feet springing up in the grass and the crowned head falling before the scythe. The female head in the background denotes social reform, the new order of things, and the uplifting of woman, and so forth.

It was perhaps this picture of a skeleton with a scythe in its bony fingers, calling up the idea of Death in the minds of those who could not understand the inner meaning of the symbolism, that caused the number 13 to be so dreaded.

If people will, however, only think, they will see that the 13 belongs to the series of 4, in the range of 4, 13, 22, 31, etc., and consequently a person born, say, on the 4th, 13th, 22nd, or 31st of a month will find all these numbers recurring in their careers, and this being so, the 13 will crop up just as often as the other numbers which make a 4.

In many hotels, even the modem ones, there is no Room 13; and a similar peculiarity characterises the seats of opera-houses in Italy.

But the dread of 13 has only a limited geographical range.

In the East and in the West the number is honoured. In the Indian Pantheon there are 13 Buddhas. The mystical discs which surmound Indian and Chinese pagodas are 13 in number, Enshrined in the Temple of Atsusa, in Japan, is a sacred sword with 13 objcets of mystery forming its hilt. Turning westward, 13 was the sacred number of the Mexicans. They had 13 snake gods.

The original States that formed the American Union were 13; its motto, *E Pluribus Unum*, has 13 letters, the American eagle has 13 feather in each wing, and when George Washington raised the Republican standard he was saluted with 13 guns.

69

THE EXTRAORDINARY EXAMPLE OF NUMBERS IN THE LIVES OF ST. LOUIS AND LOUIS XVI

ONE of the most remarkable instances I have ever come across of numbes pointing to a sequence of similar events in lives as far apart as over five hundred years, and which might be used as evidence of reincarnation, is the extraordinary case of St. Louis of France and King Louis XVI, which was published in 1852 in a book called *Research into the Efficacy of Dates and Names in the Annals of Nations.*

As history shows, there was an interval of exactly 539 years between the birth of St. Louis and Louis XVI.

If one adds this interval number to the remarkable dates in the life of St. Louis, a parallel of events, even to similarity in names, will be seen in the events in the life of Louis XVI:

ST. LOUIS		LOUIS XVI	
Birth of St. Louis 23rd April,		Birth of Louis XVI 23rd	
	1215	August,	
Add interval	539		
	1754		1754
Birth of Isabel, sister of St.		Birth of Elizabeth, sister of	
Louis	1225	Louis XVI	
Add interval	539		
	1764		1764

Death of Louis VIII, father of St. Louis,	1226	Death of the Dauphin. father of Louis XVI
Add interval	539	
	1765	1765
Minority of St. Louis commences	1226	Minority of Louis XVI commences
Add interval	539	
	1765	1765
Marriage of St. Louis	1231	Marriage of Louis XVI
Add interval	539	
	1770	1770
Majority of St. Louis (King)	1235	Accession of Louis XVI, King of France
Add interval	539	
	1774	1774
St. Louis concludes a peace with Henry III	1243	Louis XVI concludes a peace with George III
Add interval	539	
	1782	1782
An Eastem prince sends an ambassador to St. Louis desiring to become a Christian	1249	An Eastern prince sends an ambassador to Louis XVI for the same purpose
Add interval	539	
	1788	1788
Captivity of St. Louis	1250	Louis XVI deprived of all power
Add interval	539	
	1789	1789
St. Louis abandoned	1250	Louis XVI abandoned
Add interval	539	
	1789	1789
Birth of Tristian (sorrow)	1250	Fall of the Bastille and Commencement of the Revolution
Add interval	539	
	1789	1789

Beginning of Pastoral under Jacob	1250	Beginning of the Jacobins in France	
Add interval˙	539		
	1789		1789
Death of Isabel d'Angoulême	1250	Birth of Isabel d'Angouleme in France	
Add interval	539		
	1789		1789
Death of Queen Blanche, mother of St. Louis	1253	End of the White Lily of France	
Add interval	539		
	1792		1792
St. Louis desires to retire and become a Jacobin	1254	Louis XVI quits life at the hands of the Jacobins	
Add interval	539		
	1793		1793
St. Louis returns to Madeleine en Provence	1254	Louis XVI interred in the cemetery of the Madeleine in Paris	
Add interval	539		
	1793		1793

This, I believe, is one of the most curious examples of history repeating itself at a fixed interval. The addition of the interval number 539 reduced to the single digit gives the number 8, and the number of letters in the name Louis XVI gives also the 8. This number, as I explained earlier, represents the symbol of Justice and of one appealing from the brutality of Human Justice to that of the Divine.

 **70**

PERIODICITY IN NUMBERS

THE Law of Periodicity is shown in some lives in a very remarkable manner. In many cases it may last for hundreds of years, as may be noticed in the lives of St. Louis and Louis XVI in the interval of 539 years that separated these two Kings of France, and which interval, when added to the date of important events in St. Louis's life, repeated similar events in the career of Louis XVI. This is considered one of the most curious examples known in history.

Further, it will be noticed that St. Louis was born on April 23rd, the numbers added together producing a 5. Louis XVI was born August 23rd, also producing a 5.

These names worked out by the Hebrew Alphabet are:

SAINT	LOUIS
3 1 1 5 4	3 7 6 1 3
14 = 5	20 = 2
	5 AND 2 = 7
LOUIS	X V I
3 7 6 1 3	1 6
20 = 2	7
	2 AND 7 = 9

The name Saint Louis worked out to its single digit gives 7, the spiritual number. Louis XVI worked out to its single digit gives 9, the material number. Thes two single numbers added together give 16 for the compound number, the occult meaning being, as you have read in a previous chapter, A Tower Struck by Lightning from which a man is falling with a Crown on his head,' a fitting symbol in every sense for the downfall of Louis XVI.

After this date, the execution of Louis XVI , in 1793, we cannot yet trace this curious law of periodicity farther, but in adding the interval number again to 1793 we get the year 2332, in which perhaps another incarnation of St. Louis will again reign in France.

Another interesting example of a number being associated with the Kings of France is the following:

The first King of France named Henri was consecrated on the *14th* May, 1029, and the last King of the name of Henri was assassinated on the *14th* May, 1610.

Fourteen letters it will be found make the name of Henri be Bourbon, who was the *14th* King to bear the title of King of France and Navarre.

On the *14th* December, 1553, or 14 centuries, 14 decades, and 14 years after the birth of Christ, Henri IV of France was born; the figures of the date 1553 added together make also the number 14.

On the *14th* May, 1554, Henri II signed the decree for the enlargement of the Rue de la Ferronnerie. The cause of this order—the narrowness of this street—not having been carried into execution, brought about the assassination of Henri IV *in that same street exactly 4 times 14 years later.*

On the *14th* May, 1552, Marquerite de Valois, the first wife of Henri IV, was born.

On the *14th* May, 1588, the Duke of Guise opened the revolt against Henri III.

On the *14th* March, 1590, Henry IV won the important Battle of Ivry.

On the *14th* May, 1590, the main Army of Henry IV was defeated at the Fauxbourg of Paris.

On the *14th* November, 1590, 'the Sixteen' took an oath of death rather than serve Henri IV.

On the *14th* November, 1592, the French Parliament accepted the Papal Bull, which gave authority to the legate of Rome to nominate a King instead of Henri IV.

On the *14th* December, 1599, the Duke of Savoy submitted to Henry IV.

On the *14th* September, the Dauphin, who later became Louis XIII, was baptised.

On the *14th* May, 1610, owing to the narrowness of the Rue de la Feronnerie, previously referred to, the street his father Henri II had planned to be enlarged, the carriage of the King was stopped by a cart which gave Ravaillac the opportunity to assassinate him.

On the *14th* May, 1643, Louis XIII, the son of Henri IV, died, on the same day of the same month that his father was killed, and if the figures of 1643 are added together they make the Number *14*, which had played such an important part in his father's career.

Louis XIV ascended the throne in 1643, also a *14* and died in 1715, which makes a *14*. His age at his death was *77*, again making by addition a *14*.

Louis XV ascended the throne in 1715 = *14*.

Louis XVI was in the *14th* year of his reign when he convoked the States-General, which brought about the Revolution and his downfall.

The Restoration of the Bourbons took place in 1814, the number of this year added together making *14*.

The reason why this number 14 or its single number 5 appears so much associated with the destiny of France may be traced to the fact in Astrology Paris has always been represented as governed by the Sign Virgo, whose Planet is Mercury in its negative aspect, whose number is a 5.

During the period of French history I have cited, Paris was the principal point of power. The king who reigned in Paris ruled in France.

The addition of important dates often appears to bring out subsequent dates of equal importance.

The following is a striking illustration from French history:

Revolution in France and fall of Robespierre
    took place in 1794
The numbers of this date added
    together give 21

The fall of Napoleon 1815
    1815 added gives 15

Fall of Charles X and
    Revolution in France 1830
1830 added gives 12
Death of the King
    Louis Philippe 1842
1842 added gives 15

End of Crimean War 1857
    1857 added gives 21

The famous Treaty of Berlin 1878
    1878 added gives 24
Danger of War with England
over Fashoda 1902
    1902 added gives 12

World War I 1914
    1914 added gives 15
A date which was another crisis in
    French history 1929

Another curious example of the additon of dates, much commented on in both Berlin and Paris during 1914, is as follows:

In 1849, William I of Prussia fled with his mother, Queen Louise, and took refuge in England. Meeting with a woman well versed in Numerology, he asked her to tell him his future. 'Add,' she answered 'the figures of this important year together.'

1849
22
1871

In the year produced by this addition you will end a great war and will be proclaimed Emperor.'

'And then—?' asked the King.

'Add 1871,' she replied, 'and you will get the

year of your death.' The King made the addition and wrote 1888.

'And what of my country after that?' the King asked.

'Add again,' she answered, 'and see what the total is.'

The King added
$$\begin{array}{r} 1888 \\ 25 \\ \hline 1913 \end{array}$$

'In that year,' the woman said, 'the man who wears your crown will prepare another war, which will bring about his ruin and that of your country, for the time being.'

This story was repeated to me by a close relative of the ex-Kaiser when he visited me in Paris in 1904.

In Rome there is a very ancient tradition which says that no Pope who occupies the Chair of St. Peter can reign longer than 25 years. The Popes who came very near this strangely set period were the folowing:

Pius VI who reigned 24 years 6 months and 14 days

Adrian I who reigned 23 years 10 months and 17 days

Pius VII who reigned 23 years 5 months and 6 days

Alexander III who reigned 21 years 11 months and 23 days

Sylvester I who reigned 21 years 0 month and 4 days

Leo XIII entered his 25th year as Pope, but did not pass beyond the set period, although he

407

occupied the Chair of St. Peter longer than any of his predecessors.

English history also contains many equally strange examples of numbers and dates reappearing continually in remarkable lives.

On the 29th May,
> 1630, Charles II was born.

On the 29th May,
> 1660, he was restored to the Throne.

On the 29th May,
> 1672, his fleet was destroyed by the Dutch.

On the 29th May,
> 1679, the Covenanter Rebellion broke out.

On the 3rd September,
> Cromwell was born.

On the 3rd September,
> won the Battle of Dunbar.

On the 3rd September,
> he won the Battle of Worcester.

On the 3rd September,
> he died.

In a previous chapter I have related the curious influence the numbers 6 and 9 had in the life of King Edward VII.

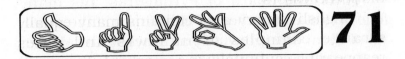

71

SOME ADDITIONAL INFORMATION

THE two schools of philosophy in regard to the subject of numbers are the Pythagorean and the more ancient one known as the Chaldean.

The Greek philosopher, Pythagoras, imbibed all his knowledge of the occult value of numbers during his residence in Egypt. On his return to Greece he established a school of occult philosophy that was eminently suited to the needs of his day. In this school only a very limited number of initiates were allowed to enter. The more involved and difficult the teachings became, the fewer were the favoured ones who could boast that they were the 'chosen of the Master,' consequently a kind of occult hierarchy was established that raised an insurmountable barrier between these students and those they were pleased to call 'the common people.'

From this the most involved and complicated system of occult philosophy became launched; nothing was allowed to be put in writing, knowledge had to be handed down by word of mouth, and most elaborate ceremonials were instituted in which initiates were sworn to secrecy, and the greatest efforts were made to conceal occult knowledge in every possible way.

After the death of Pythagoras, his many followers started school of philosophy of their own. All of them differed widely as to what 'the Master' really did teach. In the end confusion became still more confounded by the action of the early Fathers of the Christian Church condemning all occult learning as the 'work of the devil.'

One of the greatest of Pythagoras' teachings was that of the occult value of numbers. He laid down the axiom that numbers concealed and contained the secret of the universe. In this theory he was undoubtedly right, but his followers so complicated the rules he taught that in the end few could follow that great truth the underlay his wisdom.

In the study of numbers I advocate that the students should endeavour to get back to the original source; that is way I claim that in returning to the original Chaldean, Hindu, and Hebrew system, which I teach in my books, one has more likelihood of arriving at the real truth of such studies.

I could easily wirte an entire volume on the history of numbers, tracing its origin from the most remote ages; but in this practical period of humanity I realise that such an elaborate treatise in not required—that what men and women want is the practical appeal to their own personal experience and nothing more.

It is for this reason I have written this book for the masses, more than for the more limited erudite student.

Out of the many thousands of letters I have received, I shall now endeavour to answer those which appear to me as the most important.

'Should the words Mr., Mrs., or Miss be calculated when working out the complete number of a name?'

Answer : As I have explained before, it is *the name one is most known by*' that should be used in working out the number of a name.

If, for example, a young lady is always addressed or spoken of as, say, Miss Jones —as is often the case in a large business establishment— then in connection *with that business* in which she is employed, Miss Jones should certainly take that name as the one she is most known by and work out the number of the name 'Miss Jones' and use it, *but only in relation to the business she is employed in.* It is in fact, her 'trade name' but for her home life or her private affairs she should work out the Christian name she is called by or the 'pet' name she is known under. When the same young lady enters the state of matrimony and becomes 'Mrs.' she should then work out the numbers for her new title, but always keeping the numbers of her Christian or 'pet' name *for her home and private life.* The same rule applies to every woman known and called continually 'Mrs. Smith' or 'Mrs. jones,' as the case may be, in the circle of friends or acquaintances in which she is called 'Mrs.'

Men in business for themselves or in large

establishments, who are generally called 'Mr.' before their name, should also follow the above rule.

When a man or woman has many Christian names, they should only take the number made by the principal one—that they *are most known by.*

The same rule applies to every prefix or title a man or woman may obtain by *right of birth or as an honour.*

A good illustration of this is the case of the famous Melba.

The great diva's surname worked out to the compound number of 15, with 6 for the single, both being excellent for success. In one of my Press articules, speaking of the number 15, I said: 'If this number is associated with a good or fortunate single number, it can be very lucky and powerful. It is peculiarly associated with "good talkers" and 'often with gifts of eloquence, music, art and strong personal magnetism.' All these qualities were characteristic of the great Melba, as she was called all through her successful career.

Her signature, Nellie Melba, produces the number 10, also a fortunate number, and the single number 1, which is a number of strong individuality and ambition. It also denotes that people possessing this number have the desire to become the head or chief in whatever profession or occupation they take up.

If the number of her title, 'Dame,' which is the lucky number of 5, be added to the name Nellie Melba, the total of the last digits are: Dame 5, Nellie 4, Melba 6, giving again the compound number

15, so that as long as this famous woman existed good fortune always favoured her.

I will now give an example of a title which produces one of the unfortunate numbers, the curious effect if foreshadows as far as the promise of good luck is concerned.

In cases where the addition of the number of the title produces a 4 or an 8, it foreshadows that the fortunate numbers of the name have ceased their luck or power, and in such cases the title will become a detriment and not a happiness.

An illustration which may be given in connection with this is that of Napoleon. This name works out to the compound number of 41, which, as I state in my writings, is 'a magical number usually associated with combinations of peoples or nations.' The single number is a 5, also fortunate. When Napoleon became Emperor of France his name became Napoleon I, the I making his compound number 42 with the single number of 6. Both of these again are numbers of power and good fortune and he went down to posterity as the Great Napoleon.

In the case of Napoleon III the compound number becomes 44, whihc I stated in my articles 'is a number of the gravest warnings for the future; it foreshadows disasters brought about by association with others and bad advice—exactly what happened to Napoleon III. Again, the single number of his name became an 8. Even the magic of the name Napoleon was over-shadowed by it, and Napoleon III went down to posterity as 'the man who lost France.'

I think these illustrations will help to show how a prefix to a name, or a title acquired or inherited, fits in with this wonderful science of Numerology, and the number it gives added to the other numbers is a further indication of good or evil fortune for the future.

The titles given to kings and queens when they ascend the throne, especially when taken in connection with their birth number, is generally very interesting.

In the case of King Edward VII, he changed his name when he came to the throne from Albert to Edward, the name he took working out as follows:

King ....11 = 2
Edward ....22 = 4
VII ....= 7
$$\overline{13}$$

I have described this number in a previous chapter as a number of warning with its strange symbolism of 'a skeleton' or 'death.'

It was certainly a warning of great changes that were about to occur in England, and taken in conjunction with his birth number, November 9th, by adding the 4 produced by the 13 to the 9, they again made a 13, which doubled the warning and also indicated a short reign.

In the case of King George V, the numbers produced are as follows:

414

```
King..............................................11 = 2
George.......................................25 = 7
V ....................................................... = 5
                                                     ‾‾‾‾‾‾‾‾
                                                     14 = 5
```

The compound number 14 I have already described in previous pages as 'a number of movement, combinations of people and things, but danger from natural forces such as tempests, water, air, or fire, but with a strong element of risk and danger attached to it, generally owing to the actions and foolhardiness of others.'

Born on June 3rd, the late King's birth took place in the Zodiacal Sign of Gemini, which is called the Ist House of Air. Consequently the dangers foreshown by the compound number of the name and title are all the more accentuated; therefore the King's greatest danger came from anything in connection with air, even His Majesty's lungs, as the breathing apparatus of his system, come under this symbol of the Zodiacal Sign of Birth.

London, the capital of England, is also under the same sign of Gemini, and the greatest danger to it is from the air.

It is a curious fact and doubtless one charged with deep significance that not only George V but Quee Mary and the Duke of Windsor were all born under the sign of Gemini, or very close to it, in the Ist House of Air, and in the district of London, also under the same sign.

Although she had other Christian names, the

Queen was always popularly known as Queen Mary. The numbers of her name are:

Queen .... 22 = 4
Mary .... = 8

_____

12 = 3

The compound number of this name is 12. In my previous chapters I have given the symbolism of this number as 'a number indicating anxiety of mind.' It is also called 'the sacrifice.' As Queen Mary was born on May 26th, her birth number is an 8, and in the name Queen Mary the 4 and the 8 are also produced.

These illustrations of the significance of titles and prefixes to a name will, I think, be useful to my readers and will answer some thousands of letters I have received asking for information on this point.

NOTE: The Prince of Wales (The Duke of Windsor), born 10 p.m., June 23rd, 1894, at White Lodge, Richmond Park, London, is in what is called the 'cusp' of Gemini-Cancer.

The sun at this date had just passed out of Gemini and was in 2 degrees 21 of Cancer.

The qualities of Gemini will be the main influence through his life.

His Majesy King George V, born June 3rd, 1865, 1.18 a.m., Marlborough House, London, has the sun in 12 degrees 25 of Gemini.

Her Majesty Queen Mary, born May 26th, 1867, 11.59 p.m., Kensington Palace, London, is in the 'cusp' of Taurus-Gemini and has the Sun in 5 degrees 13 of Gemini.

72

HOW TO FIND THE 'LUCKY' DAY

IN answer to many letters, I take this opportunity of explaining a point of very great importance, namely, how to find the 'lucky' day.

I have stated that the birth number is the most important when the individual wants *to carry out his own plans.*

For example: a person we will say born on the Ist of a month will find *for all general purposes* that if he or she will use all dates making the Number One series, such as the 1st, 10th, 19th, or 28th of any month, especially during what is called the 'period of the 1' and 'the period of the 2,' namely, form June 21st to July 20th (period of the 2), and from July 21st to August 20th (period of the 1), they will have a far better chance of carrying out their plans successfully than if they did not follow this rule and did not know what dates to use for the best.

This is quite independent of any other rule, and I strongly recommend it.

To get a still more powerful vibration, I have advised that persons should try to make the number of their name (when they have worked out the letters of it by what is called the Mystic or Ancient Hebrew Alphabet) the same series as the number that is given by their birth date, and I have explained in a previous chapter how to do this by adding a letter to their name or taking away a letter, as the case may be. If these two numbers agree or are in harmony with one another, then they should use the date that is given to commence anything important, or endeavour to carry out their plans on that number which is indicated. They must, however, bear in mind that any number of the series they belong to is equally important.

EXAMPLE. The person born on the 1st of the month will find the 10th, 19th, or 28th of equal importance to the number 1 on which they were born, and so on with every other birth number.

Naturally, when people begin to follow this idea they must not expect to find their luck change in an instant, as if by magic. I have several letters before me as I write, where the writers expected their 'luck' to change for the better within twenty-four hours. There was one man who wrote that 'at the end of a week he had found no change in his bad luck,' but at the end of three months the same man again wrote to say that towards the middle of the third month he began to notice a distinct improvement in all his affairs.

Some of the writers have also apparently not grasped the example I gave in working out the number of the name of a man I called 'John Smith' I stated in a previous chapter that if 'John Smith' wanted to find out a favourable date to ask his employer for an increase in his wages he should add the numbers given by the name 'John Smith' together, then add the single number of the date he wanted to know about and lasly to add his Birth number. The result was a total of 15 at the last compound number with 6 as the last single number. I said, 'Look up what I have given as the symbolism of the 15, and you will find it stated "for obtaining money, gifts, and favours from others it is a fortunate number." ' and therefore the date 'John Smith' wanted to see his employer would be a favourable date for him to make his request.

This was given only as an illustration of finding out if one particular date would be likely to be favourable *for that special purpose,* but I never intended this to be employed to the exclusion of the other definite rule for *continual action all through the year* on the series given by the Birth number, such as for a number 1 person to use all dates that make a 1, as the Ist, 10th, etc.

It will be noticed that in the latter case the rule is *individual or personal;* in the 'John Smith' case another life, namely the employer, was also concerned, and in consequence the rule given would not work out with such certainty.

73

COLOURS AND NUMBERS

THERE is no reason for anyone to get confused between the colours given by the number of the month and those given by the number of the day, if one will bear in mind that the number of the month is not as *close or intimate in its relationship to the individual* as is the colour indicated by the number of birth.

Take the month of January, for example. The 'period of the number 8' as set out in Chapter 60 is from December 21st to January 20th *in its positive aspect,* and from January 21st to February 21st *in its negative aspect.* The number 8, as I stated, has for its colours 'all shades of dark grey, dark blue, and purple.' In the astrological section of this book I give the same colours with the addition of 'violet,' and under the heading of 'colours of the number 8' in the same section I have extended the list slightly by giving 'all tones of dark greys, blues, browns, and russet shades.' For the lucky jewels I have given 'all dark stones, such as dull rubies, carbuncles, and the deep-toned sapphire, which is most markedly the jewel of the number 8'. In the same section for persons born under a 4, I have given 'all shades of grey and fawn and electric shades and the minor tints of yellow and green.' In this work on numerology I have simply condensed the colours for the number 4 people to what are called 'half shades, half tones, or electric colours,' and have stated that 'electric blues' and greys seem to suit them best of all. In all this there is no contradiction of terms, as the writers of many letters to me appear to imagine. There are so many sides to the study of the occult value of numbers that one cannot put all the information in one book[1].

The following infomation will, I think, be useful, and I am giving it in order to clear up a point which I have noticed in many of the letters that have been received:

Namely: A person born on, say, January 6th will read in my astrological section that January is the 'period of the 8,' and that the colours for the number 8 are 'all tones of grey, all ranges of violet and purple, also black.' Many of those who have written to me are puzzled to know whether they should use the colours of the 8 or those belonging to the number 6. My answer is, *employ most decidedly in such a case* the colours of the number 6 as the principal, individual, and 'lucky' colours to use, but as the person was born in the 'period of the 8' he or she can use, if they wish, *but as secondary colours*, those given by the number 8.

Another illustration I will give is for those born in the 'period of the 9,' namely between March 21st to April 27th, which is *the positive period of the 9*,

---

1 The deep-toned sapphire is also the principal jewel of the number 4, and all its series.

and those born *in its negative period*, namely, between October 21st and November 27th.

If one will look up the colours I have given earlier to the number 9, they will find that they are 'all shades of crimson or red, all rose tones and pink' for the *positive period*, while for the *negative period* in my astrological section if one reads about the period October-November, one will notice I say 'all shades of crimson and blue.'

Where does blue come in? one may ask.

Because *the opposite Sign of the Zodiac* to the period October 21st to November 27th is what is called '*the House of Venus*' in her positive aspect, and as Venus, which is also the number 6, represents in this wonderful colour scheme of Nature all shades of blue, these blue rays appear to cross from one side of the Zodiac to the other and so become a favourable colour for persons born in the *negative period of the number* 9, as well as 'all shades of crimson.'

Going back to the 'periods of the number 9' for a moment we find the basic colours for both these periods are red, crimson, and pink, but the same rule applies as it did in my example for the 'period of the 8.' A person born on a 6, such as on the 6th, 15th, or 24th *in the period of the 9*, would have as his or her *principal colour* all shades of blue, with red, crimson, or pink, as his or her *secondary colours*.

The same rule applies to every month in the year and to every date of birth. It is quite simple when one has once grasped this principle and can appreciate the marvellous harmony of this wonderful universe in which we live.

74

THE VALUE OF CONCENTRATION IN REGARD TO ONE'S NUMBER

IN order to help my readers to make the best of whatever their number may be, I will now give advice which I am sure will be found of great assistance to those who want to try to make the most of their lives.

Once the principal or dominating number of the life has been found, then the next step is *to increase its power as much as possible*, the exception being those who are born under the 8, namely the 8th, 17th, or 28th of any month, to whom I will give advice on this point later.

This increase of power can be obtained by employing one of the *greatest forces* that man is endowed with, namely the Power of Concentration.

There are very few people who know anything about this extraordinary power.

All successful men and women are endowed with it, many use it unconsciously. Some are born with it, others develop it, but the majority of mankind do not use it at all.

One may often have noticed the feeble, 'wishy-washy' way most people talk. One may have tried hard to follow some rambling statement, but have found at the end that one hardly knows 'what it was all about,' or that the person who has tried to interest you has made no impression on you whatever. This has been due to the fact that the man or woman has no power of concentration, and consequently *no force behind their flow of words.*

It is the same when such people write a letter— again there may be a lot of words, even expressions and sentences well put together, but the letter has *no effect on you,* and very likely you toss it aside and think no more about it.

On the contrary, another person may say only a few words, but those *words take effect;* or they may write, and their sentences strike home — the secret of this mystery is *concentration of mind.*

The simplest way of developing this power is by the use of numbers. I will now explain.

The first thing to be done is to find one's own number, the birth number being in every case the simplest and the most certain; the next is to grasp *the meaning of that number,* and lastly to think of oneself as if that number *belonged to one,* represented one, and were *part and parcel of one's aims and plans.*

This is the sure foundation on which to build.

We will now go a step farther. The man or woman who has found his own distinct number should plan with firm determination to use that number in every way possible.

They should mentally look forward to the day or date when their number is to appear and plan that *on that day* they will take a certain course of action, and when that day or date arrives that they will go straight for what they want without shilly-shallying or hesitation of any kind.

Having read previous chapters on numbers, the reader has by now grasped the characteristics of other persons that are born under their own or other numbers. It is quite a simple matter to find out the day of the month on which the person one is going to interview was born, for if one does not ask the year of birth, even the woman most sensitive about her age will tell the date on which she was born.

A number 1 person will realise how useless it is to attempt to dominate a number 3 person. On the contrary, they must appeal to their ambition, their conscientiousness in carrying out their duties, their love of order and discipline, their sense of independence and the pride of honour and self that is the foundation principle of the number 3 person.

If they bear this in mind, *concentrating at the same time on their own plan* that made them seek the interview they will find that the number 3 person, instead of being difficult to approach, will, on the contrary, be willing to help and will most probably give ideas and suggestions that will be useful.

Having chosen a date for the interview on *one of their own numbers*, and by doing so, having concentrated their mind on this plan of action, they will find how easily they will be able to influence the person they have come to interview.

75

COMBINATIONS BETWEEN 1 HYPHEN 4 PERSONS AND ADVICE TO THOSE BORN UNDER THE NUMBERS 4 AND 8

FOLLOWING the illustrations I gave in the previous chapters on the usefulness of concentration on one's own number, so as to increase its power (except in case of those born under the 4 and 8), we will now take as an example a number 1 person meeting another of his own number. My readers have already learned from previous chapters that people born on the same series are naturally sympathetic to one another, and such knowledge gives the feeling in the first place that the other number 1 he is talking to is 'one of themselves,' as it were. This very sentiment radiating outwards destroys nervousness and allows the lines of human magnetism to vibrate in harmony from one to the other.

Let us now suppose that the number 1 person has arranged an interview with an individual born under the 2 series. In such a case he or she can select any date of the 1 or 2 series, such as the 1st, 2nd, 10th, 11th, 19th, 20th, 28th, or 29th. The number 1 person has read that number 2 persons have the feminine qualities of the number

1, and that, though opposite in character, the vidrations of both 1 and 2 persons are harmonious, and that they make good combinations. With this knowledge in his possession the number 1 person will make the effort to combine with the ideas of number 2, and so happy and good results will be obtained.

A number 1 and a number 4 person will also meet on sympathetic and harmonious vibration for the reason that in Numerology the number 1 is always associated with the 4 and these numbers are written as 1 hyphen 4, and 4 hyphen 1, but as all number 4 persons have a very decided individuality, they must not be subjugated by the 1 person, but must be allowed to keep their own distinct character and to see things from their own point of view. If the number 1 perrson will keep the peculiar temperament of the number 4 in mind, any combination with a number 4 person should be most successful.

Behind all these ideas as far as success is concerned, as I have said at the commencement is the development of the power of concentration *on one's number,* so as to *increase its influence.* This holds good for all the numbers except those born under the 4 and 8.

In previous chapters I have already warned all those under the 4's and 8's, such as the persons born on the 4th, 8th, 13th, 17th, 22nd, 26th, and 31st to avoid all numbers making an 8 or a 4 as much as possible; not to live in houses that have such numbers, and not to choose dates that make them.

In preceding pages I have gone into fuller details as to the 4 and 8 series, but briefly the rule for such persons to follow is: *Never increase the power of these numbers.* Consequently they must *not* follow the rule laid down for those born under the other numbers, but on the contrary they should do the very opposite.

As they cannot alter their Birth number, they can alter the number made by their name and cause it to produce one of the more fortunate series, especially one of a strong vibration such as a 1, 3, 5, or 6. Having definitely fixed in this way that they are going *to be represented* by the strong number they have made out of their name, they should then follow the rule I gave previously, namely, *think of themselves as that number* and do everything that is important on dates that make that number. It they do this, *and do it persistently,* the number 4 or 8 persons will get away from the bad luck such people generally experience and so become as equally fortunate as others.

They must not, however, expect the change to be seen in a few days, as so many in their impatience do, but in a reasonable space of time they will see very marked results in their favour.

76

MORE INFORMATION ABOUT PERSONS BORN UNDER THE NUMBERS 4 AND 8

I HAVE received so many letters from number 4 and 8 people, asking for advice, that I think it will be useful to devote an entire chapter to such cases.

Out of every hundred letters, fully eighty write testifying to the accuracy of my system of numbers, especially as regard the hard luck that appears to pursue persons who have the combination of 4 and 8 continually cropping up in their lives.

The 4 itself and all its series is not so much to be dreaded. Persons born on the 4th, 13th, 22nd, and 31st will find these dates and numbers the most important in their lives, but as the 4 in Numerology is always associated with the number 1, and in nearly all systems in written as 4 hyphen 1, or 1 hyphen 4, and as the 1 is a strong and powerful number, I advise the number 4 persons to use the *strong number* as much as possible and select all dates such as the 1st, 10th, 19th, and 28th for their most important efforts, and to endeavour to live in houses whose number or the addition of whose number makes a number 1. They should also remember they as what is called the interchangeable numbers of the 1 hyphen 4 series are the 2 hyphen 7 and all their series, they need not be afraid of such dates or numbers as the 2nd, 6th, 11th, 20th, 25th, or 29th.

It is only when the combination of the 4 and 8 are *continually cropping* up that those born under such numbers should do their utmost to avoid them.

EXAMPLE. A man born on either the 4th, 13th, 22nd, or 31st marries a woman born on either the 8th, 17th, or 26th. He will most certainly find that 4's and 8's will influence his life more than any other number, generally bringing sadness, ill-luck or terrible blows of fate in their train. To this number 4 man or woman, I decidedly say avoid using all 4's and 8's and use the number 1 series instead, and for the next best use the 2 hyphen 7 series.

For some reason, due probably to some law of magnetic vibration, 4 and 8 people generally attract one another, but from *a purely worldly* standpoint the combination cannot be considered 'lucky.' They often show the highest devotion to one another during illness and misfortune, and some of the greatest examples of self-sacrifice are found when 4's and 8's marry or make a combination together.

Number 8 persons belong to a still more fatalistic law of vibration and appear to be 'children of fate' more than any other class.

They can be just as noble in character, as devoted and self-sacrificing as the best of their fellow mortals, but *they seldom get the reward that they are entitled to.* If they rise in life to any high position it is generally one of grave responsibility, anxiety, and care. Such persons can become rich, but wealth seldom brings them happiness, and for love they are generally called on to pay too high a price.

My advice to them is: If they find the 4's and 8's continually coming into their lives and associated with sorrow, disappointment, ill-fate, and ill-luck, they should determinately avoid such numbers and all their series. They should, in such a case, so alter their name number, following the examples I have given in previous chapters, to produce one of the more fortunate series, such as a 1, 3, 5, or 6, and carry out their plans on dates that make these numbers. If they will do this they will completely alter their ill-luck and control as it were the curious fate that appears to follow them.

If, however, they prefer, as many do, to carry out the *full force and meaning of their number* 8, without caring what the worldly result may be, in that case they should do exactly as I have said for the other numbers and do everything important on dates and numbers that make the 8, such as the 8th, 17th, 26th, also the 4th, 13th, 22nd, and 31st.

If they do this will be equally successful, but in leading peculiarly fatalistic lives, being, if I may use the expression, 'marked' people in whatever path of life they may make their own.

Many have written to ask how to change from an unlucky or fatalistic set of numbers to more fortunate ones. This question is generally asked by people who are born under the series of 4's and 8's, and who have proved, as I have said, that all combinations of such numbers have been more or less assoicated with fatalistic events in the life. In such cases, when persons are born on the 4th, 13th, 22nd, or 31st in any month they should try to avoid doing important things on dates making the 8 or any of its combinations, such as the 8th, 17th, 26th, and *take instead the number 1 series, or the number of the Zodiacal period of the month they are born in.* For example: A person born between February 19th and March 20th being in the 'period of the 3,' if they happen to be born on February 22nd or 26th or on March 4th, 8th, 13th, 17th, or 22nd, will find it more lucky for them to use the 3 series instead of their birth number, the 4 or 8. In fact, in such cases it will be better for them to drop the birth number altogether.

The same rule will apply to all the other month periods of the year with *the exception of the period* from December 21st to January 20th, the period of the number 8 positive, and from January 21st to February 19th, the period of number 8 negative. If born in these two periods the 4 and 8 people *must not select the number of the month period,* because it they did they would only increase the power of the 4 and 8. I advise them in such cases to take the number of the month period *exactly opposite to their Zodiac period,* which is: For December 21st to January 20th, the opposite numbers are those of June 21st to July 20th, which, if they refer to Chapter 60 of this book, they will find is the period of the 2-7. For people born January 21st to February 19th, the opposite period of the Zodiac is July 31st to August 20th, the numbers of which are 1-4. By following this rule all people who have the 4 and 8 for their birth number will be able to select numbers to use to in place of the series of their 4's and 8's, and by employing the new numbers, will, in a short time, begin to notice how much more fortunate their lives have become.

They should employ also the colours and jewels which their *new numbers indicate* instead of those given for the 4's and 8's.

I feel sure this information will be useful to many hundreds who have asked questions on this extremely important point.

Many number 2 persons have written and asked me why it is that they find as well as their own number, the 2, 11, 20 and 29th, that the 8 appears to have a great importance in their lives. The reason for this is that the 8, being a very strong number, with a fatalistic tendency, tries to dominate the weaker number 2, which has a relation to itself as 4 times 2 is 8, but the 8 is not a happy combination when it comes into the lives of number 2 persons, and it should always be regarded as a warning of sorrow and disappointment or fatalistic experiences of some kind.

The 4 will also be found to have great deal of influence with number 2 persons, but this is because it not only represents the double of the number 2, but it is also one of the interchangeable numbers, such as 1 and 4 are the interchangeable numbers of the 2 and 7.

77

THE AFFINITY OF COLOURS AND NUMBERS AND HOW MUSIC AND NUMBERS ARE ASSOCIATED

NUMBER 1 persons, namely those born on the 1st, 10th, 19th, or 28th (numbers which by the addition of themselves produce the number 1), should dress themselves as much as possible in all shades of brown (light or dark) and all shades of yellow or gold colours, or at least have some of these colours about their person. If they have the freedom to select colours for their sleeping rooms, they should follow the same rule.

They will find this colour rule will have an excellent effect in soothing their nerves, and they will rest and sleep better in rooms having their own colours.

Number 2 persons, namely, those born on the 2nd, 11th, 20th, or 29th, should wear all shades of green from the darkest to the lightest shade, also cream and white.

They should avoid all heavy dark colours, especially black, purple, and dark red.

Number 3 persons, namely, those born on the 3rd, 12th, 21st, or 30th, should wear shades of mauve, violet, or the pale or lilac shades of purple, but as men cannot easily dress in such colours, they should at least employ them in the neckties, shirts, or handkerchiefs.

Number 4 persons, namely, those born on the 4th, 13th, 22nd, or 31st, should wear what are called the 'electric colours,' blue, greys, electric blues, and what are known as 'half shades'. They should avoid strong or positive colours of all kinds.

Number 5 persons, namely those born on the 5th, 14th or 23rd, should wear the light shades of all colours especially light greys, white, and glistening materials.

They should never wear dark colours if they can possibly avoid doing so.

Number 6 persons, namely, those born on the 6th, 15th, or 24th, should wear all shades of blue, from the lightest to the dark navy, what is known as the full or real blue, not 'electric blue'. For secondary colours, they can also wear shades of rose or pink, but not red, scarlet, or crimson, unless they are born between March 21st to April 24th, or between October 21st to November 24th.

Number 7 persons, namely those born on the 7th, 16th, or 25th, should like the number 2 persons wear all shades of pale green, white, yellow, and gold colours. The palest possible shades are best for them, such as what are known as 'pastel shades.'

Number 8 persons, namely, those born on the 8th, 17th, or 26th, should wear all shades of dark grey, dark blue, purple, and black; light and gaudy colours are out of place with them and should be avoided.

Number 9 persons, namely, those born on the 9th, 18th, or 27th, should wear all shades of red, rose, crimson, pink, or red purple. The darker or rich shades of these colours are best for them.

Red is the colour of the soldier, the colour of energy, restlessness and revolution. It is the chosen colour of the Revolutionist and Anarchist; hence, the origin of the 'red flag.'

On account of the magnetic rays sent off by a number 9 person, their presence often irritates people belonging to other numbers, except those born under the number 1, the 3, the 5, the 6, or their own number. People born under the other numbers are very often nervous or uncomfortable in the presence of a number 9 person.

Numbers and music show very decided affinities. The number 1, 3, and 9 persons like mertial, inspiring, or what may be called 'full-blooded' tones; number 2 and 7 persons are more partial to string and wind instruments, such as the violin,' 'cello, harp, pipes, etc.; number 6 persons like romantic, sweet music of all kinds with a lilt and rhythm; number 5 persons lean towards either extremely original or unusual music, something off the beaten track. Number 4 and 8 persons, if musical, have a special leaning for the organ and make magnificent choir or choral leaders, but in all their music there is an undertone of plaintiveness, melancholy, religious fervour, or fatalism.

The following are a few examples of countries having their own individual or what is called.

National Music, in accordance with the planet and number by which they are governed.

England and Germany, governed by Mars (number 9), martial, inspiring, or 'full-blooded' music.

Ireland, governed by Venus (number 6), romantic, sweet music, with a lilt or rhythm.

Scotland, governed by the Moon (number 2) and Saturn (number 8), string and wind instruments.

Wales, governed by Uranus (number 4) and Mercury (number 5), original music, with undertone of religious fervour, melancholy, choral and choir.

The United States, governed by the Planet Mercury (number 5), can use the qualities of that number and adapt itself to all types of music, but will always lean to what is original, new, and out of the ordinary   hence this country is the natural birthplace of what is called 'jazz' or syncopated music.

78

NUMBERS AND DISEASE, PLANETARY SIGNIFICANCE OF HERBAL CURES

IN some Press articles I gave an account of the various diseases that are associated with persons born under the numbers that make their birth date. I have received so many letters testifying to the accuracy of this system and begging me to give further information as to indications from occultism regarding the cure of diseases, that I have much pleasure in giving in this chapter the name of herbs that are beneficial to persons born under the different numbers.

To keep in good health is one of the essentials to success in life, and in following these rules I feel sure my readers can only benefit by this advice.

The same students of occultism who discovered the extraordinary influence of numbers in connection with the destiny of individuals, also discovered the sympathy of certain plants, fruits, and herbs that in the world of Nature are related to the planets and months of the year in which people are born, and so evolved a system by which pain and illness can be alleviated by the use of such herbs, or fruits which correspond to each planet and consequently to the number of birth.

I have collected this information from some of the most ancient sources of knowledge on occultism and from those who have devoted their lives to the investigation of the subject. To this I have added my own lifelong experience, in the belief that by the study of Nature we may find the secrets of Nature.

Number 1 persons, or all those born on the 1st, 10th, 19th, and 28th, of any month, have a tendency to suffer from the heart in some form or another, such as palpitation, irregular circulation, and in advanced life, high blood-pressure, They are also likely to have trouble with the eyes, or astigmatism, and would do well do have their sight carefully tested from time to time.

The principal herbs and fruits for number 1 persons, or all those whose birth number is the 1st, 10th, 19th, or 28th, are :

Raisins, camomile, eye-bright, St. John's wort, saffron, cloves, nutmeg, sorrel, borage, gentain root, lavender, bay leaves, oranges, lemons, dates, thyme, myrrh, musk vervain, ginger, barley (barely bread and barely water). Number 1 persons should eat honey as much as possible.

They will find their nineteenth, twenty-eighth, thirty-seventh, and fifty-fifth years will bring them important changes in health one way or the other.

The months to most guarded against for ill-health and overwork are : October, December, and January.

Number 2 persons, or all those whose birth

number is the 2nd, 11th, 20th, or 29th, have a tendency to suffer with the stomach and digestive organs.

The principal herbs for number 2 persons, or those born on the 2nd, 11th, 20th, or 29th of any month, are : Lettuce, cabbages, turnips, cucumber, melon, chicory or endive, rapeseed, colewort, moonwort, linseed, water plantain, and ash of willow.

They will find the twentieth, twenty-fifth, twenty-ninth, forty-third, forty-seventh, fifty-second, and sixty-fifth years will bring them important changes in health. The three months to be most guarded against for ill-health and overwork are January, February, and July.

Number 3 persons, or all those born on the 3rd, 12th, 21st, or 30th, have tendency to suffer from overstrain of the nervous system, generally brought on by overwork and their desire not to spare themselves in any thing they do.

They are inclined to have attacks of neuritis and sciatica, also many forms of skin troubles.

The principal herbs foɪ number 3 persons, or those born on the 3rd, 12th, or 30th of any month, are beets, borage, bilberries, asparagus, dandelion, endive, ewerwort, lungwort, sage, cherries, barberries, strawberries, apples, mulberries, peaches, olives, rhubarb, gooseberries, pomegranates, pineapples, grapes, mint, saffron, nutmegs, cloves, sweet marjoram, St. John's wort, almonds, figs, hazel-nuts, and wheat.

The months to be most guarded against for

ill-health and overwork are December, February, June, and September. The important years for changes in health are the twelfth, twenty-first, thirty-ninth, forty-eighth, and fifty-seventh.

Number 4 persons, or all those born on the 4th, 13th, 22nd, or 31st, have a likelihood of suffering from mysterioius ailments, difficult of ordinary diagnosis. They are more or less inclined to melancholia, anaemia and pains in the head and back.

The principal herbs for number 4 persons, or those born on th 4th, 13th, 22nd or 31st of any month, are spinach, sage, pilewort, wintergreen, medlars, icelandmoss, and Solomon's seal. Number 4 persons derive the greatest benefit from electric treatment of all kinds, mental suggestion, and hypnotism. They should be particularly careful to avoid drugs, also highly seasoned dishes and red meat.

The months to be guarded against for ill-health and overwork are January, February, July, August, and September.

The important years for their health are the thirteenth, twenty-second, thirty-first, fortieth, forty-ninth, and fifty-eighth.

Number 5 persons, or all those born on the 5th, 14th, or 23rd, have a tendency to overstrain of the nervous system. They are inclined to attempt too much mentally, to live too much on their nerves. They are likely to bring on such things as neuritis and are prone to nervous prostration and insomnia. Sleep, rest, and quietude are the best medicines they can employ.

The principal herbs for number 5 persons or those born on the 5th, 14th, or 23rd of any month, are carrots, parsnips, sea-kale, oats in the form of oatmeal or bread, parsely, sweet majoram, champignons, caraway seeds, thyme, nuts of all kinds, but especially hazel-nuts and walnuts.

The months to be most guarded against for ill-health and overwork are June, September, and December.

The important years for changes in their health are the fourteenth, twenty-third, forty-first, and fiftieth years.

Number 6 persons, or all those born on the 6th, 15th, or 24th, are inclined to suffer with the throat, nose, and upper part of the lungs. As a rule they have strong robust constitution, especially if they can live in the open or in the country, where they can have plenty of air and exercise. Women born under the number 6 often suffer with their breasts. The heart as a general rule becomes affected in the latter years and produces irregular circulation of the blood.

The herbs for number 6 persons, or those born on the 6th, 15th, or 24th, of any month, are all kinds of beans, parsnips, spinach, marrows, mint, melons, motherwort, pomegranates, apples, peaches, apricots, figs, walnuts, almonds and the juice of maidenhair-fern, daffodils, wild thyme, musk, violets, vervain, and rose leaves.

The months to be most guarded against for ill-health and overwork are May, October, and

November.

They will find that the fifteenth, twenty-fourth, forty-second, fifty-first, and sixtieth years will bring them important changes in health.

Number 7 persons , or those who are born on the 7th, 16th, or 25th, are more easily affected by worry and annoyance than any other class. As long as things are going smoothly, they can get through any amount of work, but if worried, either by circumstances or people, they are inclined to imagine things are worse than they are and get easily despondent and melancholy.

They are extremely sensitive to their surroundings; they will gladly accept any responsibility for those who appear to appreciate them; they are unusually conscientious in doing any work that is interesting to them, but as they are stronger mentally than physically, they have often frail bodies that attempt too much for their strength. They are inclined to have some peculiar delicacy in connection with the skin; it is either extremely sensitive to friction, or has some peculiarity as regards perspiration.

The principal herbs for number 7 persons, or those born on the 7th, 16th, or 25th in any month, are lettuce, cabbage, chicory or endive, cucumber, colewort, linseed, mushrooms, ceps, sorrel, apples, grapes, and the juices of all fruits. The months to be most guarded against for ill-health and overwork are January, February, July and August.

The most important years for changes in health are the seventh, sixteenth, twenty-fifth, thirty-fourth, forty-third, fifty-second, and sixty-first.

Number 8 persons, or those born on the 8th, 17th, or 26th, are as a rule liable to trouble with the liver, bile and intestines. They are prone to suffer with headaches and rheumatism. They should avoid animal food as much as possible and live on fruit, herbs, and vegetables.

The principal herbs for number 8 persons, or those born on the 8th, 17th, or 26th in any month, are spinash, winter green, angelica, wild carrot, marshmallow, plantain, sage, pilewort, ragwort, shepherd's purse, Solomon's seal, vervain, elder flowers, gravel root, mandrake root, celery.

The months to be most guarded against for ill-health and effects of overwork are December, January, February and July. They will find the most important years for changes in health are the seventeenth, twenty-sixth, thirty-fifth, forty-fourth, fifty-third, and sixty-second.

Number 9 persons, or those born on the 9th, 18th, or 27th, are more or less inclined to fevers of all kinds, measles, chicken-pox, scarlatina, and such-like. They should avoid rich food, also alcoholic drinks or wines.

The principal herbs for number 9 persons, or those born on the 9th, 18th, or 27th of any month, are onions, garlic, leeks, horse-radish, rhubarb, mustard-seed, wormwood, betony, spear-wort, white hellebore, ginger, pepper, broom, rape, madder, hops, danwort, and juice of nettles.

The months to be most guarded against for ill-health or the effects of overwork are April, May,

445

October, and November.

They will find the most important years for changes in the health are the ninth, eighteenth, twenty-seventh, thirty-sixth, forty-fifth and sixty-third.

The herbs that have been mentioned in these pages can be obtained from all good herbalists in almost all countries. Herbs are Nature's own remedies.

79

HOW TO KNOW WHAT CITY, TOWN, OR PLACE IS FORTUNATE FOR ONE TO LIVE IN

IN this chapter I intend to show how each person may more easily find if any city, town, or place is in a harmonious vibration with themselves.

Such information shold be of great value to those who find, as so many do, that a certain town or place has proved unfortunate; they may desire to make a change, but as they have nothing to guide them, they do not know what to do or how to arrive at decision. The following rules will, I believe, be of great help to all such people.

Taking the numbers 1 to 9 as the foundation numbers, which by now all those readers who have followed this book will know are the basic numbers by which all calculation on this earth is founded, I will therefore give examples of how each birth number may be found in any city, town, or place.

Work out the numbers of the name of the city or town by the numbers given to each letter by the Mystic Alphabet which I give in Chapter 62. Put these numbers under each letter and add them together until only one figure remains; if this single number corresponds to the birth number, then the vibrations of that city, town, or place will accord with the individual, and the district indicated by the number should be fortunate for the person whose birth number corresponds with it, and still more so if the person's name number is also in accord.

Number 1 persons, such as all those born on the 1st, 10th 19th, or 28th, would therefore find the following towns more likely to be favourable. We will take as an example Manchester. The name works out as follows:

MANCHESTER
4 1 5 3 5 5 3 4 5 2   = 37 and 3 plus 7
                              = 10 or the single
                                  number 1.

Other towns that make the number 1 are:

Birmingham..1
Boston..1
New York..1
Alexandria..1
Whitechapel..1

or any other town or place that will by this system produce the number 1.

Number 1 and 4 and number 2 and 7 persons have greater choice than those born under any of the other numbers, for, as I have previously explained in my chapters on this subject, number 1 belongs to the 1 hyphen 4 series whose interchangeable or sympathetic numbers are the 2 hyphen 7 series; therefore number 1, 2, 4 or 7 persons could select all places that give as their single numbr any of the series of 1, 2, 4, or 7.

Number 2 persons, or all those born on the 2nd, 11th, 20th, or 29th, can select any town whose final number makes any one of the above series, but more especially a town making their own series of the 2. We will take as an example:

LEEDS

3 5 5 4 3 = 20 =2

or any of the following places which all total to the number 2:

Plymouth..2

Los Angeles..2

Norwich...2

Brighton...2

Number 3 persons, or all those born on the 3rd, 12th, 21st, or 30th, can take as an example:

CREWE

2 3 5 6 5 = 21 = 3

or any of the following towns which add to the number 3, such as :

Dublin..3

Bath...3

Reading...3

Limerick...3

Moscow..3

Melbourne..3

York..3

Nottingham..3

Devonport 3

Bradford..3

Number 4 persons, or all those born on the 4th, 13th, 22nd, or 31st, can take as an example:

L O N D O N

3 7 5 4 7 5 = 31 = 4

or any of the following towns which add to the number 4, such as:

Paisley...4

Bristol..4

Leicester..4

Quebec..4

Montreal..4

Stockport...4

Salisbury...4

or any town indicated by the numbers of the 1, 2, 4 , or 7 series, as I explained earlier.

Number 5 persons, or all those born on the 5th, 14th, or 23rd, can take as an example :

T A U N T O N

4 1 6 5 4 7 5   = 32 = 5

or any of the following towns which add to the number 5, such as:

But as the number 5 is the only number that can associate or harmoise with any other number, they need not be so careful as to what place they select, for as they can get on with persons born under any other number almost equally as well as with those born under their own, so in the same way they get on equally well in any city or place no matter what its number may be.

Number 6 persons, or all those born on the 6th, 15th, or 24th, can take as an example :

LIVERPOOL

3 1 6 5 2 8 7 7 3 = 42 = 6

or any of the following towns, which add to the number 6, such as:

San Francisco...6

Cowes...6

Sheffield...6

Number 7 persons, or all those born on the 7th, 16th, or 25th, can take as an example :

W I G A N
6 1 3 1 5=16 =7

or any of the following towns which add to the number 7, such as:

Doncaster...7
Hollywood...7
Whitehaven...7
Auckland...7
Calcutta...7
Tiverton...7
Grimsby...7
Preston...7

or any town indicated by the numbers of the 1, 2, 4, 7 series, as I explained earlier.

Number 8 persons, or all those born on the 8th, 17th, or 26th, can take as an example :

G L A S G O W
3 3 1 3 3 7 6 = 26 =8

or any of the following, such as :

Belfast...8

Stoke-on-Trent..8
Hull..8
Bombay..8
Bournemouth...8

But, as I have explained, I advise all number 4 and 8 persons not to increase the influence of the number 8 by employing or living under this strangely fatalistic number, but instead to make their name number work out to a more fortunate vibration, such as those of the 1, 3, 5, ro 6 series.

Number 9 persons, or all those born on the 9th, 18th, or 27th, can take as an example:

```
W O L V E R H A M P T O N
6 7 3 6 5 2 5 1 4 8 4 7 5 = 63 = 9
```

or any of the following towns whih add to the number 9, such as:

Blackpool..9
Whitehead...9
St. Louis..9
Berlin...9
Rome..9
Toronto..9
Brussels...9

As I have explained previously, the series, of 3, 6, 9, if added together in any direction, produce a 9 as their final digit, so the persons born under any one of these series will find others born under any of the these series sympthetic to them, so also can they take any city or town whose final number makes a 3, 6, 9, as if they used only their own individual number.

In conclusion, it should be borne in mind that towns and places should be regarded as the *larger octave of harmony*, the number of one's house *the more intimate*, the number of the date and day of the week *the more immediate as regards events*, and the birth number of persons in relation to oneself as *the more personal* as regards out feelings, affections, and home life.

If this is born in mind, the reason and logic of this special system of Numerology is easily seen, and the harmony it makes for becomes apparent to every student of humanity.

80

HORSE-RACING AND NUMBERS

I HAVE received so many letters asking for information as to how my system of numbers could be employed in 'betting,' that I cannnot conclude this book without trying to give some advice on a subject that is of interest to so many thousands.

There is no doubt that the study of numbers can open up a new field for the successful backing of horses, but there is no saying more true than 'a little knowledge is a dangerous thing.'

My experience is that people are too much inclined to think that because they have proved that the system I teach has such a bearing on the leading events in their own individual lives, that without more preparation they are ready to plunge into racing and back any horse whose name makes the same number as their own.

The point so many people seem to forget is that horse-racing is an extremely complicated business, so much so that 'tips,' even from owners and jockeys, are as a rule as equally unreliables as the hundred and one systems that are offered daily to the public by almost every newspaper that one picks up.

Many important racing events have upset all theories as to forecsating the winner by a study of 'form,' previous running, and so forth. At many races complete outsiders have, for no apparent reason beaten the most heavily backed favourites.

Can the study of numbers be used to give a clear indication of which horses are likely to be first, second, and third?

I say most emphatically that it can, but the trouble is that it is so rare to find persons who can 'keep their heads' when it comes to such a thing as a *systematic employment of any method*, and more particularly with numbers.

If one really made up one's mind to experiment with the system of numbers as set out in these pages in connection with betting, one would have to do it on the following lines:

To attend the race meeting in person.

Select a day whose number accords with one's own.

If possible, find out the jockeys whose birth·number is the same as the number of the day.

When all these numbes are in accord, say, for example, if they all worked out to a number, such as the 9, then such horses, if they run under the numbers 9, 18, and 27 on that day would certainly be more likely to come in as first, second, and third than any others.

In such a case it would be necessary to back the three horses that are to run under the numbers, 9, 18, and 27 on the starting board for 'win and place.' If there were a greater number than 36 running in the race it would be necessary also to take in the horse under that number, but if too much money would be at stake by backing all four, a good rule is to select *the two youngest* horses out of the four and back these two for 'win and place.' If there were not much difference in age, the next rule to employ is to select *the youngest male horse* in preference to t*he youngest female*. If on the first race one lost, on the following race the stakes should be doubled, and so on systematically during the day. If this plan were carried out and the numbers selected steadfastly adhered to, one would sooner or later be rewarded by a first, second, or it may be all three, with the added chance of getting a complete outsider in some of the events.

The great difficulty is that so few persons at a race meeting have sufficient strength of will to follow such a plan systematically. They may try it for one race and, because they have not met with immediate success, they are likely to do nothing for the next even or plunge after some 'tip' they have had given them, and so on.

To those who are unable to attend the race meeting personally, I do not advise them to try to 'find the winner' by numbers, for the simple reason that if they have not got *the running number of the horse* they miss one of the principal elements for success.

81

EXAMPLES FROM THE NAME OF SOME PRESIDENTS OF THE UNITED STATES

GEORGE WASHINGTON

IN taking illustrations from the name of Presidents of the United States, I cannot do better than start with the name of George Washington.

```
G E O R G E     W A S H I N G T O N
3 5 7 2 3 5     6 1 3 5 1 5 3 4 7 5
─────────       ─────────────────────
   2 5               4 0
   ───               ─────────
    7                4 =11 =2
```

The number of the famous name of George Washington, the 1st President of the United States, worked out by the Chaldean or Hebrew alphabet, as set out in the example on Lloyd George, gives to the name GEORGE the compound number of 25, with its single of final digit of 7. On looking up the meaning of the compound number of 25 in Chapter 63, it will be found stated:

This is a number denoting strength gained through experience and benefits obtained through observation of people and things. It is not deemed exactly 'lucky,' as its success is given through strife and trials in the earlier life. It is favourable when it appears in regard to the future.

The word WASHINGTON works out to the compound number of 30, with its single digit of 4.

The meaning of this compound number is given in Chapter 63 as:

This is a number of thoughtful deduction, retrospection, and mental superiority over one's fellows, but, as it sems to belong to the mental plane, the persons it represents are likely to put all material things on one side—not because they have to, but because they wish to do so.

This is remarkably borne out by Washington's resignation of the position of Commander-in-Chief of the victorious American Army when the met his assembled Generals for the last time. His own words were, 'With heart full of love and gratitude, I now take leave of you.' Addressing the President of Congress, Washington said:

The great events on which my resignation depended having, at length, taken place, I have now the honour to surrender into their [Congress's] hands the trust committed to me and to claim the indulgence of retiring from the service of my country. Having now finished the work assigned me, I retire.

This really great man, so justly called the 'Father of the United States,' refused to accept any reward for his long years of arduous service, an thus retired to this home at Mount Vernon.

The distinguished name of George Washington

bears out in a remarkable manner the occult meaning of the numbers of this name.

If the final digits of 7 for GEORGE and 4 for WASHINGTON be added together they produce eleven (11), with the single digit of 2. This compound number 11, on being raised to its higher octave, 20, gives for this compound number (see Chapter 63) the symbol of 'The Awakening,' also 'The Judgment,' with the interpretation.

The awakening of new purpose, new plans, new ambitions, the call to action, but for some great purpose, cause, or duty.

It will thus be seen from this example how wonderfully this system of Numerology fits in with and explains the underlying qualities of the character of George Washington.

By knowing the birth date of an individual and seeing if the number of the date is in harmonious vibration with the number given by the name is of considerable help in arriving at a summing up of the general characteristics.

If the number of the birth date and the number given by the name are not in accord, the promise of the man's or woman's career will not be so definite.

Returning to the name of George Washington, as an example, the last digit is the figure 2, with 7 and 4 as the principal digits of the name.

Now, Washington's birthday is celebrated as February 22nd, which makes the double figure in this system to be written as 4 hyphen 1, with its interchangeable numbers of 2 hyphen 7. (See

Chapter 56). Some people claim that his birth date was February 11th, in the old-style calendar. Should this be the date taken, it would not alter the affect of the number of his name working out to the final digit of a 2, because, whether it was February 22nd, a 4, or February 11th, a 2, they are both interchangeable numbers with one another, and in consequence the number of the name and the number of the birth date *are in harmonious vibration together.*

Should the number of the name and the number of the birth date not be in harmony or accord, it indicates that one is likely to find a jumble or unevenness in the plans and careers of the man or woman the numbers not in vibration to one another represent.

ABRAHAM LINCOLN

Abraham Lincoln born February 12th, 1809, assassinated on the night of Friday, April 14th, 1865, died April 15th.

The Name works out as follows:

```
A B R A H A M        L I N C O L N
1 2 2 1 5 1 4        3 1 5 3 7 3 5

      1 6                   2 7
      ───                   ───
       7               9 = 16 = 7
```

In this case the birth number, the single digit 3, and the single digit of the name are not in harmonious accord.

The single digit of 3 for the birth is a powerful number, being in itself representative of the Planet Jupiter; it indicates underlying ambition, the power to rule and dictate. In describing these persons in Chapter 55, I have stated:

Number 3 people...aur decidedly ambitious: they are never satisfied in being in subordinate positions; their aim is to rise in the world, to have control and authority over others. They are excellent in the execution of commands; they love order and discipline in all things; they readily obey orders themselves, but they also insist on having their orders obeyed. Number 3 people often rise to the very highest positions in any business, profession, or sphere in which they may be found. They often excel in positions of authority in the army and navy, in government, and in life generally; and especially in all posts of trust and responsibility, as they are extremely conscientious in carrying out their duties.

The final digit of the name ABRAHAM LINCOLN, a 7, is more weak or gentle in its qualities, as I have stated in Chapter 59:

People born under the number 7... are very independent, original, and have strongly marked individuality...but in everything they do, they sooner or later show a peculiar philosophical outlook on life that tinges all their work.

I further said, number 7 people have, 'a peculiar magnetism that has great influence over others.'

The description by this system of Numerology, it must be admitted, accords closely with the well-known character of Abraham Lincoln.

Turning to the more mysterious of hidden influences indicated by the compound numbers, if we add the single digit of the birth number, the 3, to the digit of the name number, the 7, they produce the compound number of 10. In Chapter 63 we read:

10. Symbolised as the 'Wheel of Fortune.' It is a number of honour, of faith and self-confidence, of rise and fall; one's name will be known for good or evil, according to one's desires; it is a fortunate number in the sense that one's plans are likely to be carried out.

Taking the compound number of the birth, February 12th, for another indication of the occult influences governing this career, we read for this number in Chapter 63:

12. The symbolism of this number is suffering and anxiety of mind. It is also indicated as 'the Sacrifice' or 'the Victim' and generally foreshadows one being sacrificed for the plans or intrigues of others.

Now, turning to the compound number of the name, 16, we read in the same chapter:

16. This number has a most peculiar occult symbolism. It is pictured by 'a Tower Struck by Lightning from which a man is falling with a Crown on his head.' It is also called 'the Shattered Citadel.'

It gives warning of some strange fatality awaiting one.

When one considers Lincoln's sudden assassination as he sat in a box in a theatre on the night of Friday, April 14th, one cannot help being astonished at the truth underlying this system of occult significance of the compound numbers.

Further, Abraham Lincoln was the 16th President of the United, the single digit of this number, the 7, corresponding to the single digit of his name.

FRANKLIN DELANO ROOSEVELT

Franklin Delano Roosevelt, the 32nd President of the United States, was born at Hyde Park, New York, at 8.18 p.m. January 30th, 1882.

The numbers made by his name are as follows:

```
F  R  A  N  K  L  I  N        D  E  L  A  N  O
8  2  1  5  2  3  1  5        4  5  3  1  5  7
─────────────────────        ──────────────────
         2 7                           2 5
         ───                           ───
          9                             7
```

```
          R  O  O  S  E  V  E  L  T
          2  7  7  3  5  6  5  3  4
          ─────────────────────────
                    4 2
                    ───
                 6 = 22 = 4
```

It will be noticed that his birthdate, January 30th, produces for its single digit the powerful number of 3, which my readers will remember earlier in this book stands for the Planet Jupiter.

The power of the number 3 is, in his case, however, afflicted, especially through his early years, by its being in the period of the Planet Saturn, the 8 negative.

The qualities of persons born in this Zodiacal Sign of Aquarius I have described in the astrological section of this book. The foundation indications are as follows:

Persons born in this part of the Zodiac are generally very active for the public good and will often give all they have to relieve the disress of others. They are good reasoners, and are very successful in debate and argument and difficult to convince.

They are excellent in business and finance when they apply their minds to such things, but as a general rule they are more successful for others than for themselves.

They take a great interest in public meetings, large gatherings of people, and public ceremonies.

They have a quiet controlling power with their eyes, and so subdue others. It takes some sudden call of circumstances to make them 'make the most of themselves.'

In matters of health they are inclined to suffer from the nerves of the stomach in some peculiar manner that is difficult to relieve by ordinary medicine. They are prone to suffer from accidents to their teeth, pains in the knees and feet and trouble *with the middle of the spine.*

Franklin Delano Roosevelt. however, being born under the powerful number of the 3. the indicator of strong will, detemination, and ambition, was able to rise above the indications given by his Zodiacal Sign, even to conquer the spinal meningitis which attacked him in his early days.

In previous pages of this book describing the qualities of number 3 persons, I have stated:

Number 3 people, like the number I individuals, are decidedly ambitious; they are never satisfied by being in subordinate positions; their aim is to rise in the world, *to have control and authority over others.*

Number 3 people often rise to the very highest positions in any business, profession, or sphere in which they may be found. They often excel in positions of authority in the army and navy, in government, and in life generally; and especially in all posts of trust and responsibility, as they are extremely conscientious in carrying out their duties.

This appears to be a very fitting description of the 32nd President of the United States.

When we come to analyse the birth and name number, we find, however, they are not in harmony whit one another.

The birth date, January 30th, is a 3, while the name number works out to a 22, or the single digit of a 4.

President Roosevelt, being the 32nd President comes, as Head of his Nation, under a fortunate compound number, *at least as far as his country is concerned.* In dealing with the number 32, I have stated in previous pages of this book.

This number has a magical power. It is usually associated with combinations of people or nations, It is a fortunate number if the person it represents holds to his own judgment or opinions; if not, his plans are likely to become wrecked by the stubbornness and stupidity of others. It is a favourable number if it appears in connection with future events.

The compound number of President Roosevelt's name, which works out to a 22, is, however, not so fortunate *personally*. I have stated in earlier pages:

This number is symbolised by 'a good man blinded by the fooly of others, with a knapsack on his back full of errors.'

It is a warning number of illusion and delusion, a good person who lives in a fool's paradise; a dreamer of dreams who awakens only when surrounded by danger. It is also a number of false judgement *owing to the influence of others.*

President Roosevelt ran considerable danger of assassination in the course of his career. The indications were very similar to those given in the life of Abraham Lincoln, whose birth number was also a 3 in the Zodiacal Sign of Aquarius in the House of Saturn, the negative number 8.

President Roosevelt had a close call from death, when Zangara, the anarchist, fired six shots at him on February 15th, 1933, at Miami, Florida, and Mayor Cermak of Chicago was fatally wounded by his side.

467

NOTE. The title of President is not taken into account in this system of Numerology, as is that of Kings, Queens, hereditary titles, or those given for life. The reason being that the title of President is only for a term of years and is therefore a transitory one.

 **82**

THE BIBLE AND NUMBERS

IN an earlier chapter of this book, I have given illustrations of the influence of the number 7 and other numbers in connection with the Hebrew race.

One of the great wonders of the world has been the fact that, in spite of privations and persecutions such as no other race ever endured, the Jewish people have held to their religion as set, out in the pages of the volume of the Sacred Law, and furthermore, that this volume has become *the base of all law in every land and clime into which it has permeated.*

It is acknowledged to have the greatest influence for good of any book that has ever been written. It is considered the inspired message of God the Creator to the Hebrew race in the first instance, and later to all mankind.

In this book, generally called the Bible, more knowledge is at times concealed than is revealed to the ordinary reader.

For me, it will be sufficient in the short space at my disposal if I am able to call attention to one single instance—but one of radiant importance—to prove that this wonderful book not only has in its pages the evidence of Divine Design in the Creator's construction of things—but that *it contains in itself a systematic plan and design that* must carry with it incontrovertible proof that not only is the Bible inspired, but that it has within itself *the proofs of its inspiration,* so that all mankind might believe in its message.

It has been handed down to us that the first books of the Bible were written or compiled by one of the greatest men of all time, a man called Moses.

Let us consider for a moment who this man was and what his claims are for universal respect and admiration. Brielly, he was born of the priestly house of Levi. He was called Moses because Pharaoh's daughter saved him from the waters of the Nile. He was adopted by her *and became her son.*

In this position, as the child of the great Pharaoh's daughter, he received the highest education that was possible in that wonderful land of Egypt. The Bible tells us 'he was versed in all the wisdom of the Egyptians.' History tells us that he became a Master of Astrology, that he erected a great observatory in the Temple of the Sun at Heliopolis.

When his supposed mother became Queen of Egypt, Moses became Commander-in-Chief of her army; as such he conquered the Ethiopians and relieved Egypt from danger of invasion.

In this moment of triumph the Queen died, a Pharaoh came to the throne who 'knew not Moses,' and the Bible says, 'he went out unto his brethren and looked on their burdens.' The 'call of the blood' had come; he knew he was a Hebrew, the son of the priestly tribe of Levi; 'he saw an Egyptian

470

smiting one of his brethren'[1]; he slew the Egyptian and took refuge in the land of Midian.

Moses was now eighty years of age,[2] a man of experience, a man accustomed to the responsibility and power, a man of great learning, 'versed in all the wisdom of the Egyptians.' Such was the man the Lord had chosen for the delivery of His people.

I will pass over the message from 'the burning bush,' that command that has passed bown through the ages: 'I AM that I AM.'

I must leave to the imagination of my readers the humbling of Pharaoh by the ten plagues, the passover night, the outward march of that multitude of men, women, and herds of cattle. No one but Moses, who had been a Commander-in-Chief, could have organised such a march.

What a milestone in history—the first passover of the Hebrews as a nation. What a meaning it must have had for a people in slavery.

The end of four hundred and thirty years of bondage to the Egyptians, 'that night of the Lord to be observed of all the children of Israel in their generation.'[3]

The first great passover of the Hebrews took place at the full moon after the Spring Equinox in the first month of the Hebraic year, the month which is called Abib.

If one looks at an atlas containing the old Hebrew names, it is easy to see that Moses skilfully led this great multitude of people towards the most

1 Exodus ii. 11.
2 Ibid., vii. 7.
3 Exodus xii. 42.

471

fordable part of the Red Sea at the northern end of the Gulf of Suez, at a place called Pi-hahiroth, as stated in the Bible.[1]

Moses was well acquainted with this part of the country, having passed this way on his flight to Midian and his return to Egypt. He had observed the influx of the tides, and by his astrological calculations he knew that the south-eastern monsoon would arrive at a certain date to aid his plans. This is the east wind mentioned in the English version of the Bible; in the Septuagint, it is called a strong southern wind; but in both the poetical description is the same, 'and the Lord caused the sea to go back by a strong east wind all that night and made the sea dry land and the waters were divided'[2] 'and the children of Israel walked upon dry land in the midst of the sea.'

After this came that mysterious forty years of wandering in the desert which was planned and designed to purge the Israelites from the false teachings they had imbibed during their four hundred years of residence among the religions of Egypt.

If one again looks at any Old Testament map, one cannot help but remark how short the distance would have been had Moses led his people *directly across to Palestine.* Instead they were made to traverse the whole peninsula of Sinai before they

1 Ibid., xiv. 42.
2 Exodus xiv. 21.

were allowed to turn their faces towards the 'Promised Land.'

During that forty years of wandering a generation had passed away. Wisely and designedly the older race who had been contaminated by their long sojourn in Egypt had been 'gathered to their fathers.' Their place had been taken by the fresh blood of their sons and daughters, a younger generation more fitted to understand the teachings of the Great Law Giver—more fitted as 'a chosen race,' later on to hand down to posterity the pages of a sacred volume which was destined to illuminate and influence all races of mankind as well as their own.

It is this law of mysterious and wonderful Design that it is my privilege to draw attention to. It is more exemplified in the happenings and history of the Hebrew people than any other. If this race had been created for no other purpose than this, their sufferings and privations have not been in vain.

In those far-off ages when Moses collected and put together the records of God's dealings with the children of Israel, the volumes of the Sacred Law was not divided into chapters and verses.

Later still, David, the man who was specially chosen by God to be King of the Israelites, in writing the Psalms, could not by any natural means have surmised that when the Bible, some two thousand years after his death, came to be divided into chapters, the 119th Psalm would become the *longest chapter of the entire Book*, especially as scarcely one half of the Sacred Volume existed in his time.

This Psalm consists of 176 verses, every one of which directly or indirectly calls attention to the precepts laid down in the entire book.

The Psalm itself is, by some mysterious law of calculation, divided into 22 sections, the *exact number* of the letters that compose the *Hebrew alphabet*. Each section is subdivided into 8 verses, each verse being an iambic tetrameter, namely 16 syllables alternately short and long.[1]

Still more extraordinary is the first fact that every one of the 8 verses of the first section begins with the first letter of the Hebrew alphabet: Aleph.

The 8 verses of the second section begin with the second letter of the Hebrew alphabet: Beth.

The 8 verses of the third section begin with the third letter of the alphabet: Gimel.

This extraordinary precision continuing until *all the 22 letters* of the Hebrew alphabet are employed.

When this wonderful chapter thousands of years later came to be translated into other languages, it was found that no other language could fit in with this rule. Therefore the Hebrew letters were set out simply as titles at the head of each of the eight sections, as may be seen if anyone looks up the 119th Psalm.

In the millions and millions of books that have been printed, there is *not one example in the world*

---

1. I am speaking, of course, of the Hebrew original version.

of such an acrostic having ever been made, or of such an attempt having been thought of to call attention to the longest chapter of any work, especially when one considers that every verse of this chapter calls direct notice in one form of another to the good to be derived from following the precepts laid down in the volume of the Sacred Law.

Further, every verse alludes in some part of it to the Divine influence underlying the whole.

Example: The first verse contains the words 'the law of the Lord.'

2nd verse, 'His testimonies.'

3rd verse, 'His ways.'

4th verse, 'Thy precepts.'

5th verse, 'Thy statutes.'

6th verse, 'Thy commandments.'

7th verse, 'Thy righteous judgments.'

8th verse, 'Thy statutes,'

and so on through the entire 22 sections.

The mystic number of 12 appears in the root words employed, which are statutes, Ordinances, Faithfulness, Surety, Law, Name, Word, Precepts, Ways, Judgments, Testimonies, Commandments, and at least *one of these* 12 *words* are unerringly found in each of the 176 verses.

In the English version of the two longest words employed are representative of the Bible, namely 'Thy commandments' and 'Thy testimonies.' In their uses in this Psalm they present a strange coincidence with the 22 sections of the Psalm and the 22 letters of the original Hebrew alphabet. The word 'commandments' is employed either in the singular or in the plural exactly 22 *times*, while 'testimonies is used 22 *times in the plural* and once in the singular at the end of the first half of the Psalm, namely the end of the 88th verse, which number *is itself a multiple of 22*.

To sum up, then, my observations on this, the most extraordinary example of *design* in literature written or printed that has ever been known. One cannot believe that such a thing could happen by chance; equally one cannot believe that some mortal, no matter how gifted, could have created a Psalm in the form of an acrostic unmatched in the literature of the world, past or present; still more so, that this Psalm *should be designed to be* the longest chapter in a book *not then completed*.

And yet I have not exhausted all the features that call attention to this example of design.

It may not have been noticed before, by the many people who have read the Bible through from cover to cover, that both *the shortest* and the *longest chapters* of this wonderful book are placed *in close proximity to each other,* the shortest being the 117th and the longest the 119th Psalm. Now the one intermediary chapter between the shortest and the longest, the 118th, presents in itself such a number of remarkable coincidences that one is forced to the conclusion that these three Psalms *were purposely planned* to come together for a definite reason—that reason evidently being that the relation of such coincidences would sooner or later strike some searcher of truth, as an illustration of Divine Design and consequently proof of the Divine Inspiration that guided not only the writer of the Psalms, but thousands of years later *the translators of this book into other languages.*

The 118th Psalm, occupying as it does the remarkable position of being between the shortest and longest chapters of the Bible, actually contains *the middle or central verse of the entire Bible.* This, the middle verse of the Sacred Book, is the 8th verse of the 118th Psalm.[1]

Its words are significant in their meaning— they are an epitome of the great truth taught all through the preceding chapters or those that follow: 'It is better to trust in the Lord than to put confidence in man.'

Further, if one writes down in figures Psalm 118, verse 8, and puts these numbers side by side, they become 1188, which is the *exact number of chapters in the Bible,* besides the one that contains the remarkable verse above quoted and which, as I called attention to before, *is the middle verse of the entire book.*

Next to this 118th Psalm, the 117th stands out as the shortest chapter of the Bible, and not only is this a curious fact, but it is still doubly so, by being at the same time *the central chapter of* the Book, having exactly as *many chapters before it as after it.*

The most accurate way of finding out if the 117th Psalm is the central chapter of the Bible is

1. The actual form and division of the Bible is the work of different minds, widely separated by time, by countries, and by training. There can therefore be no question of collusion in the carrying out of the evident design that underlies the construction of the Bible.

to refer to the table usually printed in the beginning of the Authorised Version. This table contains six columns or 39 books of the Old Testament and 27 books of the New. By adding together the numbers of chapters given by those six columns we get the number 1189, the total number of the chapters in the Bible, the middle one must therefore be the 595th, as there cannot be anything else than 594 chapters before it and 594 following it.

The very number of 595, which is the number of the 117th Psalm, calculated as a chapter of the Bible, conveys in itself the idea of perfect symmetry, namely it can be read the same whether from left to right, or vice versa; it represents in itself *the principle of perfect equilibrium* which consists of equal disposition of the parts of both sides of a centre.

This, the shortest chapter in the Bible and the central one of the entire Book, has a striking significance of its own:

O praise the Lord all ye nations: praise Him all ye people. For his merciful kindness is great towards us; and the truth of the Lord endureth for ever.

One should not regard the extraordinary examples I have set out in these pages as isolated cases of mere coincidence, for when taken together, as they were evidently intended to be, they give the key to the construction of the Bible itself as a marvellous example of Divine inspiration. They tend to show that these three Psalms must have been written with a plan of forming these coincidences for some given purpose, and that the division and numeration of the entire Bible, so perfect in every way, *was prearranged* before even the greater part of it had been written by those who lived in later ages.

83

CONCLUSION

IT naturally follows that if a person should make a special study of any one subject, from long experience, cultivation and studious research, he will in the end unravel, at least to some extent, the so-called mysteries of the subject on which he has so concentrated his attention.

To the student of Art, Art reveals her mysteries of colour, form, design, pose, and a thousand and one subtleties that escape the ordinary observer. To the student of Biology every leaf tells its own story, every tree its age, every flower its own pedigree.

To the student of Science, what is magic to the uninitiated becomes a natural phenomenon with general laws, governed by rules or calculations that all who choose can learn and understand.

In presentir g this book to the public I need then offer no other apology for so doing, than that of having been a student of this particular branch of thought for a very long period, and having proved so-called theories by countless experiments and experiences, I feel I am at last in a position to give to the world at large the result of such studies.

It is admitted by all that the occult side of things has been the one side of life the least explored or investigated. That there is an occult or hidden part in actual relation to human life is on every side a conceded fact, but before this mystery--the greatest of all—the majority of thinkers have held themselves aloof.

In our age the physical and mechanical sciences have called for the greatest attention, yet such things as wireless communication and radium, to-day household words, have been stumbled across by so-called chance.

Already wireless communication has saved hundreds of lives, radium has done likewise, the mysteries of yesterday have become the commonplaces of to-day, and so knowledge in the eternal fitness of things becomes the servant of those who serve.

In pursuit of the laws which have controlled thought in recent centuries, man has, in earning his successes on the physical and mechanical plane, forgotten the loss he has sustained from the lack of study and observation on the occult or psychic side of humanity. He is more occupied to day in building implements for the destruction of life than he is in the problems of life itself, or in the finding out of those laws which create, control, and sustain life.

When Newton discovered gravitaion, it was not supposed for a moment that he had solved the problem of the spheres, and it is sometimes forgotten that when he came to realise that beyond our system of stars, sun, moon and planets there were again the 'fixed stars' with their countless systems, in the magnitude of the problem, he could only decide that there was again some occult law behind all, greater than any known law that could even be imagined.

I Trust my readers who have followed my theories through this book have grasped the fundamental fact underlying these pages, that the knowledge I have endeavoured to give to the public is of a *practical nature* with the decided object of helping my fellow men to make the best of themselves and render their lives as successful as possible.

Up to now occultism has been associated with the idea that its students must belong to the domain of dreamers of dreams, or those who live in some world of their own. In consequence of this idea the average "man in the street" has put aside such studies as not being useful, practical, or belonging to the money-making side of life.

It has also been drummed into his ears that all such studies bordered on witchcraft and were in some way or the other associated with the Devil.

Being brought up to go to church every Sunday and hearing every time he went that he was "a miserable sinner," doomed to punishment and torment both in this life and the worked to come, he in the end believed that he was "a miserable sinner," and so dared not seek for any knowledge that might enable him to shake off the chains of conventionality and customs that ground him down and kept him in mental and intellectual slavery.

He had perhaps no means of knowing that

some of the greatest kings of the world owed their success and wealth to advice given by their Astrologers, or that the Egyptian Magicians had greater power than either priest or potentate. He had perhaps never read that the great Queen Elizabeth consulted her Astrologer and Palmist, Dr. John Dee, on all important matters of State, and that the destiny of England had been guided from time to time by those students of occultism whom he had been taught to believe were but fit companions for black cats, and were workers of the Devil.

He had perhaps never read of that great English Astrologer, William Litty, who had, predicted the Fire of London *fifteen years before it took place,* or that the House of Commons had called him before that great assembly believing that, as the had predicted the calamity with such accuracy, he could explain to them what had caused such a catastrophe.

Further, his English History had never told him that Charles I had given the first thousand pounds his government sent him to Hampton Court the same Lilly, the Astrologer, asking him to predict his fate, and that had the King taken the warnings given to him by Astrology he might never have lost his head and descended to posterity as Charles the Martyr.

Again, it is probable he never knew that Queen Anne maintained an astrologer upon the roll of the Privy Purse, and that she had such faith in the celebrated Von Galgebrok that she asked him to predict the year of her death. This he did with perfect accuracy three years before the event, which took place on the 1st August, 1714.

Life is but the child of Mystery—we know not its origin—we know not its end. We seen "as in a glass darkly" the threads of Destiny weaving the known and the unknown—and we wonder why.

We feel there is Design in all things—but it is only in looking back on the past that the wonders of "the pattern" become manifest.

We are indeed "of little faith," we children of men. We forget that we were made "in the image and likeness of God," and, in the forgetting, we have sold our birthright for "the mess of pottage" of man-made beliefs.

We do not dare to think of ourselves, for our "teachers" alone have wisdom? But alas! they locked the doors of knowledge, and the keys have rusted for want of use.

Behind all-the Gods of patience—the God of Eternity—waits.

Slowly the ages pass: "A thousand years are but a day." Nations rise and fall. Teachers come and go. Time weaves Destiny into Design until in the end Perfection shines through the wrap and weft and *the God-thought underlying all becomes manifest.*

If, then one of the so-called "occult studies," such as I have tried to explain, has helped, in no matter how small a degree, to call attention to those hidden laws of life that illustrate the Divine Design, then when "the Call" come—I will go my way, content that the years of study I have given to this work were not wasted and were not in vain.

I have seen so many wrecked and broken lives, where, had the people possessed even a slight knowledge of their own dispositions, they might have been saved, that I have felt it a duty to publish in a cheap and simple form the indications of character and tendencies which may be easily learned by a study of these "periods of birth," as set forth in the following pages.

I believe that any aid that may help towards the observation of character is *not only useful but even essential if one wishes to keep abreast and succeed in this age of ever-increasing competition.*

Those people who have some means at their command to learn their own characters and the dispositions of others must certainly be thrice armed in the battle of life, and consequently more successful that the people who know nothing of such things. Therefore I have no hesitation in saying that with this book in one's possession, one has a means towards winning success and also happiness.

With even a slight knowledge of what I designate in these pages as Life's Natural Affinities, the road to the divorce courts would not be so crowded as it is at present, parents would more easily understand their children and children their parents, and a great deal of suffering and friction might be avoided.

In conclusion, I trust I am not presuming too much when I venture to hope that this unpretentious volume may be the means of helping a large proportion of my fellow-beings to realise that in the study of the mysteries of life we are giving praise and glory to the Creator of Life, who in His infinite wisdom created all things to be used by man for the highest development of his kind.

IMPORTANT TO READERS

It has been established by scientific observation that there are only Nine Planets in our Earth's Solar System that relate to life in this world. It has also been demonstrated by scientists that an exactly similar Solar System is repeated in the molecules revolving round all atoms in nature.

In the same way there are only Nine Numbers by which all calculations on this earth are made. Beyond the numbers of 1 to 9 the rest are repetitions, a 10 being simply as 1 with a zero, an 11 is 1 plus 1, a 2; a 12 is 1 plus 2, a 3; and so on. Every number no matter how large, can be reduced to a single figure by what is called "natural addition" adding from left to right. The final single digit that remains is called the "spirit or soul" number of the previous numbers added together.

It therefore follows that all Birthdates come into the 1-9 scale and respond to the numbers given to the Nine Planets of our Solar System. A person born on the 10th, 19th, or 28th of a month is as equally a "Number One" individual, as if they had been born on the single 1. Their characteristics vary according to the position of their month in the Zodiac.

PART THREE:
ASTROLOGY

84

ASTROLOGY AND
ASTROLOGICAL NUMBERS

TO many people the word Astrology merely stands for one of the many doubtful superstitious practices which come down to us from past ages; whereas, in fact, Astrology is the mathematical application of proved laws—laws which are no less valid than those of the complementary sciences of Palmistry and Numerology.

All sciences rest upon a very simple basis. Facts are painstakingly collected, experiments are based thereon, and deductions are made from the collected data. This same process obtains in chemistry, physics, biology and all other sciences. Once a given "law" has been established, the chemist is able to "predict" — if you like to put it that way — just what will happen in a given instance. The Astrologer works upon *exactly the same method.* He and his kind have found that if, for instance, the Planet Mars be near the eastern horizon at the *exact* time and place of birth, the individual then born will be muscular, headstrong, combative, energetic. In other words, certain known phenomena in the heavens are coincident with, or related to, certain corresponding phenomena on the earth.

How, or why this should be, is not know. The simple facts remain, and can be proved by anybody with a little mathematical and astrological knowledge, and an "Ephemeris" for their year of birth. *The basic facts of Astrology have never been disproved.* But it must be remembered that the predictions made by the Astrologer are no more "occult" than the chemist's experiment previously related. Both are based on the assumption that "Law rules the Univers," an assumption universally accepted.

It is claimed by the student of Astrology that as regards the individual human being there is a connection between that which is born and the planets at the time, hence much can be learned from the heavens concerning the individual.

All living mankind can be grouped into twelve great classes, according to the month* in which they were born. True, widely different folk are born in one and the same month. But if twenty people born (say) between the Ist and 20th of January were analysed carefully, it would be found that, however different their superficial characteristics, they were all of similar mould, similar deep down at heart. Under the veneer due to their education, environment, social position, degree of mental development, etc., they would have certain basic and common qualities in common.

I have therefore gathered up the fruits of much

---

* Note that the Astrological "month" begins about the 21st of each calendar month and runs the 21st of the next calendar month.

observation and experience, and incorporated them in a series of Readings for the various months on the following pages. These generalities of character and fortune will be found, in the main, uncannily accurate. The descriptions will not cover all the qualities of every individual, and may at times be wrong in detail. Allowing for this inevitable percentage of error due to the individual case they will be found a reliable guide.

The finer shades of character, the manifestation of genius, special ability, abnormal or subnormal qualities of mind or emotional nature, can be judged only from the individual horoscope. This depends upon the hour date and place of birth of the individual concerned. The erection and judgment of a horoscope involves recourse to personal study or a professional Astrologer.

CONCERNING THE MOON

From the dawn of history the moon has played a most important part in the life of the human race. Her changing orb has served as a time-measure, an infallible calendar in Nature, ever since men have intelligently marked the flight of time.

Reference to the Bible, or the sacred books of all times and nations, reveals the importance attached to the Lunar phases in ceremonial religion. The movable feasts of our own Church depend year by year upon the Lunar Phases.

We know that at the Full Moon animals, birds and reptiles are very much more on the move than they are during the rest of the moon's alternation.

We know well enough that the ebb and flow of the tides is partly due to the pull of the moon — wherever "men go down to the sea in ships" they must heed her times and seasons.

We know of the traditional connection between the conditions of the mentally unstable and the moon's changes.

We know of the peculiar hallucinations which are produced by exposure to tropical moonlight during sleep.

We can trace the obvious and absolute correspondence between certain feminine functions and the Lunar cycle of twenty-eight days.

Men who have studied natural phenomena in every age have credited the moon with an influence upon vegetable life, upon animal function, upon psychic activity in human beings.

The theories of the old-time alchemists have suvived many centuries of materialism, to be finally rediscovered and proved true in essentials by the modern chemist and physicist. In the same way, the teachings of the old time Astologers concerning Lunar influence (though they are loosely stated and mixed with much speculative dross) will be re-established by the enlightened Science of to-morrow.

At the moment we are concerned with the significance of the Lunar influence, and Lunar phases, *in everyday life.*

Let us briefly summarise the Astrological tradition:

All nature is assumed to be in a state of vibration, alternation, pulsation. In the human body, the muscles of the heart alternately contract and expand, pumping blood from the veins and forcing it through the arteries. The lungs inhale and exhale. The man wakes and sleeps, works and rests. Winter follows summer. The very poles swing round in an age-long cycle.

Now, in a sense, the changing moon at once symbolises and presides over the various pulsations in the life activity of the globe on which we live—the earth.

This pulsation, or ebb and flow of the life currents of the earth, occurs more or less every thirty days. The outward or positive pulsation occurs during the fourteen to fifteen days when the moon is *increasing in light* —i.e., from the time of the New Moon to the time of the Full Moon. The compensating or negative pulsation is set up *by the moon's decrease*—from the time of the Full Moon to that of the New Moon via the Last Quarter.

THE INFLUENCE OF THE LUNAR CHANGES

The period during which the moon waxes, its increase, the first half of the Lunar month, is a *period favourable to growth or expansion either material or spiritual.* The period in which the moon wanes, its decrease, is *a period unfavourable to growth or expansion; it corresponds to indrawing, lessening. decay* —on all planes. Both periods, said the old Astrologers, have their uses to mankind.

Thus any activity which calls for the maximum possible growth and expansion should be *commenced during the increase of the moon*: sowing and planting, travel, the undertaking of any new venture, animal conception, investment, and inauguration of personal relationships.

Similarly, activities of a negative kind—reaping crops, extermination of pests, either animal, vegetable or parasitic, surgical excision of morbid growths, etc.—should be undertaken *during the decrease of the moon.*

VARIOUS CONCERNS, OCCASIONS, UNDERTAKINGS, ACTIVITIES AND INTERESTS WHICH FALL UNDER THE RULE OF EACH PLANET

MERCURY ☿ - Travel, transport and communication of every kind: writing, television, radio, figuring, advertising, journalism, public speaking, education, and all things that concern the young.

VENUS ♀ - Love, courtship, mating, marriage, art, music decoration, dress, entertaining, holidays, dancing, gambling, peacemaking, pleasure of every kind, healing, social occasions of every kind, almsgiving.

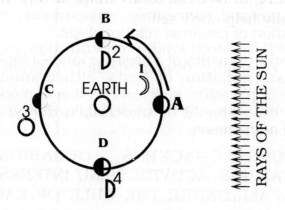

RAYS OF THE SUN

* It may be helpful breifly to illustrate here the cause of the moon's phases. Just as the earth revolves round the sun in a year, so the moon, every twenty-eight days, makes a similar revolution round the earth. As the earth itself has moved in the meantime, there is nearly thirty days between "New Moons" (or the moon reaching the sun's position). The rays of the sun (coming from the right of the diagram) always illuminate the part of the moon which is facing the sun. Thus when the moon is at A, we on earth cannot see the illuminated part at all. We see the edge of it, as a slender crescent (1) just afterwards the "New Moon." When the moon has completed a quarter of its circuit it reaches B, and it is then seen as at (2) - the "First Quarter." Just over a week later it reaches C and is seen as a fully illuminated disc (3) - the "Full Moon". Finally, the last quarter is seen at D as (4). Thus, a change, or quarter, of the moon forms the natural basis of the week of seven days.

FIG. 27

MARS ♂ - Sports, games, hunting, fighting, wresting, all that requires force, and strong and prompt action : mechanical work, "stunting," surgery, public agitations and movements.

JUPITER ♃ - Business and trading of every kind, investments, banking and dealing with Bank officials; religious ceremonies and functions, seeking favours, settlements in litigation, ceremonial and philanthropic occasions of every kind where it is desired to help others and incidentally help one's self.

SATURN ♄ - Deep study, concentration, exact and just reasoning, mining, dealing in property and real estate, farming and gardening, drawing, mathematics, occasions requiring an absolutely balanced and unemotional state of mind.

URANUS ♅ - Everything "advanced," inventions, research, occultism, astrology, telepathy, idealistic movements, photography, wireless, aviation, electrical study and research. Intense and concentrated effort which is chiefly mental.

NEPTUNE ♆ - Sea travel, bathing, sensuous pleasures, inspiration, spiritual experiences, premonitions, spiritualistic "sittings," higher forms of music and art, divination of every kind.

85

BASIC TRAITS OF CHARACTER OF PEOPLE BORN IN JANUARY

THE Zodiacal Sign of Capricorn commences on December 21st,* but for seven days, being overlapped by the "cusp" of the previous sign, it does not come into its full power until on or about December 28th. From this out it is in full strength until January 20th, and is then for seven days gradually losing its strength on account of becoming overlapped by the "cusp" of the incoming sign - Aquarius.

Persons born between January 20th and the 27th partake of the characteristics of both Capricorn and Aquarius, and the same rule applies to all persons born within the "cusp" of any sign.

People born in this period have strong mental force, but they are, as a rule, generally misunderstood by others.

They are thinkers, reasoners, and make natural heads of business organisations or any form of government work.

---

* I here speak in a symbolic and cabbalistic sense, making use of Astrological terms in order to make my meaning clear to the reader. This remark applies to all other months which are included in my psychological survey of the twelve signs of the Zodiac.

They are independent and high-minded in all their actions, and detest being under the restraint of others.

They must be leaders in whatever they are engaged, or else they are inclined to lose their interest in their work.

They have strange ideas of love, duty, and social position, and for this reason they are often considered "odd," and do not fit in easily with their neighbours.

Even when not religious they have a deep devotional nature, and make great efforts to do good to others, but generally to masses of people rather than to individuals.

They often make excellent speakers, but not so much through oratory as by plain speaking; often too much so for their own good.

They generally make their greatest mistake by espousing the unpopular cause, the "under dog" in the fight, and so often make the bitterest enemies by their actions being misunderstood.

Such people generally feel their responsibilities too keenly, and often worry themselves into bad health.

They are quick in their intuitions of people and things, but they are, as a rule, too easily discouraged, and lack self-confidence.

Although they appear cold, they have warm hearts towards suffering, and as a rule they give largely to charities, but subscribe more generously when giving to institutions than when giving to individuals.

If inclined to be religious they usually go to extremes, and become fanatical in their zeal.

They worship intellectual, clever people, and are deep thinkers; they rarely interfere with the affairs of others, but they will never stand interference from others.

They should aim for some form of public life, and in such careers they generally do best, such a as in the government and in responsible positions of control and management of others.

They are inclined to excite bitter opposition but bear up against it with a philosophic spirit. Their home and family life is very often a troubled one. They feel "lonely-hearted" and misunderstood.

FRIENDS

They usually make the most solid and best friendships with people who are born in their own period, viz. between December 21st to end of January, from April 20 to the end of May, and with their "central affinities," June 21 to July 20-27, and August 21 to September 20-27 (see Fig. 32).

HEALTH

As a rule these people are more inclined to

suffer from indigestion, rheumatism and pains in the feet.

COLOURS

The colours which give the most suitable vibrations to persons born in this period, and which are the most beneficial to them, are all tones of grey, all ranges of violet and purple, and also black. For the exact colours for people born on each individual day see Chapter 99.

STONES

The birth stones for this period are moon-stones, pearls, and amethysts.

SOME FAMOUS PERSONS BORN IN THIS PART OF THE YEAR

The Earl of Beaconsfield	Dec.	21st
Josef Stalin	"	21st
Marlene Dietrich	"	27th
Woodrow Wilson	"	28th
W.E. Gladstone	"	29th
Rudyard Kipling	"	30th
Prince Charlie (The Young Pretender)	"	31st
Clement Attlee	Jan.	3rd
Herbert Morrison	"	3rd

Joan of Arc	"	6th
Sir Lawrence Alma Tadema	"	8th
Wilkie Collins	"	8th
Lord Curzon of Kedleston	"	11th
Herman Goering	"	12th
Gamal Nasser	"	15th
Admiral, Earl Beatty	"	16th
Benjamin Franklin	"	17th
Compton Mackenzie	"	17th
David Lloyd George	"	17th
Cassius Clay	"	18th
Lord Byron	"	22nd
Francis Bacon	"	22nd
Frederick the Great of Prussia	"	24th
Wilhelm Furtwangler	"	25th
W. Somerest Maugham	"	25th
General MacArthur	"	26th

86

BASIC TRAITS OF CHARACTER
OF PEOPLE BORN IN FEBRUARY

THE Zodiacal Sign of Aquarius commences on January 21st, but for seven days, being overlapped by the "cusp" of the previous sign, it does not come into full power until on or about January 28th. From this date onward it is in full strength until February 19th. It is then for seven days gradually losing its strength on account of becoming overlapped by the "cusp" of the incoming sign - Pisces.

Those born in the "cusp" take from the qualities of both signs.

These natures generally feel very lonely in life; they are over-sensitive, and easily wounded in their feelings.

They read character instinctively, and for this reason they "see through" people too easily to be really happy.

They are not demonstrative in affection, but feel very deeply. If they "like" they fight to the bitter end for their friend; but if they dislike they are just as intense, and if they belong to the lower plane of humanity they will stick at nothing to avenge an injury or what they feel to be an injustice.

They are usually high-strung, and their nerves are generally overwrought; they often lose control of themselves and then they say or do things that they bitterly regret later.

They are generally very active for the public good, and will often give all they have to relieve the distress of others.

They are good reasoners, and are very successful in debate and argument, and difficult to convince. They generally have a scientific turn of mind.

They are excellent in business and finance when they apply their minds to such things, but as a general rule they are more successful for others, and make more money for others than for themselves.

If people born in this sign overcame their sensitiveness and developed their will-power, there is no position in life they could not attain, They generally succeed best in some large sphere of action, where they can feel their responsibilities for others. those who are "awakened" in this sign usually leave a great name behind. They have "visions," imagination and invention.

They take a great interest in public meetings, gatherings of people, and public ceremonies. They love theatres and concerts. and like to be where crowds of people congregate, and yet they always have the feeling that *they are alone in life.*

They are very contradictory in the qualities they show under the call of circumstances; although themselves very high-strung and easily overwrought, *they have the very greatest power over excitable people and over the insane, and are in the run of their lives often brought much in contact with such classes.*

They have a quiet, controlling power with their eyes. and so subdue others.

Their greatest fault is that it generally takes some sudden call of circumstances to make them "make the most of themselves".

If born with money, these people rarely show what is in them. They are inclined in ordinary conditions to let their opportunities slip, or realise them only when it is too late. If, however, people born in this period belong to the lower order of humanity they lose all sense of honour and principle, and are extremely unreliable, tricky in money matters, dishonest, and unscrupulous in gaining what they desire.

FRIENDS

In real friendship or love they get on best with those born from May 21 to June 20, and by adding the seven days of "the cusp" to about the end of the month. September 21 to October 20 or 27, and, as a rule, to November 20-27, or with those born in the centre of their triangle, as will be shown in

Chapter 98, dealing with "Life's Triangles."

HEALTH

These people are inclined to suffer most from the stomach, often through the nerves of the stomach in some peculiar manner that is difficult to relieve with ordinary medicine. Bad circulation often troubles them and there is often some delicacy of the eyes.

COLOURS

The most favourable colours for them are all shades of what are known as "electric shades," as electric blues and electric greys. These are the foundation colours for this period; for the exact colours for people born on each individual day see Chapter 99 on colours.

STONES

The birth stones for the period are sapphires, pink topazes, and moonstones.

SOME FAMOUS PERSONS BORN IN THIS PART OF THE YEAR

General Gordon	Jan	28th
Franklin D. Roosevelt	"	30th
Charles Lindbergh	Feb.	4th
Sir Hartley Shawcross	"	4th

Sir Henry Irving .... Feb.   6th

Charles Dickens............................. "   7th

Lord Carson................................. "   9th

Edison .... "   11th

Abraham Lincoln .... "   12th

Darwin .... "   12th

G.M. Trevelyan .... "   16th

Arthur Bryant .... "   18th

Copernicus .... "   19th

David Garrick .... "   20th

Lord Baden-Powell .... "   22nd

George Washington .... "   22nd

Samuel Pepys .... "   23rd

Handel....................................... "   23rd

Elizabeth Taylor............................. "   17th

87

BASIC TRAITS OF CHARACTER OF PEOPLE BORN IN MARCH

THE Zodiacal Sign of Pisces commences on February 20th, but for seven days, being overlapped by the "cusp" of the previous sign, it does not come into its full power until about February 27th. From this date onwards it is in full strength until March 20th, and it is then for seven days gradually losing its strength on account of becoming overlapped by the "cusp" of the incoming sign - Aries.

These people possess a curiously natural understanding, which they do not obtain from books or study. They easily acquire, or rather absorb knowledge, especially of the history of countries, travel, research, and like subject.

Although by nature generous, yet they are usually over-anxious about money matters, and inclined to worry about what their future position in life may be. This state 'mind is, I think, largely due to *their dislike and dread of being dependent on others more than from any love of money.*

This quality makes them, however, much misunderstood, and they are often considered close in money matters when in reality they are not.

People born in this period often go back on their promises, especially on questions of money. They promise to give, on the impulse of the moment, but if they have time for reflection then the fear of future poverty forces them, as a rule, to break their promise or give, perhaps, only one half of what they bad stipulated.

These people are also more *mentally* ambitious than otherwise. They may know their subject well in their mind, but they will hesitate and undervalue their own individuality if they find they have to put it to a test in any public manner.

They are inclined to brood and become melancholy, or to imagine all the world is against them and that they are being made martyrs of.

They have great fidelity and loyalty if trust is imposed on them, and great persistence in carrying out whatever work they have in their hands to perform, and they are generally found in positions of trust and responsibility for others.

Many artists, musicians and literary people are born in this period, but they must receive great encouragement ever to make the best of themselves.

They have great loyalty to friends or to any cause they take up, provided they feel they are trusted or looked up to. They are generally successful in all positions of responsibility, but at the same time they are not inclined to push themselves forward, and usually "wait to be asked" before giving their opinions.

They are great respecters of law and order, and uphold the conventions of whatever the social order in which they may be found.

The strongest and weakest characters are found in this sign. Some are inclined to gratify their innate sense of luxury and self-indulgence and, if this side of the nature is the one that controls, they are likely to be too easy-going, to be too receptive to their surroundings, to become influenced by false friends, to give way to fraudulent schemes and in some cases are inclined to become addicted to drugs or drink.

If, however, persons born in this part of the year find some purpose worth living for, they rise to the emergency as no others can. These are the people that one meets sometimes in life who surprise their friends by their sudden change of character.

All persons born in this part of the year have a dual element as the mainspring of their nature. It simply depnds on which of the two roads they have decided to follow.

Persons born in this sign are highly emotional. If they belong to the *weak* side of it, they are easily influenced by the people with whom they are thrown into contact, but if they belong to the stronger side, their emotional nature can lift them up to any height.

They are generally fond of the sea and large expanses of water. If circumstances do not permit them to travel, they will, if they possibly can, make their homes where they can see the ocean, or on the side of some lake, or river.

In business they are good in dealing with shipping and trade with foreign countries.

Sea captains, sailors of all kinds, also travellers, are often found under this sign.

Almost all have a curiously mystical side to their nature as well as the practical. They are often classed as superstitious, the occult in all its forms appealing to them in one way or another.

They love to search out or investigate the unknown, the philosophical, or they mysterious. Although generous, they do not allow their generous instincts to get the better of them, unless they are under the influence of someone they love. In such a case they become easily influenced and are as likely as not to give away all they possess.

If people born in this sign overcame their sensitiveness and developed their will-power, there is no position in life they could not attain.

FRIENDS

They find their most lasting friendships with people born in their own period or between June 21 and July 20, and on account of , ' the cusp" to about the end of the month (see Fig. 30); and with their "central affinities," August 21 to September 20-27, also October 21 to November 20-27 (see Fig. 30).

HEALTH

As regards health, people born in this period are mostly inclined to suffer from nerves, insomnia, despondency, and poor circulation, anaemia. They often have intestinal trouble. They should, if possible, live in bright, sunny, dry climates, and take a great amount of fresh air and exercise. They are fond of travel, are restless, and love to be continually on the move.

COLOURS

The colours most suitable to them are all shades of mauve, violet, and purple. These are the foundation colours of this period; for the exact colours for people born on each individual day see Chapter 99 on colours.

STONES

The birth stones for this period are agates, sapphires, amethysts, and emeralds.

SOME FAMOUS PERSONS BORN IN THIS PART OF THE YEAR

Joseph Jefferson	Feb.	20th
Cardinal Newman	"	21st
James Russell Lowell	"	22nd
Chopin	"	22nd
W. Dean Howells	Mar.	Ist

George Pullman ...." 3rd

Michael Angelo................................" 6th

Elizabeth Barrett Browning..............." 6th

M. Molotov.." 9th

Harold Wilson ...." 11th

Albert Einstein................................." 14th

The Prince Imperial (Napoleon)........" 16th

Rudolf Nureyev ...." 17th

Robert Donat ...." 18th

David Livingstone ...." 19th

Ibsen ...." 20th

William Lecky ...." 20th

88

BASIC TRAITS OF CHARACTER OF PEOPLE BORN IN APRIL

THE Zodiacal Sign of Aries commences on March 21st, but for seven days, being overlapped by the "cusp" of the previous sign, it does not come into its full power until about March 27th. From this date onwards, it is in full strength until. April 19th. It is then for seven days gradually losing its strength on account of becoming overlapped by the "cusp" of the incoming sign - Taurus.

People born in this section of the year have unsually strong will power and great obstinacy of purpose.

They are born fighters in every sense of the world; they have also the greatest ability as organisers on a large scale, such as in the organisation of big schemes or as the heads of big businesses, and also in the organisation of armies or development of countries.

They seem naturally to resent all criticism, and the only way to offset this in them is by quiet logic, reason, and proof.

These people are intensely independent in work. They must do everything in their own way, and if they are interfered with by others they generally make a muddle of their plans or step back and let the other person take their place.

As a rule they are unhappy in their domestic life, for they rarely meet members of the opposite sex who understand them, and if opposition does not upset them from this point it usually does through their children.

Yet these people, be they men or women, crave for affection and sympathy more than anything else, and this is generally the rock on which they are finally wrecked if they have not the good fortune to meet their right affinities.

As far as material success or power is concerned, there are no heights to which persons born in this sign cannot climb - provided they "keep their heads." Success, however, is often their undoing, praise and flattery are inclined to make from them have "swelled heads."

They are inclined to lack caution, being by nature impulsive and quick in thought and action.

They go to extremes in all things, are frank and outspoken, and inclined to make enemies by want of tact. They are enormously ambitions; as a rule they succeed in life and amass money and position.

The lower type of this sign will stick at nothing to accomplish their purpose. The higher type are good masters, but at the same time severe in discipline and more or less exacting in the service they expect from others.

Both classes have a distinct desire to peer into the future, perhaps because they are impatient for things to develop. They are inclined to prophesy what will take place, and are often very gifted in this direction.

As a general rule, the men born in this part of the year sufffer a great deal through their affections; they seldom understand women, and make great mistakes in their relations with them.

For both sexes, their greatest happiness comes from work and the overcoming of obstacles.

Persons born in this sign seldom get through life without receiving cuts, wounds, or blows to the head, either from accidents or violence.

FRIENDS

They will find their more lasting friendships and affections with those born on their own period or between July 21 and August 20-27, and from November 21 to December 20-27; and also from the centre of their triangle, September 21 to October 20-27, as I have explained in my chapter on "Life's Affinities (Fig. 29).

HEALTH

People born in this period should try to obtain more sleep than almost any other class. They overwork their brains, and are inclined to suffer from all things that concern the head, - from headache, trouble with the eyes. They are also likely to have eruptions on the face and head. And they are liable to get cuts and wounds in the head, and they usually run danger from fire. They seldom get through life without a good deal of medical attention.

COLOURS

The most harmonious colour for them is all shades of red, crimson, rose, and pink, - but when ill all shades of blue and violet are most soothing and beneficial to them. For the exact colours for people born on each individual day, see Chapter 99 on colours.

STONES

The birth stones for this period are rubies, garnets, and bloodstones.

SOME FAMOUS PERSONS BORN IN THIS PART OF THE YEAR

Arturo Tuscanini .... Mar.   25th

Robert Bunsen.................................. "   31st

Bismarck ....April   Ist

Charlemagne .... "   2nd

Lord Lister .... "   5th

David Frost .... "   7th

Albert, King of the Belgians .... "   8th

John Gielgud ....April 14th

Sir John Franklin ...." 16th

Adolf Hitler ...." 20th

Bishop Heber ...." 21st

Yehudi Menuhin ...." 22nd

James Anthony Froude ...." 23rd

Shakespeare ...." 23rd

Oliver Cromwell ...." 24th

Sir Stafford Cripps ...." 24th

89

BASIC TRAITS OF CHARACTER
OF PEOPLE BORN IN MAY

THE Zodiacal Sign of Taurus commences on April 20th, but for seven days, being overlapped by the "cusp" of the previous sign, it does not come into its full power until on or about April 27th. From this date onwards it is in full strength until May 20th, and is then for seven days gradully losing its strength on account of becoming overlapped by the "cusp" of the incoming sign - Gemini.

People born in this section of the year have a curious power of dominating others, *even when not conscious of trying to do so.*

They are very unyielding in their determination, and are often called "stiff-necked" and obstinate, but when they love they are the most yielding and pliable of all, but only to those to whom they are attracted.

They have great power of endurance, both physical and mental, and can pass through enormous strains of fatigue as long as the excitement or determination lasts.

They have great ability to commit to memory from books, and are often very successful in literary work, but as a rule they love pleasure and society too much to make the best use of their gifts.

They make wonderful hosts and hostesses, and have great taste about food, and in the management of their houses they can make much out of little.

They make excellent directors, have good business intuition, but are generally considered richer than they really are, as they always dress well and look well.

They are governed by their sensations and by their loving nature, *but affection has a greater hold on them, than passion.*

If they love, they are generous to the last degree, and will consider no sacrifice too great for the person they care for; if they are enemies, they will fight with the most determined obstinacy. But they always fight in the open, for they hate trickiness, double-dealing, or deceit.

They are easily influenced by their surroundings, and become morbid and morose when trying to live under uncongenial conditions.

Neither men nor women born in this period *should marry early; their first marriage is usually a mistake.*

They should always decide all important questions when they are alone, for they seem to be so much in touch with the minds of those around them that they get confused, and often imagine other people's thoughts and ideas are their own. They are also too easily misled by their emotions, sensations, or affections.

As a rule both sexes are jealous in their disposition, and their jealously often drives them into acts of violence or sudden exhibition of temper, which they bitterly regret when the storm is over.

They forgive at the slightest show of feeling or kindness, and this side of their nature makes them do all kinds of things that the world calls stupid.

As leaders in any cause they inspie love and devotion, and often have great responsibility forced upon them.

They have an innate sense of harmoney, rhythm and colour, and often succeed well in music, poetry and art.

Those born in this sign make the most faithful, loyal friends; also excellent public servants, officials, or as heads in Government positions or in the Army. They also make good, patient nurses and healers, and almost all have a keen love of gardening and flowers.

HEALTH

In health, although, as a rule, endowed with a splendid constitution, they suffer with all things that affect the throat, nasal cavities and upper part of the lungs.

FRIENDS

They will find their most lasting friendships with people born between August 21-27, and September 20-27, December 21 and January 20-27, and with their "central affinities," October 21 to November 20-27 (Fig. 32).

COLOURS

The colours most favourable to them are all shades of blue. Red is an exciting colour for them, and they should use it as little as possible. For the exact colours for people born on each individual day see Chapter 99 on colours.

STONES

The birth stones for this period are emeralds, turquoises, and lapis lazuli.

SOME FAMOUS PERSONS BORN IN THIS PART OF THE YEAR

Sir Thomas Beecham .... April   29th

Haydn .... "   30th

The Duke of Wellington .... May   Ist

Bing Crosby .... "   2nd

Thomas Huxley .... "   4th

Lord Rosebery .... "   7th

Robert Browning .... "   7th

Harry S. Truman ....May   8th

Sir James Barrie..............................."   9th

Sir Arthur Sullivan ...."   12th

Alphonse Daudet ...."   13th

Margot Fonteyn..............................."   18th

Sir Laurence Olivier ...."   22nd

Thomas Hood..................................."   23rd

Queen Victoria ...."   24th

Duke of Marlborough ...."   24th

90

BASIC TRAITS OF CHARACTER OF PEOPLE BORN IN JUNE

THE Zodiacal Sign of Gemini - The Twins - commences on May 21st, but for seven days, being overlapped by the "cusp" of the previous sign, it does not come into its full power until on or about May 28th.

From this date onwards it is in full strength until June 20th, and is then for seven days gradually losing strength on account of becoming overlapped by the "cusp" of the incoming sign - Cancer.

People born in this part of the year, namely, from May 21st to June 20th, and in the "cusp" to June 27th, have the characteristics of Gemini - The Twins - and are dual in character and in mentality.

The twin sides of their nature are perpetually pulling in opposite directions.

Their brains are subtle and brilliant, but they usually lack continuity of purpose.

Of all people they are the most difficult to understand; in temperament they are hot and cold almost at the same moment. They love with one side of their nature, and they are often critical or dislike with the other.

They are mentally very quick and keen, and in all matters where a subtle mentality is needed they can out distance all rivals.

They are excellent in diplomacy, and dazzle their listeners by their wit and brilliancy, but they usually leave them no wiser than they were at the start.

They seldom, themselves, know what they want to achieve. At heart they are ambitious for social position; but when obtained they have already tired of it, and are ready to go in for something else or for something totally opposite.

If taken as they are, in their own moods, they are the most delightful people imaginable, but one must not attempt to hold them or to expect them to be constant to their ideas or plans.

They believe they are truthful, constant, faithful, and so they may be at the moment, but every moment to them has a separate existence.

They are always employed doing someting, but they are restless, and as a rule want the thing they have not got.

They see quickly the weak points in those they meet, and can reduce all to nothing by wit, sarcasm, or mimicry.

They make clever actors, lawyers, lecturers, and a certain class of public speakers, all those who play a changing role in life's drama; but if endowed with unusually strong will power, and if they can *force themselves to stick to one thing, then they generally make brilliant successes of whatever they undertake in any sphere of life.*

They often succeed the best, as far as money is concerned, on the Stock Exchange or as Company Promoters or in the invention of new ways to get wealth in business, but their more suitable career is generally that which requires diplomacy, tact, and finesse.

In all matters of affection they are human puzzles. They can love passionately and yet be inconstant at the same moment, and it is only their shield of diplomacy and exquisite tact that keeps them from often making a mess of their lives.

They are more generous to individuals than to institutions, for they act on impulse in giving as in everything else they do.

In appearance these people generally have a rather long, narrow head and face; good, keen, sharp-looking eyes. The hands, as a rule, are long, thin or bony; restless or always doing something. In nature they are inclined to have to many "irons in the fire" at the same moment.

The higher types are clever, capable, witty, subtle, with an odd sense of humour quite their own. As a rule they are very intellectual with a keen mentality that shows itself in anything they serioulsy take up. Worry, annoyance or undue mental strain breaks them down very rapidly, producing nervous prostration, brain exhaustion, and in some cases insanity.

The lower types are unscrupulous in finance and untruthful. They often make successful gamblers and company promoters of "get-rich-quick" schemes.

Either type make hosts of friends and are kind-hearted and generous to the person who fills their thoughts at the moment, but "out of sight, out of mind" explains their fits of "foregetfulness" as nothing else can.

FRIENDS

Both types make their most lasting friendships with people born either in their own period of the year of from September 21 to October 20-27, January 21 to February 18-27, or with people born in the centre of their own triangle, from November 21 to December 20-27 (Fig. 31).

HEALTH

They are more inclined to suffer from what concerns the nervous system than anything else; both men and women are likely to have delicacy with the digestive organs. They are rather inclined to have chest trouble.

COLOURS

Their colours are silver, glistening white, and all shimmering things. For the exact colours for persons born on each day see Chapter 99 on colours.

STONES

The birth stones for this period are white and red cornelians, sapphires, diamonds and all glittering jewels.

SOME FAMOUS PERSONS BORN IN THIS PART OF THE YEAR

John F. Kennedy	May	29th
Charles II	"	29th
Bob Hope	"	29th
Sir Edward Elgar	June	2nd
Thomas Hardy	"	2nd
Richard Cobden	"	3rd
George V	"	3rd
Jefferson Davis	"	3rd
George III	"	4th
Sir Anthony Eden	"	12th
Gounod	"	17th
Earl Haig	"	19th
Julian Hawthrone	"	22nd
Sir Rider Haggad	"	22nd
Ralph Waldo Emerson	"	15th
Lord Louis Mountbatten	"	25th

91

BASIC TRAITS OF CHARACTER
OF PEOPLE BORN IN JULY

THE Zodiacal Sign of Cancer commences on June, 21st, but for seven days, being overlapped by the previous sign, it does not come into full power until on or about June 28th. From this date onwards it is in full strength until July 20th, and is then for seven days gradually losing its strength on account of becoming overlapped by the "cusp" of the incoming sign - Leo.

The Sign of Cancer, or the Crab, was so called by the ancients because the sun at this time of the year appears to advance and retreat in the heavens like the actions of a crab.

People born in this section of the year are full of contradictions, they have deep home interests, but are at the same time restless, and have a decided longing for travel and change, they are always making homes, rarely keeping them, and usually have more than the usual trouble in the homes they do succeed in making and in their domestic life.

They are generally over-anxious in financial matters, and make great efforts to gather in money, as a rule, they have unusual ups and downs in their early life, and it takes all their hard work to keep ahead, but once they get on their feet they generally keep there.

They are inclined to speculate, so as to make money quickly, but in all gambles they generally lose, whereas in business *they are as a rule most successful.*

They are industrious and hardworking in all they undertake, but from the standpoint of chance or luck they are seldom fortunate, but the most extraordinary and unexpected changes, for good or evil, seem always ready to come into their lives.

They are generally gifted with strong imaginations, and often make excellent artists, writers, composers, or musicians. At heart they are romantic and of a very loving and affectionate disposition.

They have a great dislike of being dictated to, but are most devoted and faithful when treated with confidence.

They have, however, most sensitive natures— perhaps more so than any other class of people— and if not understood they quickly give up or get depressed and melancholy. Above all, they require encouragement and appreciation.

The often make excellent psychics, and usually have a yearning after the mysterious.

They should never marry young, *for their nature seems to change at different stages of life.*

Like the symbol of "the Crab," which this part of the Zodiac represents, they advance and retreat both in work and ideas; they may reach a certain point in some definite plan or career, and then surprise everyone by stopping, or turning back at the most critical point.

People born in this part of the year often reach very high exalted positions. In their home lives, however, they usually go through a great deal of trouble, and are seldom surrounded by great happiness, no matter how successful they may appear in the eye of the world.

Although of a deeply affectionate disposition they-are seldom demonstrative, and are wrongly considered cold and un-emotional.

Generally, they have splendia memories and store up knowledge of all kinds in their minds.

They have deep love for what they call "their own people," for family customs and for tradition.

HEALTH

They are chiefly inclined towards gastric troubles, and they should be extremely careful in regard to shellfish and such things. Inflammatory diseases, such as rheumatism, are also likely to attack them, and trouble with the legs and feet.

FRIENDS

Their affections or friendships last longest with those who are born in their own period, June 21 to July 20-27, or from October 21 to November 20-27, or from February 19 to March 20-27, and also those who are in the centre of their triangle, December 21 to January 20-27, which I have explained in a subsequent chapter on "Life's Triangles." (Chapter 98).

COLOURS

The colours most in harmony for them are all shades of green, and cream and white. For the exact colours for persons born on each day see Chapter 99 on colours.

STONES

The birth stones most favourable for this period are pearls, diamonds, opals crystals, cat's-eyes, and moonstones.

SOME FAMOUS PERSONS BORN IN THIS PART OF THE YEAR

James I of England	June	28th
Charles Laughton	July	1st
Gluck	"	2nd
Nathaniel Hawthorne	"	4th
Gertrude Lawrence	"	4th
Cecil Rhodes	"	6th
Edward Heath	"	9th

John Calvin	July	10th
John Quincy Adams	"	11th
Sir Joshua Reynolds	"	16th
Lord Balfour	"	25th
George Bernard Shaw	"	26th
Mussolini	"	29th

92

BASIC TRAITS OF CHARACTER
OF PEOPLE BORN IN AUGUST

THE Zodiacal Sign of Leo commences on July 21st, but for seven days, being overlapped by the " cusp" of the previous sign, it does not come into its full power until on or about July 28th. From this date onwards it is in full strength until August 20th and is then for seven days gradually losing its strength on account of becoming overlapped by the "cusp" of the incoming sign - Virgo.

People born in this period always aim to get above the common herd of humanity, and they themselves in turn are naturally attracted to strong personalities - in fact, they will forgive any fault in the people they like so long as they have individuality and purpose.

These people represent what might be termed the heartforce of humanity. They are overflowing with sympathy, and are generally generous to a fault.

They will defend a friend in the face of a million foes, and disloyalty and deceit are the only things that can break their great hearts.

They are themselves exceptionally truthful and honest, but they often get terribly deceived, and have a tendency in the end to become bitter, severe, and over-critical.

They are usually luckly in money matters, often having money given to them from unthought-of sources ; but they crave love above all, and this is the one thing they seldom get.

They have the power to inspire others, and as leaders - like Napoleon, born in this Sign - they can lead their men through fire or death. They are intensely proud, and often are easily wounded at this point in their nature.

They have an extremely independent spirit; they detest control or being dictated to. They have great tenacity of purpose and will power and if once they put their mind on some plan, purpose or position, they usually reach their goal in spite of every difficulty or obstacle.

Such persons must, however, be always actively employed. If forced by circumstances out of the heart and stress of life, they often become morbid and despondent.

As a rule they are extremely patient and long-suffering, but if once roused, they know no fear and do not even know when they meet defeat, or acknowledge it when they do.

They make enemies by their frankness of speech and their hatred of anything underhand or that savours of subterfuge.

They have great tenacity of purpose,

determination, and will power if they once put their mind on some purpose, but they usually attempt the most daring and difficult things.

Great soldiers, leaders in finance, and public men are often born in this period.

As a rule, people born in this period feel isolated and lonely in life, and if not actively employed in some work or purpose they become melancholy and despondent.

FRIENDS

They would find their most lasting friendships with people born in their own period or from March 21 to April 19-27, with their "central affinities" January 21 to February 18-28 (Fig. 29), and November 21 to December 20-27; and strange to say, all those people born on the 1st, 10th, 19th, or 28th of any month, for the reason that these numbers accord and have a sympathetic attraction to the Number of the Sun, *which is the number of this period.* These numbers and dates are fully explained elsewhere in this book.

HEALTH

These people are inclined to suffer from the heart, palpitations, pains in the head and ears.

COLOURS

Their most suitable colours are all shades of yellow orange, pale green, and white. For the exact colours for persons born on each day see chapter 99 on colours.

STONES

The birth stones for this period are topazes, amber, and rubies.

SOME FAMOUS PERSONS BORN IN THIS PART OF THE YEAR

Alexandre Dumas	July	28th
Henry Moore	”	30th
King Haakon VII of Norway	Aug.	3rd
Sir Harry Lauder	”	4th
Neil Armstrong...............................	”	5th
Alexander Fleming	”	6th
Field-Marshal Sir William Slim	”	6th
Dean Farrar	”	7th
President Hoover............................	”	10th
George IV, of England	”	12th
Napoleon I	”	15th
Louis XVI..	”	23rd
Bret Harte.......................................	”	25th
Prince Albert, Consort of Queen Victoria...............................	”	26th
George Hegel..................................	”	27th

535

bar

BASIC TRAITS OF CHARACTER OF PEOPLE BORN IN SEPTEMBER

THE Zodiacal Sign of Virgo commences on August 21st, but for seven days, being overlapped by the "cusp" of the previous sign, it does not come into its full power until on or about August 29th. From this date onwards it is in full strength until September 20th, and is then for seven days gradually losing its strength on account of becoming overlapped by the "cusp" of the incoming sign - Libra.

People born in this period are as a rule generally successful in life. They have keen, good intellects, are very discriminating about those with whom they associate, and in all business matters they have, good judgment, and are not easily imposed upon or deceived.

They are usually materialistic in their views of life, and analyse and reason everything *from their own way of thinking outwards.*

They make good literary critics, being quick to see the weak points, and at the same time they are rapid readers and endowed with wonderful memories.

They are extremely fond of harmony in their

surroundings, have excellent taste about their house and dress, and always want things in good taste, and elegant.

They are not so apt be originators as they are to carry out some plan or work that appeals to them and which others have failed to finish, and in the execution of almost all things to which they put their minds they achieve success.

They are fastidious about their personal appearance, have great respect for rank and position, and are great supporters of the law and the law's decisions.

They make excellent lawyers and debaters, but they tend towards supporting precedents more than originating any new law.

They succeed well in business, but more from their steady, industrious persistency than from evolving new ideas.

They are inclined to become wrapped up in themselves and their own ideas, and often become selfish in the close pursuit of their aims.

They are more capable of going to extremes in good and evil than any other type. If they develop a love for money they will stick at nothing to acquire it, and this type is often considered cunning and crafty at the expense of others.

They can adapt themselves to almost any pursuit in life.

In love they are the most difficult to understand, they very best and they very worst of men and women being born in this part of the year.

In their early years nearly all are intensely virtuous and pure-minded, as might be expected, being born in the Sign of Virgo - the Virgin.

If they change they do so with a vengeance and become the exact reverse, but, on account of their inborn respect of the law and their natural cleverness, they succeed in covering up their lapses better than any other class They have often a tendency to indulge in drugs or drink.

HEALTH

In health, as a rule, they are less liable to diseases than persons born in any other part of the year, yet the strange thing about them is that they are always imagining themselves to have evry illness that they may happen to read about.

They are very refined in their tastes as far as food is concerned, and must have things nicely put before them or they will lose their appetites.

They are extremely sensitive to their surroundings; the least inharmony or annoyance affects their nervous system and upsets their digestive organs.

They have a tendency to have chest trouble, and to suffer from neuritis in the shoulder and arms.

As this sign of the Zodiac appears to be intimately associated with the Solar Plexus, people born in this part of the year need sunlight and fresh air more than any other class of individual.

They should live as much as possible in the open air, and when run down or ill a few weeks in the country will work marvels with them.

As a rule, they retain their youth through life in the most wonderful manner.

If badly mated, or living under inharmonious marriage conditions, they easily fall into ill health or get extremely despondent.

They should never drink alcohol, as it seems to be more a poison to them than to any other class.

FRIENDS

They will find their most lasting friendship with those born in their own Sign, also from April 20 to May 20-27, and with their "central affinities," February 19 to March 20-27 and December 21 to January 20-27 (Fig. 32).

COLOURS

Their most suitable colours are all very pale shades and silvery, shimmering materials, For the exact colours for persons born on each day see Chapter 99 on colours.

STONES

The birth stones for this period are emeralds, diamonds, and pearls.

SOME FAMOUS PERSONS BORN IN THIS PART OF THE YEAR

Goethe	Aug.	28th
Oliver Wendell Holmes	"	28th
Queen Wilhelmina of Holland	"	31st
Henry George	Sept.	2nd
Sir Charles Dilke	"	4th
Sir Norman Birkett	"	6th
Queen Elizabeth I	"	7th
Lord Oxford and Asquith	"	12th
Chateaubriand	"	14th
President Taft	"	15th
President Diaz	"	15th
Bonar Law	"	16th
Sir Edward Marshall Hall	"	18th
Greta Garbo	"	18th
Peter Sellers	"	19th
Twiggy	"	20th
Sophia Loren	"	21st

94

BASIC TRAITS OF CHARACTER OF PEOPLE BORN IN OCTOBER

THE Zodiacal Sign of Libra commences on September 21st, but for seven days, being overlapped by the "cusp" of the previous sign, it does not come into full power until on or about September 28th. From this date onwards it is in full strength until October 20th, and is then for seven days gradually losing power on account of becoming overlapped by the incoming sign— Scorpio.

This sign of Libra is represented in symbolism as The Balance.

People born in this Sign are positive and decisive in their thoughts and actions. They have great foresight and intuition, and are generally seen at their best when acting on first impressions.

They are often very psychic, have curious presentiments, and would make very devout spiritualists, theosophists, and occultists, and yet so strongly endowed are they with the desire to reason out everything that their *love of exact proof* usually overwhelms their psychic powers.

They are often very successful as speculators, but they have little regard for the value of money, and have as a rule great ups and downs in their careers.

In symbolism they represent a "balance." They seem always trying mentally to balance things and get an even judgment.

Large numbers of them seem to drift naturally into the study of law, and in it they generally make a name as lawyers, barristers, or judges.

They are also often found in public life, but again it is with their innate desire to adjust the balance of things by making laws for the betterment of their fellows.

They have great reverence for knowledge, and often spend their lifetime in study and research in some particular subject, again weighing and balancing every side of the question in the most conscientious manner. For this reason they make excellent doctors, but generally make their name as masters of some particular line of study more than as general practitioners.

In all careers that require depth of study, thoughtfulness, and balance they succeed best, but all professional walks of life are as a rule well suited to them.

In marriage they are seldom happy. In affection they appear to weigh and balance matters too much.

They crave for the peace and happiness of home life, but in doing so they generally become too exacting, and the result is more often than not, disaster. They have the compensation, however, of making large circles of friends and acquaintances, and are largely sought after as companions.

FRIENDS

They would find their most lasting friendships and unions with persons born between January 21 and February 18-27, May 21 and June 20-27, and with those born in their own Sign or with their "central affinities," March 21 to April 19-26, as shown by Fig. 31.

HEALTH

People born in this period are inclined to suffer most from nerves and depression of spirits, also from pains in the back and kidneys and severe headaches.

COLOURS

The most suitable colours for them are all shades of blue, violet, purple and mauve. For the exact colours for persons born on each day see Chapter 99 on colours.

STONES

The birth stones for this period are the opal and the pearl.

SOME FAMOUS PERSONS BORN IN THIS PART OF THE YEAR

Julius Caesar	Sept.	23rd
Brigitte Bardot	"	28th
Lord Roberts	"	30th
Marshal Foch	Oct.	2nd
Mahatma Gandhi		2nd
Sir Alfred Munnings	"	8th
Christiaan Barnard	"	8th
George II, of England	"	10th
Ralph Vaughan Williams	"	12th
General Eisenhower	"	14th
P. G. Wodehouse	"	15th
Oscar Wilde	"	16th
Frederick III, of Germany	"	18th
President Adams	"	19th
Samuel Taylor Coleridge	"	21st
Martin Luther	"	22nd
Faraday	"	22nd
Sarah Berndardt	"	22nd

95

BASIC TRAITS OF CHARACTER OF PEOPLE BORN IN NOVEMBER

THE Zodiacal Sign of Scorpio commences on October 21st, but for seven days, being overlapped by the "cusp" of the previous sign, it does not come into its full power until on or about October 28th. From this date onwards it is in full strength until November 20th and is then for seven days gradually losing its strength on account of becoming overlapped by the "cusp" of the incoming sign—Sagittarius.

The Sign of Scorpio is represented by two symbols, that of the Scorpion and the Eagle.

People born in this section of the year see to be a mass of contradictions. The best and the worst seem to make this period their chosen battlefield.

Up to nearly twenty years of age they are usually extremely pure-minded, virtuous, and religious, but once their nature is roused they are often found to swing in the opposite direction. At the same time the greatest saints have been found in this period.

All remain, however, intensely emotional, which is the very keynote of their character in all its phases.

They have great magnetic power, and as speakers appeal to the emotions and sentiments of their public more than to logic, but they sway their audiences as they choose.

They have excellent power in writing, are intensely dramatic in their gift of description, and are unusually versatile in their talents.

In dangers and in sudden crises they are cool and very determined, and many of the very best surgeons have been found in this period.

Their worst fault is that they are too adaptable to the people with whom they come in contact.

They are often great humanitarians, with great plans for making the world right, and praise will often force them on to do great things in the world fellow-men.

They nearly always, however, lead double lives— one for the eyes of the world and another for themselves.

They have clever ideas in business and politics, but they are best as advisers of others. They should be warned against "putting off things until tomorrow," for procrastination is one of their besetting sins.

They are mental fighters, and are most subtle in arguments. They make good organisers and generals on paper, but detest bloodshed and strife in actual life.

For this reason they gain a reputation as peacemakers, and in fact, they usually excel in settling other people's quarrels and bringing enemies together to shake hands.

No class of people make more friends or have more enemies than those born in this period, but their strong personality carries them through like a resistless wave.

The sex quality is an enormous factor in their lives. The women attract men and the men attract women; but in cases where the will and ambition are dominant these people can keep the curb on their strong sex-natures.

People in this Sign should, above all, be encouraged to have ambition, *for it is the one thing that will save them; for it they will make any sacrifice or deny themselves any pleasure,* and so accomplish more work than any other class.

They are inclined to be selfish and to sacrifice everything to the need of the moment; but, in contradiction to this, if they succeed there are no people more generous in paying back tenfold for any help they may have received.

In their home life the men are inclined to be dogmatic, and expect to rule; but their influence over women is so great that they are almost always forgiven.

With their strong magnetic influence they possess generally a strange psychological power over others; they make natural healers, for they give of their great vitality to others, and when their emotions or sympathies roused they love to give and to help, and will face my danger to be of assistance.

Sooner or later, they generally become interested in occult matters, they readily develop unusual clairvoyant powers, and quite often gain fame and distinction as writers, painters or poets. They are natural philosophers, deep students of Nature, and observe and analyse other persons' characters better than any other class.

They are generally loved and adored by those who know them, but there are very few born under this sign who at some stage in their career escape being attacked by calumny of scandal.

Persons born in this sign generally have, or make, two sources of income. As a rule they go through a great deal of trouble, difficulty and often privation in their early years; such trials seem to increase their will-power and ambition, and sooner or later success and fame nearly always crown their efforts.

FRIENDS

They will find their most lasting friendships and unions with people born in their own period and between June 21 and July 20-27, from February 19 to March 20-27, and with the centre of their "Life's Triangle" (Fig. 30), namely, those born from April 20 to May 20-27.

548

HEALTH

These people as a rule are very slight and thin in thin in their early years, but put on weight and are inclined to corpulency after reaching middle life. Later the heart is inclined to be their weakest organ, and they should be careful not to overstrain it in exercise, or in work.

COLOURS

The colours most suitable for persons of this period are all shades of crimson and blue. For the exact colours for persons born on each day see Chapter 99 on colours.

STONES

The birth stones for this period are the turquoise, the ruby, and all red stones.

SOME FAMOUS PERSONS BORN IN THIS PART OF THE YEAR

Pablo Picasso .... Oct.   25th

President Roosevelt .... "   27th

Captain Cook .... "   28th

Generalissimo Chiang Kai-Shek ..... "   31st

"Cheiro" .... Nov.   1st

Marie Antoinette of France .... "   2nd

President Harding .... "   2nd

Vivien Leigh	Nov.	5th
Billy Graham	"	9th
Richard Burton	"	7th
William Hogarth	"	10th
Saint Augustine	"	13th
Sir William Herschel	"	15th
Field-Marshal Lord Montgomery	"	17th
President Garfield	"	19th
Charles I, of England	"	19th
Thomas Chatterton	"	20th
George Eliot	"	22nd
Charles de Gaulle	"	22nd
Grace Darling	"	24th

96

BASIC TRAITS OF CHARACTER OF PEOPLE BORN IN DECEMBER

THE Zodiacal Sign of Sagittarius commences on November 21st, but for seven days, being overlapped by the "cusp" of the previous sign, it does not come into its full power until on or about November 28th. From this date onwards it is in full power until December 20th, and is then for seven days gradually losing its strength on account of being overlapped by the incoming Sign—Capricorn.

This sign of Sagittarius is symbolically represented either by the figure of an archer, or by a half-horse, half-man, the man part shooting an arrow from a bow.

Those born in this section of the year are executive, fearless and determined in all they undertake.

They are apt to be too decisive and too outspoken in their speech, and so are often misjudged in their criticism, and make bitter enemies.

They concentrate all their attention on whatever they are doing at the moment, *and seem to see no other way but theirs until their effort is made.*

They are, however, the great workers; they never seem to tire until they drop with fatigue.

They are generally very honourable, but chiefly when they feel others are placing implicit confidence in them. Brutally truthful, they resent deception, any unmask and attempt to deceive others even when such action is against their own interests. There are two distinct classes that exist in this period. The people of one section have their ideals of life extremely high, and any appeal to do good is met with an immediate response.

Those of this first class are the salt of the earth in their care for their employees and people under them.

They have great enterprise in business, but never feel themselves confined to any one line; because they have been successful in some one thing is no reason whatever that they must follow it through life. For this reason one often finds the men of this period change from clergymen to stockbrokers, or from professors to followers of trade; while the women successful in one line of work will just as quickly throw themselves heart and soul into some entirely new study.

As a rule, perhaps from their intense concentration and will power, they are successful in whatever they do, and they should *always be allowed a free hand in chossing their vocation.*

The people of the second class born in this period are easily recognised; first, by their sharp criticism of every one else's efforts for good and by their petty meanness in all matters that concern money.

People of this second class are eaten up with selfish ambition. In any country in which they live they force their way into government positions. They toady to titles and are snobs beyond description. They are also hypocrites and religious bigots of the worst class, but the simplest student of humanity, after a little observation, will never confound them with those of the other class in the same Sign.

Nearly all classes in this Sign are devoted to music. They often make brilliant musicians.

They are, however, inclined to go to extremes in all things, and make sudden decisions, or change their minds rapidly, for which they may have regrets, *but they are too proud to acknowledge their error.*

The men of this Sign nearly always marry on impulse and regret it afterwards, but they are too proud to show their regrets and too conventional to appeal to the courts for assistance, so they often pass for models of married happiness even when they are the most wretched.

The women born in this Sign are, as a rule, the nobler of the two; they love to make their husbands successful and will sacrifice everything to that end. They are generally chaste and have an intense love of home, and even when unhappily married they make the best of a bad bargain.

They are great Church-goers.

They venerate law and order and make the best of mothers.

People born in this period, even when successful, should never cease to be actively employed—inactivity for them would mean despondency and an early decay.

FRIENDS

Their most lasting unions and friendships would be made with people born from March 21 to April 19-26, and July 21 to August 20-27, or in their own period, and they will also find excellent companions in those born in the centre of their triangle - namely, from May 21 to June 20-27 (Fig. 29).

HEALTH

They will be more inclined to suffer from rheumatism than from any other disease, also from a delicacy of the throat and lungs, and skin troubles. They also, especially in their latter years, suffer from the nervous system.

COLOURS

Their most suitable are all shades of violet and mauve and violet-purple. For the exact colours for persons born on each day see Chapter 99 on colours.

STONES

Their most favourable stones are amethysts and sapphires.

SOME FAMOUS PERSONS BORN IN THIS PART OF THE YEAR

Sir Winston Churchill	Nov.	30th
"Mark Twain"	"	30th
Queen Alexandra	Dec.	1st
Thomas Carlyle	"	4th
Maria Callas	"	4th
Sir Hamilton Harty	"	5th
Henry VI	"	6th
Admiral, Lord Jellicoe	"	6th
Sir Walter Scott	"	6th
Warren Hastings	"	6th
Joseph Conrad	"	6th
Sir Osbert Sitwell	"	6th
Field-Marshal Lord Alexander	"	10th
Frank Sinatra	"	12th
John Osborne	"	14th
Noel Coward	"	16th
Sir Humphry Davy	"	17th
H.R.H. Prince George	"	20th
Andrew Carnegie	"	25th
Malene Dietrich	"	27th
President Woodrow Wilson	"	28th

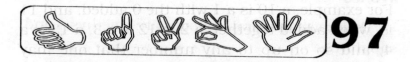

97

OCCULT SIGNIFICANCE OF NUMBERS WITH BIRTHDATES

AT first sight it may seem extravagant to say that people may easily and quickly learn whether or not they will be in harmony with those they meet by applying the following few simple rules which I have found, by long experience, cover one of the mysterious sides of occultism in regard to Numbers.

Even a few tests will prove to those who care to try that there is a great deal in the curious theory which I am about to lay before the readers of this book.

When dealing with such subjects I endeavour to write in such a clear and simple way that even those who have had no experience whatever in occult studies may be able to understand and act on my remarks, and make experiments for themsleves.

ONLY NINE NUMBERS

In the first place, it is necessary to grasp the idea that there are really only nine Numbers, that is to say, that the foundation numbers of all science and all calculation lie between the Number 1 and the Number 9, and that all others are only a repetition of these numbers, and nothing more. For example, a 10 is a 1 with the 0 added, and 11 is, when added together, a 2, a 12 is a 3, a 13 is a 4, and so on up to any number that one may examine.

The occult side of this may be found in the fact that man has been called into being by the Seven Creative Planets. Beyond these seven planets there are two others, namely Uranus and Neptune, whose domain is considered to rule the mental or spirit plane of things, and the numbers representing them have been from time immemorial incorporated with the numbers of the Sun and Moon (the only two planets that have been given double numbers), as follows: Mars, 9; Mercury, 5; Jupiter, 3; Venus, 6; Saturn, 8.

In this way the entire nine numbrs on which life has built all its calculations are accounted for, and so are also all the planets of our solar system, from the earth itself up to the "fixed stars," behind which, the ancients said, the Creator of all creates.

BIRTHDATES

Taking the above explanation as a starting basis, the reader may now be able to follow my theory—a theory, by the way, that has taken me years to work out and prove, which is that *independent of what part of the year one may be born in, a curious sympathy and attraction will be found to exist between all those who have the same number for their birthdate.* For example, a person born, say, on the Ist of any month will find others that are born on the Ist, 10th, 19th, or 28th, of any month more sympathetic than people not born on these dates.

An exception must, however, be made for all people born under the Sun's and Moon's numbers, which are, Sun, 1-4, and Moon, 2-7, as such people are always attracted and "natural friends" to one another; but all other numbers attract, as it were, their own class.

AFFINITIES IN HUMAN BEINGS

Such attraction is, however, *more mental than physical*. It is, as it were, that the planets of the same numbers rule the mind and make those born on the same dates have a similarity *and sympathy of thought to one another.*

Physical attraction takes place if the birth date of two people should be in certain months of the year (see chapter on "Life's Affinities"), and if in such a case the numbers should also be found to be in sympathy then we would have both mental and physical attraction, which would make a union of friendship unbreakable. This is an illustration of that often misused expression that "marriages are made in heaven."

Such marriages are, in fact, made in the heavens by the planets and places of the year creating affinites in human beings, which has been so eloquently expressed in the following well-known verse:

"Two shall be born the whole wide world apart

And speak in different tongues, and take no thought

Each of the others' being, and no heed,

And these o'er unknown seas to unknown lands

Shall cross, escaping wreck, defying death,

And all unconsciously shape every act,

And bend each wandering step unto this end

That one day out of darkness they shall meet

And read life's meaning in each other's eyes."

In the following chapter I shall deal with this curiously interesting subject, and also show the affinities of those born in certain months with others.

LIFE'S TRIANGLES AND AFFINITIES

AS I stated in the previous chapter, independent of what part of the year one may be born in, a sympathy and attraction will be found to exist between all those persons who have the same number for their birthdate. For example, a person born, say, on the 1st of any month will find others born on the 1st, 10th, 19th, or 28th of any part of the year sympathetic and attractive to him, because, as explained in the preceding chapter, all these numbers, by natural addition, have the number 1 for their root. A 10 is simply a 1 with a 0; a 19 is also a 1, for 1 added to 9 would make 10, which, as before explained, is a 1. And so on with any number whose parts must be added together to get what is called the "spirit of the number."

The next rule is that the double numbers of the Sun and Moon, which are Sun, 1-4, and Moon, 2-7, are sympathetic to one another, as they are also to their own series when taken as single numbers, such as a person born on the 2nd is sympatheitc to those born on the 7th, 11th, 16th, 20th, 25th and 29th. which make, as explained earlier, all twos and sevens.

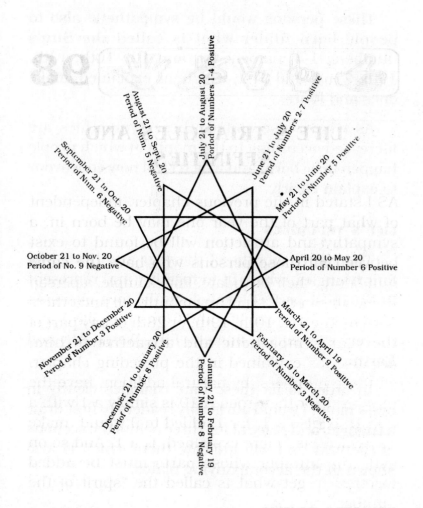

July 21 to August 20
Period of Numbers 1-4 Positive

June 21 to July 20
Period of Numbers 2, 7 Positive

August 21 to Sept. 20
Period of Num. 5 Negative

May 21 to June 20
Period of Number 5 Positive

September 21 to Oct. 20
Period of Num. 6 Negative

October 21 to Nov. 20
Period of No. 9 Negative

April 20 to May 20
Period of Number 6 Positive

March 21 to April 19
Period of Number 9 Positive

November 21 to December 20
Period of Number 3 Positive

February 19 to March 20
Period of Number 3 Negative

December 21 to January 20
Period of Number 8 Positive

January 21 to February 19
Period of Number 8 Negative

FIG. 28

LIFE'S TRIANGLES

561

These persons would be sympathetic also to people born under what is called the Sun's numbers, 1-4, namely, Ist, and 4th, 10th, 13th, 19th, 22nd, and 31st, which, as explained, make ones and fours.

As I have also stated, these sympathies are increased according to the month in which people happen to be born, and which I will now endeavour to explain clearly.

LIFE'S TRIANGLES

The twelve months of the year are divided by four triangles, which fit in together and represent in the most perfect symbolism the four elements necessary to human life, and from which life draws its very existence,—namely, Fire, Water, Air, and Earth.

In order to fix these four triangles clearly in one's mind, I would advise my readers to first draw a triangle, and place at its three points the sections of the year as I will indicate them which is also shown in the accompanying plates.

TRIANGLE OF FIRE

Taking the triangle of Fire place March 21 to April 19 at the top, July 21 to August 20 at the second point, on the left-hand side, and November 21 to December 20 on the third point, on the right base of the triangle. You will then have what are called the "Fire affinities" in their proper places.

If the lines of your triangle are of equal length, and if you draw a line from each apex to cut the centre of the line at its base, the months thus indicated, which would necessarily be a period equally distant in that part of the year from the two sections at each point, you would then get what I call "the central affinity," which as a rule is equally strong although totally *opposite in character* (Fig. 29).

Now if you were to find that a person born in any of these four sections is also born on a sympathetic number, as earlier explained, you would then have *a mental and physical affinity attracted in every sense to one another.*

THE WATER TRIANGLE

The symbolic triangle representing the element of water is formed in the following manner: Place the section June 21 to July 20 at the top, the section October 21 to November 20 at the left lower angle, and the section February 19 to March 20 at the lower right angle, and the Water triangle becomes complete. You again draw the apex lines from each point, as indicated in the illustration, and work out the sympathetic attaction of the numbers to one another (Fig. 30).

THE AIR TRIANGLE

The symbolic triangle of the element of Air is formed in the following manner: Draw a triangle as before. Place at the top the section May 21 to

563

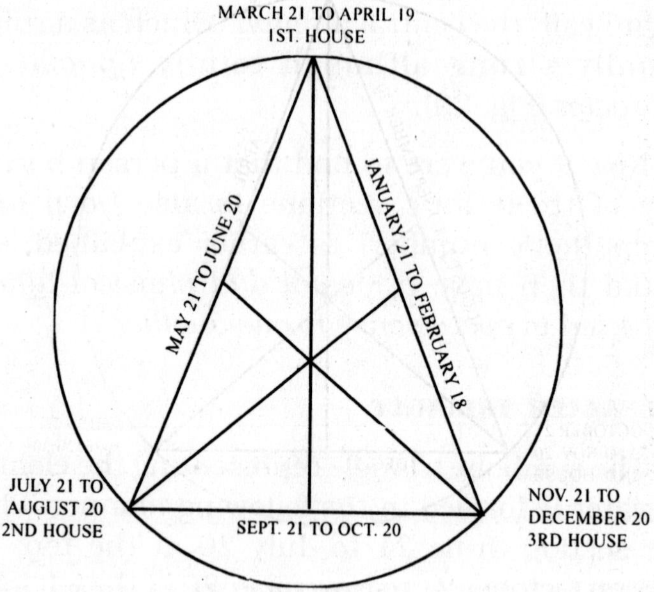

The Fire Triplicity

Explanation

First House : March 21 to April 19 and "cusp" to April 26.
Second Hose : July 21 to August 20 and "cusp" to August 27.
Third House : November 21 to December 20 and "cusp" to December 27.

Central Affinities

Of First House : September 21 to October 20 and "cusp" to October 27.
Of Second House : January 21 to February 19 and "cusp" to February 26.
Of Third House : May 21 to June 20 and "cusp" to June 27.

FIG. 29

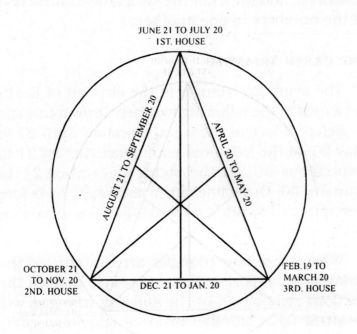

JUNE 21 TO JULY 20
1ST. HOUSE

AUGUST 21 TO SEPTEMBER 20

APRIL 20 TO MAY 20

OCTOBER 21
TO NOV. 20
2ND. HOUSE

DEC. 21 TO JAN. 20

FEB.19 TO
MARCH 20
3RD. HOUSE

The Water Triplicity

Explanation

First House : June 21 to July 20 and "cusp" to July 27.
Second House : October 21 to November 20 and "cusp" to Nov. 27.
Third House : February 19 to March 20 and "cusp" to March 27

Central Affinities

Of First House : December 21 to January 20 and "cusp" to January 27.
Of Second House : April 20 to May 20 and "cusp" to May 27.
Of Third House : August 21 to September 20 and "cusp" to September 27.

FIG. 30

565

June 20; at the left-hand point place September 21 to October 20; at the right, January 21 to February 18. Draw lines from each apex as before described, and work out the sympathetic attraction of the numbers to one another.

THE EARTH TRIANGLE

The symbolic triangle of the element of Earth is formed in the following manner: Draw a triangle as before. Place at the top the section April 20 to May 20; at the left-hand point place August 21 to September 20; at the right, December 21 to January 20. Draw lines from each apex as before described, and work out the sympathetic attraction of the numbers to one another.

When these four triangles are constructed the entire year is represented and people born in the sections symbolised by the different triangles will be attracted as affinities to one another, *especially their numbers should also be found to harmonise.*

People born, however, in such triangles as are symbolised by Air and Water are favourable to one another, although one could not call them affinities. It is the same with the Air and Earth triangles, and with the Air and Fire, but in all such cases the Air people will dominate the others more by their mental than by their physical attraction.

The Earth and Water people can also blend, and make, as it were, solid material things together; but the mixture will be more that of the material than of the spiritual.

Fire and Earth people can also get on together, for in this symbolism the Fire will warm the Earth and make it fruitful.

NOT TRUE AFFINITIES

All these cases cited may, as I say, get on together, and even be helpful to one another; but still these are not what one can call true affinities, and, such being the case, they are always liable to separate, whereas those born on the same triangles, and especially when having the sympathetic numbers when once they come together can never part, or if they do (under some unusual stress of circumstances) they generally come together again in spite of every influence that may try to keep them as under.

People under the symbolism to Fire and Water will, however, never blend, and if forced to live together by necessity or marriage they will just as certainly separate, and are likely in the end to become enemies.

In the following chapter I will deal with the exact colours for people born on every day of the year, and tell how their colours and numbers are harmonious to one another.

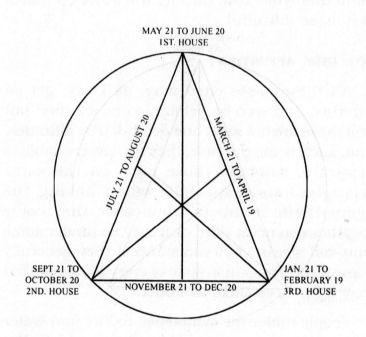

MAY 21 TO JUNE 20
1ST. HOUSE

MARCH 21 TO APRIL 19

JULY 21 TO AUGUST 20

SEPT 21 TO
OCTOBER 20
2ND. HOUSE

NOVEMBER 21 TO DEC. 20

JAN. 21 TO
FEBRUARY 19
3RD. HOUSE

The Air Triplicity

Explanation

First House : May 21 to June 20 and "cusp" to June 27.
Second House : September 21 to October 20 and "cusp" to October 27.
Third House : January 21 to February 19 and "cusp" to February 26.

Central Affinities

Of First House : November 21 to December 20 and "cusp" to December 27.
Of Second House : March 21 to April 19 and "cusp" to April 26.
Of Third House : July 21 to August 20 and "cusp" to August 27.

FIG. 31

568

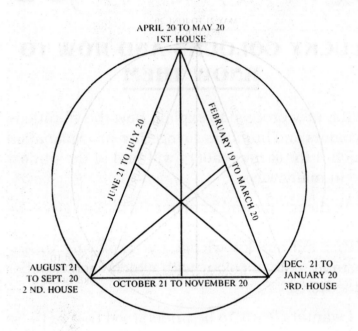

APRIL 20 TO MAY 20
1ST. HOUSE

FEBRUARY 19 TO MARCH 20

JUNE 21 TO JULY 20

AUGUST 21
TO SEPT. 20
2 ND. HOUSE

OCTOBER 21 TO NOVEMBER 20

DEC. 21 TO
JANUARY 20
3RD. HOUSE

The Earth Triplicity

Explanation

First House : April 20 to May 20 and "cusp" to May 27.
Second House : August 21 to September 20 and "cusp" to September 27.
Third House : December 21 to January 20 and "cusp" to January 27.

Central Affinities

Of First House : October 21 to November 20 and "cusp" November 27.
Of Second House : February 19 to March 20 and "cusp" to March 27.
Of Third House : June 21 to July 20 and "cusp" to July 27.

FIG. 32

569

99

LUCKY COLOURS AND HOW TO KNOW THEM

I WILL now proceed to explain how the vibrations of colours and numbers go together, an explanation which, I think my readers will find of the utmost use in many ways.

As the main number of our Birth Sign gives the principal note of characteristic of our lives, we can further aid our knowledge by employing with it the main note of colour with which each number is identified.

I want it clearly to be understood that in these chapters I am dealing more with *the material side of existence* than with the spiritual, and consequently I am not treating such sides of the question as the astral number or the astral colour, I consider such points too complicated for any but advanced students of occult subjects. Further, the lessons contained in this book are intended for the larger proportion of the people, *who are more concerned with their material welfare and their success on the earth's plane.* I believe that, by demonstrating that there is a side to occultism which is helpful in a material way, a wider and larger circle of people may be induced to see that there is something of immense practical purpose in such studies, and once this point is grasped they will proceed to examine further all such questions for themselves.

TRUE VIBRATIONS

No matter how beautiful a piano, harp, or other musical instrument may be to look at, if the vibration of its strings is not in accordance with its proper scale, the instrument will be considered out of tune *and useless for all practical purposes.*

It is the same with human beings; if their vibrations are not true in the harp of life, their thoughts and actions will cause discords and the unseen force of Nature prefers to leave them silent, or inactive, *rather than have inharmony in the great scheme of harmony*, which it has always been and ever will be Nature's purpose to attain.

As time is of so little importance to Nature, it follows that she does not worry about such infinitesimal things as human lives, with their odd three score years and ten of sorrow or happiness. But to the human being his span of life is of the greatest importance; it is thus compulsory for us *to learn Nature's secrets as quickly and as early as possible, so that we may fit in with her plan* instead of demanding that Nature take that trouble for us, which I find so many people expect.

Without going further into this question, I will now proceed to show what are the principal colours associated with each birth number and month of birth.

HOW TO USE COLOURS

Although the earth would look for brighter if we were to dress in our true colours in ordinary life, as do the flowers of the earth, yet as I cannot expect to effect this drastic changes all at once in our conventional appearance, I must content myself with hoping that my readers may commence to make the changes I suggest in some slight form, or at least in those working rooms or studios where they evolve their plans, write their letters or see their friends. If they do even this I honestly believe they will see quickly the advantage they will gain in their material success and also in their own personal happiness.

COLOURS OF THE NUMBER 1

Persons born under the sign of the number 1, such as on the 1st, 10th, 19th, or 28th of any month, have for their main number, as I stated in previous chapters, the 1-4; and they can blend or use their colours with those given to the number 2-7, and vice versa. The 1-4 and 2-7 are the only double numbers that have to be considered in this way. The number 1-4 and its colours are more important to all those born in the "House of the 1-4," namely, from July 21-28 to August 20-28.*

Their main colours are all shades from the palest yellow to deep orange or golden hues, and

*In making these calculation I have added the seven days previously mentioned to the beginning and ending of the Zodiacal periods shown on Fig. 3.

572

they can also use the colours of the 2-7, which are all shades from the palest green to the darkest, also creams and whites. All purples, blues, crimsons, and rose colours are favourable to them, *but they, are not what are called the main colours,* and should only be used as accessories.

The number I people should have as much as possible of the main colours around them, at least in their rooms or studios and in their dress, and they should also wear topaz or amber as much as possible in their jewellery.

COLOURS OF THE NUMBER 2

The persons who have this number for their Birth Number are all those who are born on the 2nd, 11th, 20th, or 29th of any month, but this number and colour are of still more importance if they are born in what is called the "House of the 2-7," namely from June 21 to July 20-27.

Their main colours are all shades from the palest green to the darkest creams and whites, but they also can use the colours of the 1-4 sign as described above. Rose and pink tints and pale blues are also favourable to them, but only as accessory colours, and the number 2 people should endeavour to wear and use all the lighter shades and *avoid deep tones of colour as much as possible.* The stones favourable for them to wear are pearls, cat's-eyes, and moonstones.

COLOURS OF THE NUMBER 3

The persons who have this number for their Birth Number are all those born on the 3rd, 12th, 21st, or 30th of any month, but this number and colour are of still more significance if they are born in what is called the "House of the 3," namely from February 19 to March 20-27 or from November 21 to December 20-27.

Their main colours are all shades of mauve, violet, and purple, which they should have around them in their rooms or with them as much as possible, and they should also wear some jewel containing an amethyst, on account of its colour vibrations.

All shades of blue, crimson, or rose and yellow are favourable for them, but only as accessories.

COLOURS OF THE NUMBER 4

The persons who have this number for their Birth Number are all those who are born on the 4th, 13th, 22nd, or 31st of any month, but this number and colour are of still more significance if they are born either from July 21 to August 20-27, or from January 21 to February 19-26.

Their main colours are all shades of grey and fawn, and electric shades and the minor tints of yellow and green. They would also find the sapphire the most favourable stone to wear, on account of its colour vibrations.

COLOURS OF THE NUMBER 5

The persons who have this number for their Birth Number are all those who are born on the 5th, 14th, or 23rd of any month, but this number and colour are of still greater significance if people are born in what is called the "House of the 5," namely, form May 21 to June 20-27, or from August 21 to September 20-27.

Their main or principal colours are all shades of silver grey, glistening white, or silvered, glittering materials, and as accessory colours *the pale or light shades of all colours.*

These people are far more magnetic if they do not wear or surround themselves with major colours or dark shades. They should also wear some jewel or ornament made of platinum or silver and diamonds, if possible.

COLOURS OF THE NUMBER 6

The persons who have this number for their Birth Number are all those who are born on the 6th, 15th, or 24th of any month, but this number and its colours have greater significance for all those born in what is called the "House of the 6," namely from April 20 to May 20-27, or from September 21 to October 20-27.

Their main colours are all shades of blue, from the lightest to the darkest. *They have more accessory colours than any other class, and their range runs through all colours, except black and dark purple.*

The turquoise and emeralds are the most favourable stones for these persons to wear, on account of their colour vibrations.

COLOURS OF THE NUMBER 7

The persons who have this number for their Birth Number are all those who are born on the 7th, 16th, or 25th of any month, but especially if they happen also to be born in what is called the "House of the 7-2"—namely, from June 21 to July 20-27. Their main colours are exactly similar to those given to people born under the number 2, which I described a little earlier, with this difference— that, as *they are more positive in character* than the numbr 2 people, so can they also wear stronger or more positive colours, but all shades of green and yellow remain their foundation or principal colours.

The jewels most personal and most favourable to them are moonstones, all white stones, and cat's-eyes, but these people should remember to avoid deep or dark colours, both in stones and materials.

COLOURS OF THE NUMBER 8

The persons who have this number for their Birth Number are all those who are born on the 8th, 17th, or 26th of any month, but especially if they happen also to be born in what is called the "House of the 8," namely, from December 21 to January 20-27, or from January 27 to February 19-26.

The first mentioned period is the Positive of their number, while the second is the Negative.

These people, with their invariably strong personality, should be exceptionally careful of their surroundings and of their colours.

These seem "out of place" and irritable when surrounded by light, bright, or garish tones, and they easily become silent, moody and despondent under such circumstances.

As they are at heart grave, serious, and solid people, they should remember that all grave and serious colours *are theirs by right of birth.*

Even children born under the influence of this number (which has always been considered the number of mystery), especially if they are also born in the "House of the 8," seem strangely "out of the picture" if dressed in light, garish colours—and as they grow up this becomes more and more accentuated. On the contrary, all dark shades suit them and seem in harmony with their personality and with their "atmosphere."

They would be especially fortunate in all tones of dark greys, blues, browns, russet shades, and so forth.

For example, take some men belonging to this

577

number, dress him in light clothes and he will immediately look like a baker out on a holiday, whereas put the same man in *the colours that belong to him* and every one will speak of his personality and his charm.

In their houses or business offices the same rule will again apply. Such people look "at ease" and "at home" when surrounded by oak panels and bark woodwork, and equally "out of place" when some unthinking architect gives them a Louis XV background.

For the same reason the jewels most fortunate and favourable for such types are a*ll dark stones*, such as dull rubies, carbuncles, and, best of all, the deep-toned sapphire, which is most markedly the jewel of the number 8.

COLOURS OF THE NUMBER 9

The persons who have this number for their Birth Number are all those who are born on the 9th, 18th, or 27th of any month, but this number and its colour are of still more significance if people are born in what is called the "House of the 9" namely, from March 21 to April 19-26, or from October 21 to November 20-27. Their main colours are all shades of crimson or red, and their accessory colours are rose and pink, but they are more fortunate when they avoid the darker shades of these colours. All shades of blue are, however, very favourable for them.

They should wear red stones, such as rubies', garnets, and bloodstones.

If people will follow even in some degree the rules I have given about numbers and colours, and heed the information in the previous chapters, they will very quickly be astonished by the good results they will notice in their daily lives.

There is no guesswork or mere theory about the rules I have laid down. They have been, in the first place, taken from ancient writings of the highest authority, all the dross or super fluities weeded out of them, and experimented on by myself in thousands upon thousands of cases before I have allowed them to pass.

The law of the "vibrations of things" *is as great as the law of gravitation.* It has, however, a wider and higher scope, for it concerns our thoughts as well as our actions. Professor Proctor, in his great work on astronomy, has laid down the rule that not the slightest vibration in the smallest atom in the farthest planet of our solar system but is intimately felt and associated with our human life on this planet, and, although many of these vibrations may be beyond our limited observation, as colours beyond the ultra-red and the ultra-violet are beyond our range of vision, yet, on that is no proof that they are not equally as powerful as those we can more readily examine.

It is well-known fact that there are tones and vibrations in music that are beyond our range of hearing, yet there are other animals that as readily perceive these sounds as we do those that come within our scope.

We receive light and heat only by a certain tension of vibration, and scientists have declared that even life is only a question of vibration—that when it falls below a certain point it ceases to exist.

By following out the simple rules set forth in this book one comes into harmony with Nature, there is less friction, as it were, in the vibrations of the human machine, and so one *will be able to accomplish more and so become more successful.*

Success and happiness are, after all, the principal pivots on which so much depends, both for ourselves and for those with whom we are brought into contact in our short journey from the cradle to the grave.

Notes

....

....

....

....

....

....

....

....

....

....

....

....

....

....

....

....

....

....

....

....

....

....

....

....

....

....

....

....

....

Notes